FLY-FISHING
in Northern New Mexico

FLY-FISHING
in Northern New Mexico

Edited by: Craig Martin
Written by: Van Beacham
Barrie Bush
Jerral Derryberry
Marcus Garcia
Jan Gruber
Mark Gruber
Joe Hussion
Gerald Jacobi
Dirk Kortz
Craig Martin
Martha Noss
Taylor Streit
Bert Tallant
Bob Widgren
Richard Wilder
Illustrated by: Ron Lujan

The Sangre de Cristo Fly Fishers

University of New Mexico Press • Albuquerque

Library of Congress Cataloging-In-Publication Data

Fly-fishing in northern New Mexico/
edited by Craig Martin.
    p.   cm.
  Includes bibliographical references and index.
  ISBN 0–8263–1290–X
  1. Trout fishing—New Mexico—Guide-books.
1. Fly fishing—New Mexico—Guide-books.
I. Martin, Craig, 1952– .
SH688.U6F58   1991
799.1′755—dc20   91–11440

Fishing Localities Map © 1989 by Andrea Kron, Los Alamos.
All rights reserved.
Illustrations by Ron Lujan.
Photos by Richard Wilder.
Grateful acknowledgment is made for permission to quote from *If
Mountains Die*, by John Nichols, © 1982 by Alfred A. Knopf, Inc.

Designed by Whitehead & Whitehead

Contents

Maps

Tables

Selected Illustrations

Preface

Fly-Fishing in Northern New Mexico was born in November 1988 following a summer of frustrating fly-fishing experiences. All season long I had heard reports of fantastic fishing on this river or that lake; but by the time I got to the spot, the excitement was over. I was always a week or two behind. Why hadn't someone written a book of the essential fly-fishing information for New Mexico so I could plan to be on the Rio Grande for the thick April caddis hatch, at the Jicarilla Lakes just after ice-out, or on the Chama during perfect flow conditions below El Vado Dam? What I needed was a source of reliable information to help me pick the right streams at the perfect times, to know when the best hatches occurred, or to find the best stretches of a big river. I gave some thought to writing the book myself but realized it would take me ten years to acquire the knowledge of streams, runoff conditions, seasonal patterns, and hatches that would be necessary to make the book a truly valuable tool.

The inspiration came at a meeting of the Sangre de Cristo Fly Fishers: I was sitting in a storehouse of fly-fishing information! Surely there were fly fishermen who knew other areas as well as I knew my local waters in the Jemez Mountains. Why not make the book a cooperative effort? Each chapter would come from an author who had extensive knowledge of his favorite stream. Working together, the book could be written!

The Sangre de Cristo Fly Fishers heartily endorsed the project. As I had hoped, club members freely volunteered their time as authors and contributors, and the governing board offered financial support. It was agreed that money from book sales would be used by the club for fly-fishing projects designated by the board.

Through my most valuable resource, club members Mark and Jan Gruber of High Desert Angler in Santa Fe, I was able to enlist the help of other excellent anglers from northern New Mexico: Van Beacham, of Los Rios Anglers in Taos; Dirk Kortz, formerly of Troutfitters of Santa Fe; Bob Widgren of Los Piños Rods; and Taylor Streit, of Taylor Streit Guide Service in Arroyo Seco. This book could not have been written without the generous donation of knowledge and time from these business owners. Singled out for special recognition are the Grubers for their endless supply of good cheer, unshakable support, fly-fishing knowledge, editorial comments, authorship, and continual willingness to help. Their assistance has been invaluable.

This guidebook is the product of countless hours on the streams and lakes of New Mexico. Most of the information is firsthand, but everyone who has fished with us or told us a fishing story has contributed to this volume. It is truly a cooperative work. A group of special people deserve to be mentioned and thanked. All of the contributors to this book worked as volunteers, sacrificing many hours of their spare time to share their expertise. In addition to writing, Van Beacham, Barrie Bush, Jerral Derryberry, Marcus Garcia, Mark and Jan Gruber, Joe Hussion, Dirk Kortz, Marty Noss, Taylor Streit, Bert Tallant, Bob Widgren, and Richard Wilder each endured my repeated phone calls, constant questions, and editorial changes. Ron Lujan worked tirelessly on the beautiful illustrations that grace these pages. There are others who provided valuable help: Michael Hatch, New Mexico Game and Fish Fisheries Biologist, patiently answered my questions about stocking patterns, Rio Grande cutthroats, and other technical matters; Andrea Kron, cartographer from Los Alamos, produced the complex "Fishing Localities" map and worked many more hours than she was paid for; William Black, physician and angling author from Albuquerque, shared his detailed knowledge gathered during many years of fishing the Rio Guadalupe; Kevin Kopriva took the time to supply much of the information on the Rio Brazos; Bert Tallant read an early draft of the manuscript and his generous praise provided the inspiration to continue; Richard Wilder and Marty Noss carefully reviewed the entire manuscript, correcting errors in grammar and information, eliminating many of my mistakes; and June Fabryka-Martin, my wife, also reviewed the complete manuscript, and even though she can't tell a Grey Wulff from a grey wolf, she has a knack for spotting an awkward sentence and suggesting ways to make it right.

When I took the manuscript for this book to the publisher, I thought my work was over. How naive! My sincere thanks to my editor, Jeff Grathwohl, for skillfully leading me through the maze of bookmaking, for his enthusiastic encouragement, for suggesting changes and inclusions, and for accepting the fact that my job as full-time father always came first.

As I received each contribution from my co-authors and sat at my desk entering their words into the computer, I could barely contain my excitement, eager to go to the places they described. During the summer of 1990, I took the opportunity to field test much of the information and can happily report that my fly-fishing was highly successful! I hope the readers of this book find the same excitement in these pages and on the enchanting trout streams of northern New Mexico.

Craig Martin
November 1990

CHAPTER ONE

New Mexico Fly-Fishing: Undiscovered Treasure

Jan Gruber, Mark Gruber and Craig Martin

THE WATERS OF NORTHERN NEW MEXICO HOLD some of fly-fishing's best-kept secrets. Within this small region of the southern Rocky Mountains are over 4,000 miles of cold-water streams suitable for trout, along with an untold number of lakes, both natural and man-made. Here the fisherman can find a stream matched to every style of fly-fishing. Abundant backcountry creeks flow through wildflower-covered meadows, rewarding those who are willing to hike a few miles with solitude and plenty of wild trout. On summer evenings, freestone streams host swarms of mayflies and caddis. Also waiting are crystal clear, quiet creeks to test the skills of a seasoned fly fisherman. Roiling pocket waters, hiding trout in deep holes, frequently pour from the highest mountains. For the big-water fly fisherman, the Rio Grande and the San Juan River provide the opportunity to net truly large trout. Alpine lakes nestle beneath high peaks, offering still-water fishing in a spectacular setting.

Most fishing waters in New Mexico are little known. National magazines have brought the San Juan River to the attention of the outside world, but the high quality of water in the rest of the state remains unrecognized. This is true not only for the smaller trout streams, but also for the trophy trout waters on the Rio Grande and, just over the state line in Colorado, on the Conejos River. What has kept the world from discovering New Mexico's fly-fishing potential? Perhaps it is simply the state's location in the desert Southwest. With some justification, nonresidents believe that New Mexico is entirely a desert landscape. They are not far from the truth. The existence of trout streams within such a large arid region is a result of complex geologic forces that gave birth to the three mountain ranges that dominate the cold-water trout streams in northern New Mexico and southern Colorado. The Sangre de Cristo Range, the southernmost extension of the Rockies, rises from the Great Plains to 13,000 feet, feeding the headwaters of the Rio Grande and the Pecos River. Across the Rio Grande from the Sangre de Cristos lie the Jemez Mountains. This small range was once a single, massive volcano rising to at least 15,000 feet. Today, the remains of the volcano feed the streams of the Jemez watershed. The highest and most extensive range in the region, the massive San Juan Mountains of Colorado, feeds large rivers on both sides of the continental divide: the San Juan, the Rio Grande, and the Conejos.

These pages contain descriptions of fly patterns and techniques that will help readers stalk trophy trout and have 50-fish days, but this book is not primarily a teaching tool. It is a guide to help fly fishermen make the best use of their limited and valuable time on the water. New Mexico offers anglers a delightful but bewildering assortment of streams and lakes. This book will help fly fishermen get to the best fishing locations at the best possible times.

New Mexico residents who use this book will also find new fishing areas to explore and different hatches to fish. Visitors planning to fish in northern New Mexico will be able to make better decisions on when to come, where to go, and what to bring. The book will assist all readers in selecting the best places to fish in each season of the year by identifying important insect hatches and detailing where, when, and how to fish them. On the often confusing larger rivers, such as the San Juan, the Rio Grande, and the Pecos, fly fishermen will be able to select the best locations to cast their flies. For anglers seeking a variety of places to fish, each offering a different type of fly-fishing experience, this book will be invaluable.

As readers can well imagine, writing a guidebook creates a serious dilemma for the authors. If we enjoy our favorite waters so much, why write a book that threatens to increase the number of fly fishermen on our streams? Why let other anglers in on our secrets? It may come as a surprise to learn that our love of the streams has prompted us to convey this information in an effort to call attention to some of the problems that our streams, lakes, and the trout must face.

The Pecos, the Rio Grande, the Jemez streams, and the San Juan are often crowded and in places overfished. By detailing some of the attractions of the lesser-known rivers and lakes in New Mexico, we hope to disperse the angling pressure on our overused streams, creating more favorable conditions for both fishermen and trout. We also hope to increase anglers' awareness of sensitive populations of trout. Releasing all native Rio Grande cutthroats is a central theme in these pages, and we have a special concern for wild brown trout.

As the state's expanding human population and swelling number of visitors place more pressure on our rivers and lakes, it takes a larger number of dedicated and hard-working individuals to protect our waters from environmental threats. The more people that are aware of the bountiful nature of New Mexico's smaller rivers, the more supporters we will have in the battle for their protection. The willingness to fight for our rivers and streams comes only with a love of them. If through this book more fly fishermen come to love New Mexico's streams, then there will be a better chance of preserving and improving the high quality of fisheries in our state.

Our discussion of fly-fishing in New Mexico begins with the trout found in the state. An outline of a typical fishing year follows, along with a stream calendar summarizing the best times to be on New Mexico's major rivers. We recommend that all anglers carefully read the

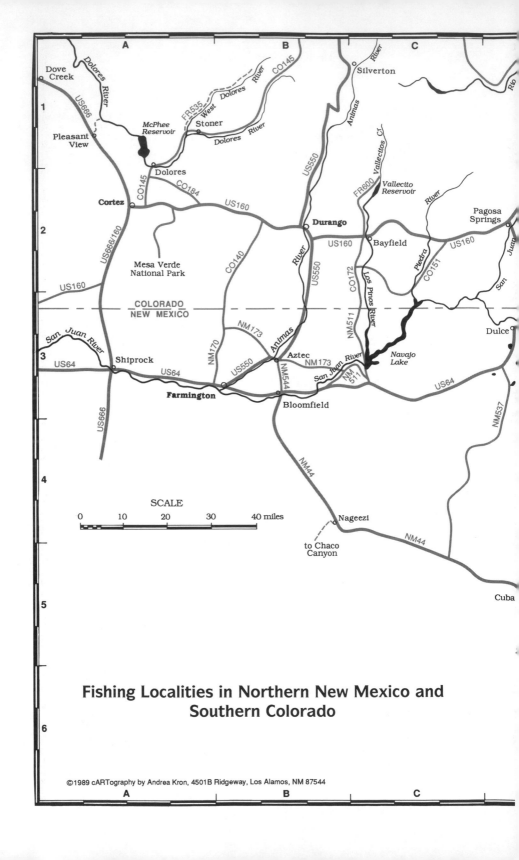

Fishing Localities in Northern New Mexico and Southern Colorado

SCALE

0   10   20   30   40 miles

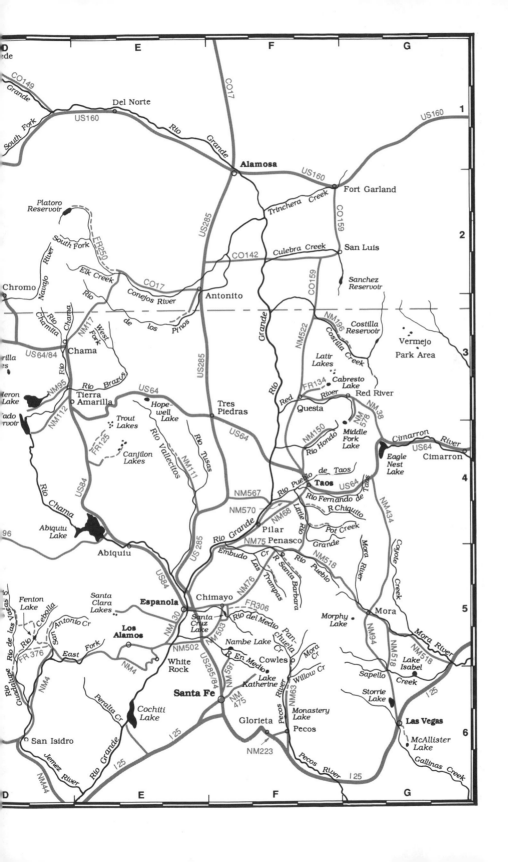

chapter on how to fish safely and comfortably. Chapters 5 and 6 provide information for all anglers, especially those who have a strong desire to help maintain high quality fishing in New Mexico. Please read those chapters thoughtfully. Chapters 7 through 20 cover New Mexico's waters in the detail necessary for successful fly-fishing. Summary boxes at the beginning of each description tell at a glance important information about each water, including the coordinates for finding the stream's location on the "Fishing Localities" map found on pages 4 and 5. For each stream and lake, we describe its location and access, the characteristics of the water, the difficulty of wading and casting, the kinds and sizes of trout, the major insects in the water and the timing of hatches, successful patterns for the water, and the best times to fish there. Chapter 21 lists aquatic insects that are important to fly-fishing in New Mexico, and suggests fly patterns to match each insect.

Although this book is about fly-fishing in northern New Mexico, we have included a chapter on the Conejos River of southern Colorado. Southern Colorado and New Mexico are linked historically by their common Spanish settlement. Geographically, the Conejos, like the majority of the streams described in this book, is part of the Rio Grande watershed, and it is much closer to New Mexico's population centers than to Colorado's larger cities. Most important, the Conejos is a superb trout stream that many New Mexicans love to fish.

Three abbreviations are used in the text and on the maps, in reference to roads: NM for New Mexico State Road, CO for Colorado State Road, and FR for Forest Road.

To be consistent, the editor has adopted the use of the word "fisherman" throughout the book. Please read this as a generic term that is not meant to imply gender.

Take this book into the field, to the streams and lakes of New Mexico, and use it as a starting point for your own explorations. Use as much or as little as you like, but please don't let our information place any limitations on your fishing. There is much more to be learned about the trout waters of New Mexico, and we hope that you will use this book as a foundation on which to build a storehouse of your own knowledge about fly-fishing in New Mexico.

Streams	County	Managed by
Alamitos Creek	Taos	Carson National Forest
Canjilon Creek	Rio Arriba	Carson National Forest
Comanche Creek	Taos	Carson National Forest
Costilla Creek	Taos	Carson National Forest, private
Cow Creek	San Miguel	Santa Fe National Forest
East Fork of the Brazos	Rio Arriba	Carson National Forest, private
La Junta Creek	Taos	Carson National Forest
Lake Fork of Cabresto Creek	Taos	Carson National Forest
Nabor Creek	Rio Arriba	New Mexico Game and Fish
Peralta Creek	Sandoval	Santa Fe National Forest
Ponil Creek	Colfax	Private
Rio Chiquito	Taos	Carson National Forest
Rio del Medio	Santa Fe	Santa Fe National Forest
Rio Santa Barbara	Taos	Carson National Forest
Rito Peñas Negras	Sandoval	Santa Fe National Forest
Lakes		
Cabresto Lake	Taos	Carson National Forest
Canjilon Lakes	Rio Arriba	Carson National Forest
Horseshoe Lake	Taos	Carson National Forest
Latir Lakes	Taos	Private
Nabor Lake	Rio Arriba	New Mexico Game and Fish
Pecos Baldy Lake	Mora	Santa Fe National Forest

Table 1. **Native Cutthroat Waters in New Mexico**

CHAPTER TWO

Trout of Northern New Mexico

TROUT ARE FAR AND AWAY THE MOST POPULAR game fish pursued by fly fishermen in New Mexico. Four species of trout inhabit the state's northern waters: cutthroat, brown, rainbow, and brook. The cutthroat is the region's native salmonid, but the most common quarry of fly fishermen is the non-native species.

Cutthroats are the only native trout that live in the waters of the southern Rocky Mountains. Before competing trout species were introduced, cutthroats lived in all suitable streams and lakes in New Mexico and Colorado; today, their distribution is limited to small headwater streams. Three major factors have contributed to the rapid decline of native trout during the twentieth century. First, the destruction of suitable habitat for cutthroats is an important factor throughout the Rio Grande watershed. Second, non-native species simply out-compete cutthroats for food, cover, and holding water. Finally, cutthroats easily hybridize with rainbow trout. Most of the "cutthroats" caught now are cutthroat-rainbow hybrids that exhibit characteristics of both species. Because almost every watershed has been planted with rainbow trout, cutthroats have been genetically diluted until virtually every population shows some signs of hybridization.

Rio Grande and Colorado River cutthroats are the two native subspecies of cutthroat trout that are present in the lakes and streams of
the San Juan Range and the southern Rocky Mountains. In addition,
two non-native subspecies, Yellowstone and Snake River cutthroats,
have been introduced to some of New Mexico's waters. In many locations, the gene pool of the native subspecies has been substantially
diluted by hybridization with introduced fish.

The beautiful Rio Grande cutthroat trout is found only in small,
high country tributaries of the Rio Grande watershed. In New Mexico,
over fifty populations of relatively pure strains of Rio Grande cutthroats
exist, and many additional populations are found in the mountains
surrounding Colorado's San Luis Valley. Some of the more isolated
strains have survived on their own. Protection by New Mexico Game
and Fish has ensured the survival of other populations, and native trout
have been reintroduced to specific areas within their former range.

Once found in the Rio Grande and the Pecos River, cutthroat
trout are now found only in upper, colder headwater streams and in
high mountain lakes. (A partial listing of cutthroat waters is found in
Table 1.) Because they have adapted to the smaller waters, cutthroats
rarely grow to over 11 inches long. Cutthroat streams can be quite
small, but there is a lot of action when fly-fishing for these fish. Fishing a stable population of Rio Grande cutthroats, like that in Peralta
Creek in the Jemez Mountains, can bring a dozen fish per hour. **Because of their threatened status and vulnerability to fishing pressure, anglers are encouraged to return all the Rio Grande cutthroats
to the water.**

Colorado River cutthroats are found in rivers west of the Continental Divide. This subspecies is native to the San Juan watershed
and to a broad area that extends north into Wyoming. Like the Rio
Grande subspecies, Colorado River cutthroats have seen their range
severely restricted over the last century. Careful management policies
applied to Colorado River cutthroats have begun to reverse the trend.

Brown trout were introduced into the waters of New Mexico in
the early twentieth century. Browns of catchable size are rarely stocked

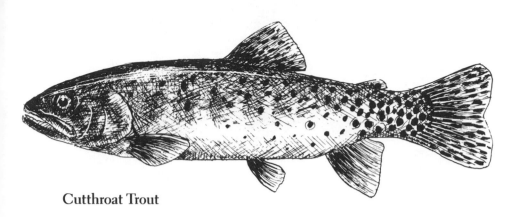

Cutthroat Trout

anymore, but many locations throughout the state receive an occasional planting of brown trout fry. Self-sustaining, healthy populations of brown trout are found in many rivers and lakes. Surprisingly, large browns often lurk in streams that are heavily stocked with small, easy-to-catch rainbows. Many small mountain streams are filled with fat, hungry, little wild browns that are a joy to tempt with a well-cast dry-fly. The state's best brown trout waters include the Cimarron River, Mora Creek, the Rio Guadalupe, and the Rio Grande Gorge.

Rainbow trout are the most heavily stocked fish in New Mexico and Colorado. Feeding mostly in the subsurface, these trout grow quickly, and 12-inch rainbows are not unusual in the pools of even the smaller mountain streams. For truly large fish, the quality water on the San Juan River is ideal. Protected by regulations designed to maintain a trophy fishery, rainbows in the cold water below Navajo Dam sometimes reach 22–26 inches. A population of wild rainbows in the Conejos River in Colorado also produces enormous fish. Eagle Nest and McAllister lakes give the stillwater fly fisherman the opportunity to challenge trophy-sized rainbows.

For a different angling experience, fly fishermen can cast a line on New Mexico's streams and lakes that hold eastern brook trout. (A list of brook trout waters is found in Table 2.) A regular feature of early twentieth century stocking programs, this colorful fish remains in a few wild populations. Because of the brookies' intolerance of water temperatures above 70–75 degrees, stream fishing for these fish involves hiking to the cold, clean headwaters of the Pecos or the Rio Grande

Streams	County	Managed by
Cabresto Creek	Taos	Carson National Forest
Lake Fork of Cabresto Creek	Taos	Carson National Forest
Rio Frijoles	Sandoval	Bandelier National Monument
Jarosa Creek	Rio Arriba	Carson National Forest
Osha Creek	San Miguel	Santa Fe National Forest
East Fork of the Red River	Taos	Carson National Forest
Red River	Taos	Carson National Forest
Soldier Creek	San Miguel	Santa Fe National Forest
Wolf Creek	Rio Arriba	Carson National Forest
Lakes		
Trout Lakes	Rio Arriba	Carson National Forest
Cabresto Lake	Taos	Carson National Forest
Middle Fork Lake	Taos	Carson National Forest
Hopewell Lake	Rio Arriba	New Mexico Game and Fish
Lagunitas Lakes	Rio Arriba	Carson National Forest

Table 2. **Brook Trout Waters in New Mexico**

systems. In waters that experience little fishing pressure, such as the Rio Frijoles in Bandelier National Monument, brook trout are very vulnerable to any fly that floats on the stream. Fishermen have easier access to brook trout at Jack's Creek near Cowles, the Red River above the townsite, and the diminutive Lake Fork of Cabresto Creek. Hopewell, Cabresto, and some of the Vermejo Park lakes have sizable populations of brook trout, with fish that reach over 20 inches.

CHAPTER THREE

The Fishing Year

IT IS NO SECRET THAT NEW MEXICO HAS A WON-
derfully mild climate, with warm sunshine each
month of the year and year-round fly fishing. There is
no closed fishing season, no opening day, and, happily,
no opening day crowds. Elevations in the New Mexico-
Colorado border region range from 5,500 to over 13,000 feet,
so at any time of the year there is always someplace where it is warm
or cool enough to fish.

Warming temperatures and melting snow in March, April, and
May mark the beginning of the fishing year in northern New Mexico.
Like the weather, spring fly-fishing can be unpredictable, depending
on winter snowfall and spring temperatures. If spring comes early, a
heavy runoff brings high and muddy water, putting an end to easy
fishing. Larger rivers, like the Rio Grande and the Rio Chama, turn
into boiling, muddy torrents, and small rivers can be so loaded with
sediment that they look more like rivers of chocolate milk than trout
streams. If the spring weather is cold, runoff can be delayed until April,
providing a rare opportunity to fish the early spring hatches. A winter
of low snowpack brings a short spring runoff, quickly clearing the streams
and creating good dry-fly-fishing during the late spring caddis and stone-

fly hatches. After a winter of undependable surface fishing, these heavy hatches can provide welcome excitement.

With the exception of one or two weeks, observant fly fishermen can always find a clear stream to fish during spring runoff. Each watershed has its own characteristics, often with one drainage running clear while others nearby are high and muddy. The smaller headwater rivers, with their smaller watersheds, progress through the high water cycle first. Runoff in the Jemez Mountain and Little Rio Grande Watershed streams begins in March, while high mountain areas such as the Pecos are snowbound and clear. By late April, when runoff clouds the Pecos and other large watersheds, the Jemez and Taos streams begin to clear. Runoff on some north-facing watersheds and the larger rivers continues into the early days of summer.

Lakes, tailwaters, and lake-fed streams are alternative places to fish in order to avoid spring runoff. The San Juan below Navajo Dam and the Cimarron River flow high but clear in the spring. The fast water makes dry-fly-fishing difficult, but nymphs and high-floating dry flies will usually tempt a hungry trout. Ice-out in most lakes between 7,000 and 9,000 feet occurs in mid-April, providing another way to avoid high water. These lakes present an exceptional opportunity to fly-fish for some large trout that will retreat to much deeper water during the warm summer months. The fish seek out the warmer water margins and lurk under receding ice edges, waiting for food to drop from the melting ice. Casting from a float tube, a small fly dragged off the ice edge will often bring a rise from these hungry fish. Fenton, San Gregorio, McAllister, Eagle Nest, and the Jicarilla lakes offer some of the best spring lake fishing in northern New Mexico.

In June, reliable dry-fly-fishing arrives at most rivers in New Mexico. The water clears, temperatures increase, and aquatic insects and trout become more active. Exciting hatches occur just after runoff: large stoneflies on the Pecos, Cimarron, and Guadalupe and large mayflies on the Rio de los Piños and the Conejos. As even the highest valleys begin to green, fly fishermen will relish the wildflowers and

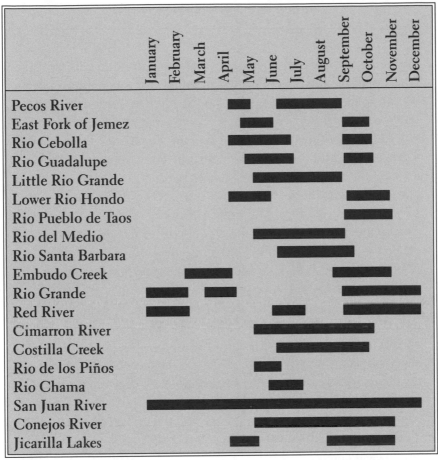

■ Best times to be on the stream. See individual chapters for details.
Table 3. **Fishing Calendar for Northern New Mexico Waters**

hummingbirds along the streams. Days are sunny and warm, making an ideal time for fishing and relaxing.

July and August are the premier months for summer dry-fly-fishing on many mountain streams. Hatches of mayflies, small stoneflies, and caddisflies bring feeding trout regularly to the surface. Terrestrial insects—such as ants, crickets, beetles, and, in late summer, grasshoppers—supplement the surface food supply and add excitement to top-water fly-fishing. Subsurface flies imitating the nymphal stages of aquatic insects are also dependable patterns, especially for deep-feeding, large brown trout. During July and August, intense afternoon thundershowers can muddy streams for a few hours, but the storms are often so localized that fishing conditions on a nearby stream are unaffected.

During the height of summer, many streams are too warm for feeding trout, and they must be fished in the early morning or late evening. Successful anglers seek out colder waters in the high streams. Streams like those in the Valle Vidal Unit of the Carson National Forest are at their peak during July and August. North-facing watersheds, such as the Santa Barbara, remain cold throughout the summer and offer an excellent opportunity to catch summer trout. Prolific hatches of Blue-winged Olives, Pale Morning Duns, and small brown caddis provide superb dry-fly-fishing on the San Juan.

September and October are favorite months for many fly fishermen in the southern Rockies. The days are generally fair, warm, and windless with an unlimited supply of sunshine. The streams run low, and the trout are accessible. Mayfly and caddis hatches continue, and dry flies can still easily lure the hungry trout. As spawning season approaches, brown trout become more aggressive and are vulnerable to streamers fished in riffles and pocket water. The Rio Grande, muddied since spring by snowmelt and summer thundershowers, now begins to clear and at last provides excellent fishing. Northern tributaries to the Rio Grande—the Rio Hondo and the Red River—consistently produce large fish throughout the fall. The San Juan continues to be excellent for dry flies.

Fishing opportunities in New Mexico do not end with the first frost and the disappearance of most hatching insects and terrestrials. The water temperature cools considerably, but fishermen using nymph imitations will still find success in deeper riffles and heads of pools. Late in the season, there is no advantage in arriving at the stream early in the day. Water temperatures warm throughout the afternoon, reaching a daily peak near sunset, and fishing later in the day brings the best chances for success. Even adverse weather conditions can signal excellent fishing: on the Rio Pueblo de Taos, with the first snowstorms of October and November, fishermen can take over 20 fish in an afternoon.

Throughout the winter, when the lakes and streams of mountain areas are locked in snow and ice, the tailwaters of Navajo Dam on the San Juan and the lower section of the Rio Grande Gorge provide exciting fishing for rainbows and browns. On the Rio Grande, dry-fly-fishing is best during the winter, when the water is consistently clear and low enough for wading. In the late afternoon, trout rise to mating swarms of tiny black midges; both browns and rainbows readily take midge cluster imitations. Excellent fishing continues on the San Juan, a location that has been ranked with exotic Christmas Island and New Zealand as one of the world's three best places to fly-fish during the winter.

Zug Bug

CHAPTER FOUR

Comfort and Safety: Climate, Altitude, and Wildlife

A NEAR-PERFECT CLIMATE GREETS THOSE WHO fly-fish in New Mexico, where sunshine is plentiful, rain is infrequent, and cloudy days are a rarity. But on any day, the differences in elevation create an extreme range of temperatures. Weather in the high desert is generally pleasant, but extremely variable and unpredictable.

In the mountains, summers are mild with daily temperatures reaching the 70s and 80s, while it may be near 100 degrees in the Rio Grande Gorge. The nights are cool in the high country. At lower elevations, winters are mild but variable, with highs in the 50s during warm spells and the 30s when arctic air masses force the jet stream far to the south. One general rule to remember is that temperatures will drop about 5 degrees for each 1,000 feet of ascent.

The weather can create special safety and comfort problems for anglers. In winter, the temperature during the day may remain above freezing but will drop below zero at night. The days may seem mild when standing in the sun, but temperatures drop rapidly after the sun disappears behind mountains or canyon walls. Water temperatures in winter are frigid, and anglers must be aware that repeatedly getting wet can lead to hypothermia. It is wise to listen to a weather forecast before beginning a winter fishing trip. Winter storms can quickly hit from the west, dropping temperatures 25 degrees in an hour and filling the air with snow. When heading for the San Juan or Rio Grande in winter, take plenty of warm clothing, chest waders (preferably neoprene), blankets, matches, hot drinks, and a complete set of dry clothes.

Mild temperatures can make spring days perfect for fly-fishing, if you catch one of the rare days when the wind is calm. During the spring an endless string of fronts moves west across the mountains, and strong winds usually blow between 10 a.m. and 5 p.m. Then casting is difficult, and sometimes even impossible on small, brush-lined streams. Some fronts encounter enough moisture to produce precipitation, and spring snowfalls in the mountains are common.

Summer fishing is pleasant in the mountains, although it can get up to 100 degrees between the walls of the Rio Grande Gorge in the afternoon. But the mornings and evenings are cool, and it is necessary to have a light jacket for comfort. Summer brings its own special weather conditions. Mornings are generally cloudless, and by noon each mountain range has a large thunderhead growing above it. The frequent afternoon thundershowers are often accompanied by hail. Usually of short duration, the storms are intense and quite violent. New Mexico ranks second only to Florida in the number of lightning strikes each year, and anglers should seek shelter during thunderstorms. Raingear is an important part of the summer fly fisherman's equipment.

The high elevation of the fishing locations in northern New Mexico creates a set of special problems. With abundant sunshine and a thin atmosphere, the incidence of skin cancer in the mountain Southwest is very high. The problem is compounded for fly fishermen who stand within the water's reflective surface. Special precautions should be taken to protect against ultra-violet light. Fishermen should wear a long-sleeved shirt and wide-brimmed hat and apply sunblock to face, lips, ears, and hands. Sunblock should be applied before starting the day's fishing; don't wait until your skin turns red. If you choose to wear insect repellent, apply it after the sunblock. It is also essential to wear sunglasses that block at least 95 percent of the sun's ultra-violet rays.

Inadequate eye protection can result in burned retinas, "snow" blindness, or, at the least, painfully sore eyes after a day's fishing in the sun's glare.

The high altitude also means thin air and lower concentrations of oxygen. Hiking to streams and wading them can be exhausting. When you fish in the mountains, slow down and avoid heavy exertions.

Rapidly ascending to a high altitude (usually above 10,000 feet) can lead to a potentially severe medical problem called mountain sickness. The symptoms include headache, nausea, weakness, shortness of breath, and general achiness; discomfort is usually worse in the morning. A gradual ascent into the mountains, with time spent at an intermediate altitude, will help reduce the possibility of this condition. If the symptoms do occur, dropping to a lower elevation will usually relive them. If the symptoms persist, medical assistance is required.

In a dry climate at high elevation, you must drink plenty of fluids to prevent dehydration. Be sure to carry drinking water while on the streams and drink at least a half-gallon of liquid each day. Using water from streams and lakes is not recommended because of the presence of giardia, a protozoan parasite that causes a severe intestinal disorder.

Fly fishermen need to be aware of a potentially harmful snake that inhabits the New Mexico-Colorado border region. Western Diamondback rattlesnakes are common during the warm months along streams below 8,000 feet. Particularly in the morning and evening, keep a sharp lookout for snakes while walking the banks of the Rio Grande, the Rio Pueblo de Taos, the Rio de los Piños, the Rio Embudo, the Jemez, and the Rio Guadalupe. As a simple precaution when walking or climbing, always check for snakes before placing feet or hands.

Ticks commonly live in the tall grasses at streamside during the spring and early summer. These tiny, blood-sucking insects can transmit at least three diseases. Rocky Mountain spotted fever is a serious disease, whose symptoms are high fever, flu-like aches, and a red rash. Colorado tick fever is less severe but also causes flu-like symptoms. The presence of Lyme disease has not yet been confirmed in New Mexico or southern Colorado, but it may appear soon. Check for ticks after each trip, and be on the watch for the symptoms of serious illness.

Each year several cases of plague are reported from New Mexico. Plague is transmitted by fleas living on host animals. Avoid handling any wild animals, particularly squirrels, gophers, and other rodents. Try to keep pets away from wildlife, too, and be sure they wear a flea collar or powder.

CHAPTER FIVE

Regulations and Conservation

New Mexico Fishing Regulations

ALL ANGLERS IN NEW MEXICO OVER THE AGE OF 12 must have a license in order to fish. Trout validations are required to fish the cold-water areas of northern New Mexico. Currently, fees are $14 for an annual license, $41 for nonresidents. Short-term licenses, ranging from one to five days, are also available for residents and nonresidents. In general, there is an eight-trout daily limit. For specific regulations, read the information given to anglers when they purchase a license.

Beginning on April 1, 1991, the New Mexico Department of Game and Fish has implemented the Sikes Act throughout the state. The act requires anglers who use public land managed by the Bureau of Land Management and the U.S. Forest Service to buy a habitat improvement stamp, which costs $5.25. The money generated by sale of the stamps goes into a special fund that the BLM and USFS will use for habitat improvement projects in the state. Because the overwhelming majority of fishing waters described in this book are located on public land, anglers should ask for the stamp when purchasing a fishing license.

Special regulations are in effect on New Mexico's Special Trout

Waters. In general, the regulations limit angling to the use of flies and lures with single, barbless hooks, and they impose minimum size and maximum bag limits. Unfortunately, the regulations encourage the taking of the very fish that make the waters special. Minimum size limits allow the harvesting of larger fish only: 20 inches on the San Juan and 12 inches in other waters such as the Pecos and the Rio Grande. By mid-summer 1989, waters like the Rio Cebolla, which were downgraded from catch-and-release to Special Trout Water in April of that year, had experienced a significant drop in the average size of trout. For specific information on Special Trout Waters, see the chapters on each of the streams or the New Mexico Fishing Proclamation, which is available where you buy your fishing license.

Sadly, New Mexico's only catch-and-release waters are in the first quarter-mile of the San Juan River below Navajo Dam and the streams of the Valle Vidal in the Carson National Forest.

Conservation

Why are there fly fishermen? Answers to that question are as numerous as hackles on a grizzly cape. The reasons for fly-fishing are as individual as an angler's casting style or selection of favorite flies. Ours is a unique sport, steeped in a long history and a rich tradition. It is one of the few recreations that dares to even ask questions that require thoughtful answers of a philosophical nature.

Answers to the question have certainly changed over the last century. In the not-so-distant past, fly-fishing was an effective method of taking fish for food. An angler's success was measured solely by the number of fish that ended up in his creel. Today, it is a rare angler who fishes because he needs meat. Fly fishermen today are more apt to measure success in intangibles: the feeling of relaxation, the time spent in solitude, a return to nature, and matching carefully honed skills against the trouts' instinct.

But the reasons for becoming a fly fisherman are not all that have changed over the last century. Few streams remain in their original condition. Our watersheds are victims of logging, mining, overuse by recreationalists, and the damming of streams. Cutthroat trout have vanished from the major rivers, forced out by competition from introduced non-native species. Where trophy trout once were caught, now only small stocked rainbows are found. For every angler on the water in 1900, there are 100 today. The very foundation of trout fishing— the streams that hold trout—has been dramatically changed.

As we head toward the year 2000, every fly fisherman has a responsibility to his sport to help conserve our streams and reverse changes of the twentieth century. Each of us needs to work for the improved regulation of our trout waters to protect species that are disappearing from our waters; to protect trout habitat by fighting against unnecessary dam projects, poorly planned road building, and unregulated mining and logging operations; to contest permits for increasing the amount of pollutants dumped into our trout waters; and to fight against the dewatering of streams for irrigation, industrial, or poorly planned municipal development. Fly fishermen have two ways to meet their responsibility to the future: conservation and self-regulation.

By informing public officials of their feelings on important issues, individuals *can* make a difference. One person who writes a letter to a congressman, a senator, a governor, or an editor of a newspaper is worth 100 people who remain silent. Anglers are encouraged to take every opportunity to express their opinions to officials at all levels of government.

Another constructive way to add clout to your voice is to join fly-fishing organizations that seek sensible fisheries management and fight for habitat preservation. National groups such as Trout Unlimited and the Federation of Fly Fishers will make certain that your dues money is spent wisely on political action. On the local level, groups such as the Sangre de Cristo Fly Fishers, the Rio Grande Flyfishers, and New Mexico Trout will help you stay abreast of regional issues and add to your power in the state capitol.

Self-Regulation

An increasing number of fly fishermen are finding other pleasures in the sport than catching and killing trout. Fly-fishing is the only hunting or fishing sport where the quarry can be released unharmed. Enjoyment can come simply from being on a stream or lake, high in spectacular country. Satisfaction is found in the challenge of selecting the proper fly, in the act of casting, and in the sipping of the fly by the fish. And after the fight, there is that special moment when you watch a released fish shake his tail and swim back into the current.

Everyone who fly-fishes must make a simple choice: kill or no-kill. In unregulated waters, the choice belongs to each individual who lands a fish. Catch-and-release fishing is not for everyone, and many anglers see killing the fish as the ultimate tribute to a trout. Some may still find a creel filled with dead trout to be the measure of a man's fishing ability. Most trout fishermen would not deny the satisfaction gained from eating the catch, especially fresh trout grilled over a campfire.

Yet, living in a modern world has forced us to learn to deny at least some of those pleasures. As more people take to the water each year, the shrinking number of trout streams face ever-increasing pressures. Without some regulation, trophy trout waters would not exist. But is state-mandated regulation enough? Not likely.

More and more fishermen are finding that the regulations of state management agencies do not meet their personal aims. These anglers take the opportunity afforded by the nature of fly-fishing to release all or the majority of trout they catch. Voluntary catch-and-release has a few simple goals:

1. *To protect species of trout that are threatened, no matter what their official status.* Rio Grande and Colorado River cutthroats are examples of trout with shrinking populations that require protection. While no special regulations currently apply to the species, the fragile balance of their populations demands that each angler take special care with these fish.

2. *To preserve quality fishing waters.* Harvesting the larger fish in a trophy trout water only leads to a decline in the size of the fish caught there. A full-grown trout deserves to be treated with re-

spect, and other anglers deserve the opportunity to try to catch it.

3. *To protect wild trout waters.* Self-sustaining populations are not uncommon, but they provide more challenging fishing. With no source of new fish other than natural reproduction, these streams should be treated as no-kill areas.

4. *To maintain trout populations at adequate levels in those areas that experience heavy angling pressure.*

5. *To reduce the need for stocking inferior, non-wild fish.*

Although the need to release native trout is easy to recognize, it is not so obvious for brown trout. Although browns are non-native, most populations are predominantly wild fish that have survived for many years under difficult physical and biological conditions. Browns that are caught and killed are not replaced by stocking, but by the growth of fry or the slow process of natural reproduction.

If you plan to keep some of your fish, carefully consider each individual fishing situation. Some simple but important guidelines can help with your decision on whether to kill or release:

• Release all Rio Grande cutthroats
• Release all big fish
• Release large brown trout in wild trout waters
• Limit your kill to stocked fish (typically rainbow trout)

Evaluate each catch. A 12-inch brown trout in the Rio Grande may be a keeper, but the same fish from the wild water in Rio Guadalupe should be released. A 10-inch rainbow that shows signs of recent stocking in the Rio de los Piños may be a prime candidate for the frying pan; the same-sized brown trout should be released. In overfished water such as the Pecos, even a 9-inch brown trout deserves to be returned to the water.

New Mexico's lack of catch-and-release water is lamentable. With the state's current management policies, maintaining quality fishing on many rivers depends entirely on self-regulation by fly fishermen. Many rivers in the state deserve a catch-and-release designation. The quality fishing in the Special Trout Waters on the Rio Grande, the Rio Cebolla, and the Pecos and Cimarron rivers, for example, should be protected by no-kill management. Cutthroat populations on the Rio Chiquito, Comanche Creek, Peralta Creek, and the Rito Peñas Negras also warrant protection from angling pressure.

Another regrettable aspect of fisheries management in New Mexico is the lack of special protection for wild trout populations. Whether through no-kill policies or maximum size limits, wild populations should be included in the state's regulated waters. A number of high quality wild fisheries need to be added to the list of protected waters: the Rio de los Piños; the Cimarron River from the current Special Trout Water boundary to at least a mile farther downstream; and Mora Creek a mile above the Pecos.

CHAPTER SIX

How to Catch and Release

RELEASING A HEALTHY FISH BACK TO THE WATER is not as easy as it sounds. Simply removing the hook and throwing the trout back into the current is *not* the proper technique. Lactic acid accumulates in a fish's muscles as it struggles during the process of playing and landing, leaving the fish exhausted. A carelessly handled fish may swim quickly out of sight, only to lose its equilibrium, roll over, and float away to die.

The proper way to release a fish starts even before you reach the stream. Purchase barbless hooks, or simply smash the barb with a pair of pliers. (When tying your own flies, smash the barb **before** you tie the fly; if the hook point breaks off, you have not wasted time tying the fly.) Barbless hooks offer three advantages: it is easier to release fish unharmed; the smaller wedge created by the smashed barb results in more hooked fish; and it is easier to remove a barbless hook that is accidentally cast into clothing or skin.

Once a fish is hooked, it is important to land it as quickly as possible. This does not mean that you should force the fish in before the fight is over; it is better that the fish fight on the end of the line than risk injury by wriggling out of your hands and flopping on the ground.

Try to limit the use of a net to larger fish, and be careful not to entangle the fish in the mesh.

Try to keep the fish in the water. Make sure your hands are wet when handling the fish to protect the mucus layer on the fish's skin. *Never* put your fingers into the gills of a fish, an act akin to someone grasping your lungs! Hold the fish with one hand, slipping the hook out with the other and taking care not to squeeze the fish. For a deeply hooked fish, use needle-nose pliers or hemostats. Grasp the hook with the tool and push it back toward the tail, turning it at the same time. If this fails to remove the hook, cut the leader and leave the fly in the fish. Trout have a natural mechanism for dissolving the hook, and it will be gone in a few days.

Once the hook is removed, you must revive the fish. In calm water, face the fish upstream. With one hand, hold the fish by the tail and use the other hand to support the body from underneath. Gently move the fish back and forth so that oxygen-carrying water flows over the gills. Don't let the fish swim away the first time it tries. Make sure it seems strong enough to hold its own in a quiet current. After a lengthy fight it may take a half an hour to properly revive a fish, but it usually requires only one to 5 minutes. Remember that the survival of the fish depends on your doing the job correctly. You caught the fish, and only you can revive it. By doing so, you can give yourself and other anglers the opportunity to once again catch it or its offspring.

CHAPTER SEVEN

Fly-Fishing the Wilderness: The Pecos Area

PECOS RIVER
Marcus Garcia

Location: Sangre de Cristo Mountains, Santa Fe National Forest
Altitude: 6,300 to 11,200 feet
Type of Water: freestone stream, pocket water, pools
Best Times: April to early May, mid-June to August
Hatches: Giant Stonefly, Golden Stonefly, Red Quill, caddisflies
Patterns: Whit Stone, Sofa Pillow, Red Quill, Elk Hair Caddis
Localities Map Location: F5, F6
USGS Quadrangle Maps: Rosilla Peak, Cowles, Elk Mountain, Pecos Falls

BENEATH THE 13,000-FOOT PEAKS OF THE SANGRE de Cristo Mountains in the Pecos Wilderness Area are the many headwaters of the Pecos River. From its beginning as a tiny cutthroat stream in a wilderness accessible only by hiking or horseback, the Pecos flows south, gathering tributaries as it tumbles through a scenic canyon. As the river grows in volume and leaves the wilderness, the Pecos becomes excellent brown and rainbow trout water. Leaving the mountains, the Pecos flows across the high plains of eastern New Mexico to finally meet the Rio Grande deep in the state of Texas.

Throughout the mountain section of the Pecos, the river holds some fine trout water. This is particularly true of the section from the confluence of the Pecos with Panchuleta Creek above Cowles south to its junction with Holy Ghost Creek. Within this section, the most popular and productive waters for fly fishermen are the canyon areas from the Terrero General Store to the confluence of Willow Creek and the Special Regulations water within the Pecos Box.

The upper Pecos is in extreme northwest San Miguel County. From Santa Fe or Albuquerque, access is via Interstate 25. Take NM 50 at the Glorieta exit, about 18 miles east of Santa Fe. Follow the signs 6 miles to the town of Pecos. Then turn left onto NM 63, traveling north. At this point, NM 63 parallels the river. A few miles above town the river enters the Pecos Ranger District of the Santa Fe National Forest, but there are several sections of private inholdings where access to the river is restricted. Please respect the rights of the property owners. Public fishing is permitted for short stretches around the Forest Service Recreation Areas of Dalton, Field Tract, and Windy Bridge and at the Bert Clancy Fishing and Wildlife Area managed by the New Mexico Department of Game and Fish. At the Terrero General Store, the road becomes improved dirt, easily passable with any vehicle except during winter and following heavy summer thundershowers. The dirt road parallels the Pecos until you reach Cowles. Above Cowles the road crosses the river and winds uphill to Jack's Creek Campground, and the river heads deep into the wilderness.

The Pecos River canyon is loaded with excellent campgrounds, all of which can be quite crowded during the summer. Forest Service campgrounds at Panchuleta, Holy Ghost, Field Tract, and Jack's Creek all charge a moderate fee. No fee is charged at a small and often jammed New Mexico Department of Game and Fish campground at Mora Creek.

Twenty miles of the Pecos River above Cowles has been designated a National Wild and Scenic River. Access to this part of the river and its tributaries is by trail only. The smaller headwater creeks—

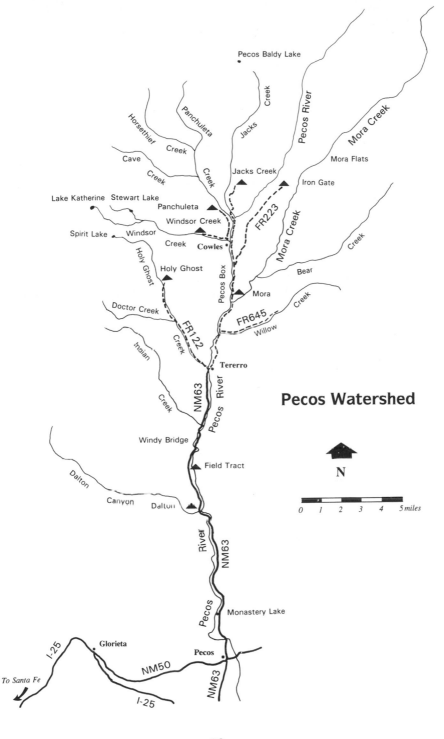

Pecos Baldy Lake

Pecos River

Mora Creek

Jacks Creek

Panchuleta

Horsethief Creek

Cave Creek

Creek

Mora Flats

Jacks Creek

Iron Gate

Lake Katherine   Stewart Lake

Panchuleta

FR223

Windsor Creek

Spirit Lake   Windsor

Creek   **Cowles**

Holy Ghost

Mora Creek

Holy Ghost

Creek

Bear

Pecos Box

Doctor Creek

Mora

FR645

Creek

FR122

Creek

Willow

Indian

Tererro

NM63

Pecos River

Pecos Watershed

Creek

N

0 1 2 3 4   5 miles

Windy Bridge

Field Tract

Dalton

Canyon   Dalton

River

NM63

Pecos

Monastery Lake

I-25   **Glorieta**

NM50   **Pecos**

NM63

To Santa Fe

I-25

33

Panchuleta, Jack's, Cave, and Horsethief—and the upper Pecos itself hold plenty of small brown and cutthroat trout in the 6–9-inch range. The tributary streams and the Pecos above Cowles are small streams that average 3–6 feet across. The hike-in water offers unbounded solitude on trails leaving from Jack's Creek, Iron Gate, and Panchuleta campgrounds. For details on how to hike into these locations, consult one of the hiking guides listed in the bibliography.

The best rainbow and brown trout fishing on the Pecos is in the two canyons between Terrero and Cowles. The mile-long stretch from Terrero is best fished by hiking in from the store or by parking across the river along the road to Holy Ghost Campground. The upper canyon, better known as the Pecos Box, is reached by hiking in from the parking area along the river just above the Mora Creek Campground.

In the canyons, the Pecos River is a moderate-sized stream ranging from 10–30 feet in width, averaging about 12 feet. As you might expect, the river in the canyon bottoms is narrower than in the valley bottoms. The fast-flowing freestone stream has a mixture of pocket water, pools, and some riffles. The stream bottom is composed mainly of gravel and medium-sized rocks. The gradient is gentle, but the river often falls through a series of rapids. Stream banks are lined with willows, firs, and sod-forming native grasses.

Except during spring runoff, most of the Pecos River can be easily waded. Because of the irregular stream bottom, however, caution is advised. Chest waders are not needed, but hip waders are recommended for ease of mobility. During the summer months, it is possible to wet wade during the heat of the day. Boots should be felt-soled for positive footing on the slippery bottom. During high runoff years, the river can be dangerous from May to mid-June and it is wise to forego any attempts at wading. It is safer to fish the small pockets next to the bank than to attempt to wade to or fish the larger pockets in midstream.

Casting can be difficult in the canyon areas due to overhanging vegetation. Where the stream widens, casting is much easier. Casting distances are always between 10 and 20 feet. In tight locations, a straight upstream or downstream presentation is necessary.

The Pecos is one of New Mexico's most heavily stocked streams, receiving frequent summer plantings of rainbow trout from the Lisboa Springs Hatchery near the town of Pecos. Bait fishermen catch many of the rainbows during their first few days in the river, and the remaining fish quickly become selective feeders. Most rainbows caught in the river are between 9 and 14 inches.

Even though rainbows are abundant in the Pecos, one of the attractions of the river is the large number of wild brown trout. These beautiful, olive-orange fish range in size from 6–12 inches, with most of them in the 10–12-inch range. This fishery does not often produce oversized fish, and anything over 15 inches is considered a prize. Although the potential does exist, current management is not interested in producing trophy trout. The river is not regularly stocked with brown trout, and most browns are pure stream-bred trout that will not hesitate to smash a properly presented fly.

There is a problem with the browns in the Pecos. They live in the small upper portion of the watershed, close to the headwaters, where there is not much opportunity for nutrients to collect in the water. Because the river flows through a young, narrow canyon, the water remains cold throughout the year and relatively unproductive. The low nutrient level combines with stress from competing with large numbers of stocked rainbows, producing brown trout that are long and thin and have noticeably oversized heads.

Most of the river is under ice throughout the winter, and the Pecos is rarely fished from December to March. Ice-out varies greatly from year to year, but usually by mid-March adventurous anglers can try their luck with standard nymph patterns, such as Hare's Ears and stoneflies. The water is still cold and the fish are sluggish, so successful anglers cover the water thoroughly. Fishing action picks up by mid- to late April, when the water is warmer.

The first major hatch of the season is the well-known and well-

35

loved (both by anglers and the trout) giant stonefly (*Pteronarcys californica*) hatch that occurs between late May and mid-June. Depending
on the previous winter's snowpack in the watershed, the runoff could
be extremely high and fishing this hatch can be difficult. When the
river is a muddy torrent of whitewater and debris, it is possible to fish
this hatch along pockets next to the bank. At these times, the roar of
the river is so overwhelming it is difficult to hear yourself think. During other years (1989 quickly comes to mind), wading and fishing the
pockets at the middle or other side of the river is easy. The hatch gradually progresses up river, usually reaching the middle section from about
the later part of May to the first week in June.

A second stonefly species, the Golden Stonefly (*Hesperoperla*), is
also found on the Pecos. These insects are every bit as large as Giant
Stoneflies (up to two inches in length), and seining samples show that
Golden Stoneflies are more abundant than Giants. Golden Stones hatch
later in the summer, usually during the first two weeks in July.

Two basic but different patterns successfully imitate the nymphs
of both Pecos stoneflies. During the peak emergence, when the fish
are exposed to a great number of nymphs, try the Whit Stone designed
by Dave Whitlock. The Whit Stone is a realistic imitation and is likely
to fool the most selective trout. The second successful nymph pattern,
the Poor's Helgy, is an attractor used at those times of the year when
the nymphs are not actively hatching. Poor's Helgy was first tied to
imitate hellgrammites of Colorado's intermountain region, but it is
a fine imitation of the *Hesperoperla* nymphs and, when tied with slightly
darker materials, it is also a good *Pteronarcys* imitation. Tie these
patterns on weighted 3X or 4X long hook shanks in sizes 6–12. These
nymphs are most effective when they are allowed to bounce along the
rocky stream bottom. To cut down on the number of snags, tie the
pattern with the hook upside down, so that the hook point is over the
rear of the abdomen. Fish them with a three-quarter upstream cast,
and then mend the line several times to allow the imitation time to
sink. Remember, the key to successful stonefly fishing is having the fly
right on the stream bottom.

Adult imitations of the stoneflies don't have to be elaborate; a size 8–12 Bucktail Caddis or Elk Hair Caddis tied on longer hook shanks will do the trick. The adult imitations should be heavily hackled and have deer hair wings, which will aid in floating the heavy wire hooks. Adult patterns should be fished directly upstream, three-quarters downstream, or directly downstream. Drag-free floats are the rule, but sometimes a slight twitch of the fly may be all that is needed to stimulate a fish to rise to it.

After spring runoff subsides, during the latter part of June through early August, an important mayfly hatch occurs when insects of the genus *Rhithrogena* begin emerging. In other parts of the country, members of this genus are called March Browns, but in this area they are known as Red Quills. Because of their large numbers, this is the top mayfly hatch on this stretch of the Pecos. The nymph stage is best imitated with a size 12 or 14 cream or natural Hare's Ear Nymph. The best adult pattern is the Dorato Hare's Ear. This pattern is tied with a grizzly hackle fiber tail, upright divided wings of wood duck flank feathers, a thickly dubbed body of natural hare's ear, and mixed brown and grizzly hackle.

In the late 1970s, a fly-fishing friend told me about a mayfly hatch that occurred on the Pecos about the first week in July and lasted to the end of the month. I had never before noticed the small, light-colored mayflies hovering just off the river and up in the trees. I luckily swatted a dun with my cap and managed to get a close-up look. It is a cream-colored mayfly with light gray wings, similar to a Pale Morning Dun. Although this insect has never been properly identified, it is easily imitated with a size 16 Light Cahill for both the nymph and dun stages.

Two important caddisflies inhabit the Pecos: the free-living *Rhyacophila* and the cased *Brachycentrus*. They emerge from mid-June to late August, and hatches vary from year to year. *Rhyacophila* is light green, and the *Brachycentrus* varies from olive to tan. A selection of weighted and unweighted Hare's Ear Nymphs in various colors and in sizes 12–18 will match the larval stages of these insects. The same

37

patterns will work for the pupal stages if the angler uses the Leisenring lift. The adults are best imitated by Elk Hair Caddis, size 12–16.

Another aquatic insect that is worth imitating on the Pecos is the cranefly. Craneflies are abundant, and larval imitations are often an excellent choice of searching pattern. Use a pattern with a cigar-shaped body dubbed with cream fur and gold wire ribbing on a 2X or 3X long hook in sizes 10 or 12.

If there is no obvious insect activity on the water, especially during the high-water period of late spring and early summer, approach the river with a weighted stonefly nymph tied to the tippet. During non-hatch periods later in the year, search the water with an attractor pattern. Two attractor patterns are important on the Pecos; what they imitate is not important, as the fish don't seem to care. Both patterns are of the trude style, with calf hair tied over the back of the fly's body. One favorite, the Royal Trude in sizes 12–18, is best used in clear and quiet water; the smaller sizes work best as the water gets increasingly clear and shallow. You should also carry a selection of Humpy Trudes in sizes 8–18 to use in faster currents on the river.

The Pecos Box, just upstream from the river's confluence with Mora Creek, is currently managed as Special Trout Water by the New Mexico Department of Game and Fish. The special regulations area begins at a point one-half mile above the junction of the Pecos and Mora Creek and continues through the Box to a point one-quarter mile above the Cowles Bridge. On this stretch of river, only flies and lures with single, barbless hooks are permitted. Special limits are also in effect: only two trout 12 inches or longer are allowed each day or in possession. As in all Special Trout Waters, anglers are encouraged to help maintain the high quality of the fishery and release their entire catch of brown trout, no matter what size.

MORA CREEK
Craig Martin

Location: Sangre de Cristo Mountains, Santa Fe National Forest
Altitude: 8,200 to 10,000 feet
Type of Water: deep pools, riffles, runs
Best Times: June, September
Hatches: Giant Stonefly, Red Quill, caddisflies
Patterns: Brooks Stone, Red Quill, Humpy, Adams,
  Elk Hair Caddis
Localities Map Location: F5, F6
USGS Quadrangle Maps: Cowles, Elk Mountain

ONE OF NEW MEXICO'S PREMIER BROWN TROUT STREAMS—MORA Creek—is found within the Pecos watershed. Although the lowest mile of this small river is often lined with campers and bait fishermen, the upper river is a fly fisherman's dream of solitude, scenery, and excellent trout water. For backpacking fishermen, the Mora offers the chance to fish for days without seeing another soul.

Mora Creek—also known as the Rio Mora or the Mora-Pecos River—ranges from 20–30 feet wide as it approaches the Pecos, but it is a small stream 6–10 feet wide upstream in the Mora Flats area. The river changes constantly from a riffle and pool structure to a freestone stream. The riffles are often a foot deep and offer trout many protective lies. Shallow runs with 18-inch channels are common, and deep holes can be up to 10 feet deep. Throughout, the water is extremely clear and clean. Wading is easy but often tiring in the fast currents; hip waders and felts are recommended. The river's banks are forested for the entire lower section of river, but the stream is large enough to allow for easy casting. The river flows through a large meadow in the Mora Flats area, but the stream itself is mostly willow-lined and casting can be difficult.

You can get to the Mora in two ways. The easiest entry is from the New Mexico Game and Fish Campground on NM 63 at the junction of the Pecos and the Mora, about 2.5 miles north of Terrero. Don't let the crowds that inhabit this spot during the summer discourage you. A hike along the road that parallels the stream will soon take you away from the crowds. Just beyond the end of the campground, the road turns into a trail that follows the north bank of the Mora. Fishing can be good anywhere along this trail, but it is best beyond the first stream crossing, about a mile from the campground. The trail crosses the stream many times for the next mile, until it reaches the river's junction with Bear Creek. From here the trail climbs away from the river, but wading the now smaller Mora continues to provide access to fishing there. North of Bear Creek, the Mora enters a wild canyon section that extends 5 miles to Mora Flats. This section of the Mora is rarely fished, but it holds some excellent brown trout for those who are willing to make the long hike in.

Reaching the upper Mora at the Flats also requires a hike. The trailhead is located at Iron Gate Campground at the end of FR 223, a 4-mile, rough, steep dirt road that in dry weather can be carefully negotiated in a passenger car. Follow Trail 249 toward Hamilton Mesa for a half mile and then branch right at the trail marker on Trail 250 to Mora Flats, about 3 miles in from the campground. Mora Flats is a popular spot for camping that provides access to the upper 4 miles of the Mora. The area is filled with a quiet beauty and is well worth the hike, even without the attraction of fine fishing.

On the lower-most mile of the Mora, stocked rainbows are the most common trout, usually in the 8–14-inch range. Further upstream, the river becomes prime brown trout water where most of the browns run from 8–12 inches. Larger fish are found under rocks in the deep water near the many small waterfalls along the stream.

The Pecos and the Mora are streams of similar size and character. They share major insect hatches: *Pteronarcys* stoneflies in May and June, *Rhithrogena* mayflies in July, and an abundance of caddis hatches throughout the summer. On the brown trout water more than a mile from the road, the fish see few flies and are less selective than those in the main Pecos. Because of this, using highly visible flies make fishing this swift stream easier. Attractor patterns such as Adams, Grizzly Wulff, Humpys, trude-style flies, and Elk Hair Caddis all work well in the moving water. To tempt the larger browns lying in the deep pools, try black and olive Woolly Buggers, Muddler Minnows, or large, dark stonefly nymphs. Be aware that it is difficult to cast and retrieve a fly undetected in the pools where the water is so clear that details of the bottom are easily seen to depths of 10 feet.

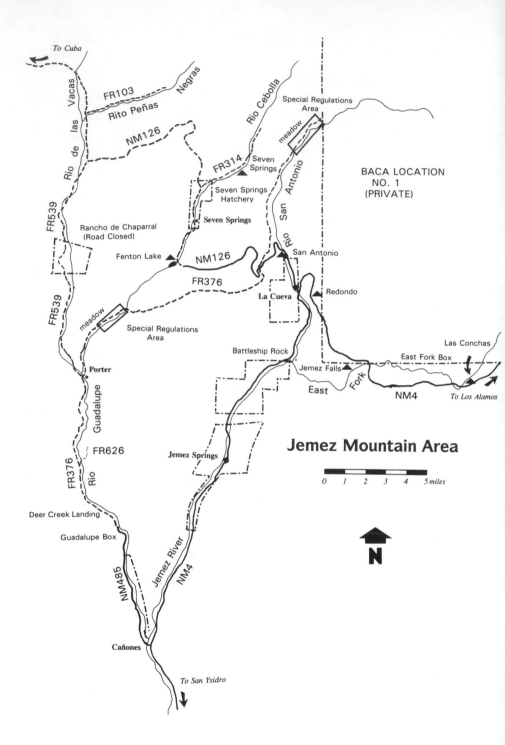

Jemez Mountain Area

0   1   2   3   4   5 miles

N

To Cuba

FR103

Rito Peñas

Negras

Rio de las Vacas

NM126

Rio Cebolla

Special Regulations Area

meadow

FR314

Seven Springs

Rio San Antonio

BACA LOCATION NO. 1 (PRIVATE)

Seven Springs Hatchery

FR539

Seven Springs

Rancho de Chaparral (Road Closed)

Fenton Lake

NM126

San Antonio

FR376

La Cueva

Redondo

meadow

Special Regulations Area

Battleship Rock

Las Conchas

East Fork Box

Jemez Falls

Porter

Guadalupe

East Fork

NM4

To Los Alamos

FR626

Jemez Springs

FR376

Rio

Deer Creek Landing

Guadalupe Box

NM485

Jemez River

NM4

Cañones

To San Ysidro

CHAPTER EIGHT

Under the Volcano: Jemez Area Streams

Craig Martin

THE JEMEZ MOUNTAINS OFFER FLY FISHERMEN AN unexpected number of delightful trout streams. Each of the major streams has a distinct personality, giving anglers a diversity of intimate settings for fly-fishing. There are the high meadows of the San Antonio; the deep, quiet canyon of the Guadalupe; still-water fishing on the East Fork; fast pocket water in the canyon of the San Antonio; 7X-tippet fishing on the Rio de las Vacas; and the year-round water of the Jemez River. There is also an impressive variety of trout species; wild browns flourish in the riffles and pools of the Guadalupe; rainbows are stocked on the East Fork; a relatively pure strain of Rio Grande cutthroats survive in Peralta Creek; and brook trout thrive in the Rio Frijoles.

The Jemez Mountains are located north of Albuquerque and west of Los Alamos. Because of their easy access to over a half-million people, the Jemez streams are often crowded with picnickers, hikers, bait fishermen, and fly fishermen. To avoid sharing the water, evenings and weekdays are the perfect time to head to the Jemez. Some stretches of the rivers are more heavily used than others: all road crossings of the East Fork, the upper San Antonio along Forest Road 376, the Cebolla above Fenton Lake, and the Jemez River below the town of

Jemez Springs. Even on a sunny summer weekend you can avoid the crowds and catch more fish by visiting some of the lesser-known areas, such as the San Antonio above Battleship Rock, the East Fork above Las Conchas Campground, or the Rio de las Vacas.

Overnight trips to the Jemez country are made easy by many fine campgrounds maintained by the Forest Service. From their locations on or near NM 4 and NM 126, these campgrounds offer easy access to any of the rivers. Las Conchas Campground (tent camping only) is located on the East Fork. The newly rebuilt Jemez Falls Campground is an easy walk from the East Fork in the upper canyon section. Redondo Campground, just east of La Cueva on NM 4, provides a good base for fishing the East Fork and San Antonio. San Antonio Campground, a mile above La Cueva, is on the Rio San Antonio. Seven Springs Campground, an undeveloped site above the Seven Springs Hatchery, is within walking distance of the upper Cebolla. Primitive camping is permitted in most areas of the National Forest, and the upper San Antonio and lower Cebolla are lovely (and popular) locations to set up camp. For directions on how to reach these areas, refer to the Jemez Area map.

The geology of the Jemez Mountains creates two problems for fly-fishing streams in the Jemez. Many of the headwater streams flow across ancient lake bottoms that are poorly drained and cannot support tree growth, resulting in the extensive meadows of the Valle Grande and the Valle San Antonio. The meadows are vast basins that collect large quantities of rain. Muddy runoff from summer thunderstorms often clouds the Jemez waters for days. Adding to the problem of murky water is the soft nature of the rocks that make up the largest part of the surface. Volcanic ash is easily eroded into the streams, giving the water a grayish cast and increasing the water's turbidity. Jemez streams are almost always murky.

A large portion of the Jemez Mountains is privately owned. The huge Baca Location Number One covers most of the Valles Caldera and, hence, most of the headwaters of the Jemez streams. The borders on Baca land are fenced, well-marked, patrolled regularly, and no trespassing is permitted. Respect the property owner's rights, and stay off private land.

With a wide variety of streams to choose from, the Jemez area offers unlimited fishing potential. Because of the varying size of individual watersheds and the amount and direction of their exposure to the sun, spring runoff comes at different times to different rivers. Even during March and April, fly fishermen can always find some water to fish, and playing the runoff game can be almost as much fun as fishing itself. While the San Antonio and Cebolla are muddy-red and the upper East Fork is still frozen, the lower East Fork just above Battleship Rock is clear and its trout hungry. As snows melt in the Valle Grande, runoff begins on the East Fork at about the same time the Cebolla begins to run clear. By early April, the upper meadows of the San Antonio and Cebolla are clearing and fishable, but the Guadalupe and Jemez are high and brown. With some educated guesses and stream-hopping, patient anglers can always find the right stream.

The rich diversity of insects in the Jemez waters accounts for the area's fine fishing potential. Species vary little from stream to stream. Table 4 lists major insects of the Jemez streams.

The remainder of this chapter discusses the individual streams in the Jemez area, beginning with the large, popular waters and moving to the small, lesser-known streams. No matter where anglers choose to fish in the Jemez, there are plenty of trout to take their flies.

JEMEZ RIVER

Location: Jemez Mountains, Santa Fe National Forest
Altitude: 5,600 to 6,700 feet
Type of Water: freestone with riffles and pools
Best Times: April to late May, September and October
Hatches: Giant Stoneflies, Pale Morning Duns, caddisflies
Patterns: Bird's Stonefly, Brooks Stone, Adams, Grizzly Wulff,
     Green Caddis Larva
Localities Map Location: D6
USGS Quadrangle Maps: Jemez Springs, Ponderosa

At Battleship Rock the Rio San Antonio joins the East Fork of the Jemez to form the Jemez River, the largest river in the Jemez Mountains. From Battleship Rock to Jemez Pueblo, the Jemez River flows through an arid sandstone canyon that is quite atypical for a trout stream. The lower walls are deep red and orange; above is a light tan rock that is the volcanic ash deposited during the eruptions that created the Valles Caldera. Excellent riparian habitat is found along the stream: huge cottonwoods, willow thickets, and stands of alder. The Jemez is one of New Mexico's lowest elevation trout streams, flowing entirely below 7,000 feet. The altitude allows fine winter fishing in the upper miles of the river; but below the river's junction with the Guadalupe near the town of Cañones, conditions are marginal for trout.

Getting to the Jemez River is almost too easy. Coming to the Jemez area from Albuquerque on NM 44 and NM 4, it is the first trout stream encountered. From Los Alamos, the Jemez is only 33 miles west on NM 4. The river never flows more than 50 yards away from NM 4, and pull-offs for parking are everywhere. The result is very heavy fishing pressure from early spring through the fall.

Private property is common along the Jemez River, and boundaries are often unmarked and ambiguous. In general, public water is found in the 4 miles between NM 485 and the south end of Jemez Springs, on a short stretch from the north end of Jemez Springs to the Soda Dam, and in the mile just below Battleship Rock.

A medium-sized stream, the Jemez ranges between 12 and 30 feet wide. For much of the river's length, it is freestone in nature, with a few pools as deep as 4 feet. In-stream boulders are common, as are submerged ledges below Jemez Springs. The stream bottom is composed of gravel, pebbles, and silt, and wading is never a problem during normal flow levels. Wet wading is perfect in the summer, but hip boots are recommended for the rest of the year. Banks are heavily vegetated with willow and alder and there are many overhanging branches. Casting from the middle of the stream can eliminate snagging during the backcast.

A paved road parallels the Jemez for its entire length, making the

Common Name	Genus	Dates of Hatch	Time of Hatch	Type of Water
Mayflies				
Grey Drake	*Siphlonurus*	late summer	mid-morning	pools
Blue-winged Olive	*Baetis*	spring to fall	all day	riffles, pools
Pale Morning Dun	*Ephemerella*	summer	morning	riffles
Red Quill	*Paraleptophlebia*	summer	all day	riffles
Tiny White Wing	*Tricorythodes*	summer	mid-morning	pools, runs
Pale Evening Dun	*Heptagenia*	summer	evening	riffles
Blue-wing Red Quill	*Cingymula*	early summer	morning	riffles
Stoneflies				
Golden Stonefly	*Hesperoperla*	spring, summer	evening	riffles
Giant Stonefly	*Pteronarcys*	spring	evening	riffles
Winter Stonefly	*Capnia*	winter, spring	all day	runs, riffles
Sepia Stonefly	*Zapada*	spring to fall	all day	riffles
Little Yellow Stone	*Isoperla*	summer	evening	riffles
Caddisflies				
Green Rock Worm	*Rhyacophila*	summer	afternoon	riffles
Spotted Sedge	*Hydropsyche*	summer	evening	riffles
American Grammon	*Brachycentrus*	summer	evening	riffles
Other				
Cranefly	Tipulidae	summer	all day	all
Midge	Chironomidae	all year	all day	all
Mosquito	Culicidae	summer	evening	slow
Damselfly	Zygoptera	summer	all day	all
Dragonfly	Anisoptera	summer	all day	all

Table 4. **Jemez Area Aquatic Insects**

river popular for bait fishermen. The heavy use demands frequent stocking with catchable-sized rainbows. Some wild browns are found in the river, especially above Jemez Springs. Trout average 8–12 inches, with a rare fish reaching as much as 18 inches.

Runoff on the Jemez begins in late February and continues through late April or early May. Fishing is impractical during runoff, when the bright red water matches the color of the surrounding sandstones. Conditions often improve in time for the *Pteronarcys* stonefly hatch in early to mid-May. This hatch makes any large (size 6–10) stonefly nymph pattern an excellent choice throughout the month of May. Adult stonefly imitations, such as Sofa Pillow or Bird's Stonefly in sizes 8–12, will often bring the largest trout to the surface. In late spring, sporadic occurrences of black cicadas can add to the excitement. Use black stonefly nymphs or Woolly Worms to imitate the cicadas floating beneath the surface. By late May, attractor mayfly patterns are effective in the riffles and along the banks of the shallow runs.

Fishing quickly slows as summer heats up. Water levels are often very low and water temperatures high. Another feature of summer fishing is that frequent runoff from thunderstorms turns the water muddy red. As a result, fishing is generally slow from mid-June through early September. Fishing the cool hours shortly after dawn or close to sunset offers the best chance for success. Mayfly patterns, particularly Pale Morning Duns or Grizzly Wulffs sizes 14–18, are the best choice in the morning; caddis patterns are the most effective in the late evening.

Fishing improves as temperatures cool in the fall, when the fish seem to lose most of their selective nature and will take almost any carefully floated fly. Try the usual attractor patterns, such as the Adams or any of the Wulffs, Humpys, or grasshopper imitations. Early morning and late afternoon fishing is the most productive, as air temperatures in the canyon may still reach the 80s into October.

For many anglers, winter is their favorite season to fish the Jemez River. Even when the banks of the river are covered with snow, the lower Jemez can brighten a winter's day with a few trout. The river rarely freezes, and a few warm springs help keep water temperatures high. The springs fill the air with the smell of sulfur, reminding travelled anglers of fishing in Yellowstone. To add to the chances of catching a fish, the river below Jemez Springs is regularly stocked with catchable rainbows throughout the winter.

Cold-weather fishing is best with nymphs and streamers. Attractor nymphs like the Gold Ribbed Hare's Ear and Pheasant Tail in sizes 12–16 should be fished deep through all the pools and around the in-stream boulders. Streamers should be fished with a slow twitch retrieve through the pools. Try bright and flashy patterns, such as Little Brown and Rainbow Trout Streamers or Muddler Minnows. Snowfly (midge) hatches occur on the warmest days, and fish will take mating clusters in the late afternoon. Look for rises in quiet water where the midges accumulate. Cast size 20 Griffith's Gnats or midge cluster patterns to rising fish.

EAST FORK OF THE JEMEZ RIVER

Location: Jemez Mountains, Santa Fe National Forest
Altitude: 6,800 to 8,500 feet
Type of Water: small riffles, shallow pools
Best Times: May to mid-June, September to October
Hatches: Giant Stonefly, *Trico*, *Siphlonurus*, Pale Morning
    Duns, caddisflies
Patterns: Bird's Stonefly, Green Caddis Larva, Adams, Light Cahill
Localities Map Location: D5, E5
USGS Quadrangle Maps: Redondo Peak, Jemez Springs

THE FIRST CAST I EVER MADE WITH A FLY ROD LANDED AN ADAMS ON THE East Fork of the Jemez River. With a borrowed bamboo rod that had spent too many years lying in a dry southwestern closet, the size 12 Adams landed about 10 feet from where I had intended it to be. On my fourth awkward cast, a trout rose to take the fly. In the excitement of the moment, I yanked back enthusiastically. The 7-inch fish became airborne, flying out of the water on the end of the line. The tip of the desiccated rod broke off, and I was left with a small trout and a broken rod. That experience, although burdened with technical errors and bad luck, hooked me on fly-fishing. The next day, I took my friend's bamboo rod for repairs and bought a new graphite one for myself.

The East Fork of the Jemez River is an unusual trout stream. There is a special feeling that comes over anglers when they are fishing inside the remains of a volcano. The East Fork drains most of the Valles Caldera in the Jemez Mountains, a huge crater 14 miles in diameter that originated in a series of explosive eruptions about a million years ago. The headwaters of the East Fork are on the private Baca Grant in the scenic Valle Grande. The public water is in the Santa Fe National Forest, where it flows through a narrow canyon lined with volcanic cliffs and spruce-fir forests. At 8,500 feet, alpine meadows, colored with summer wildflowers and populated with elk, add to the area's appeal. In 1990, in recognition of the importance of this section of the Jemez, the East Fork was given National Wild and Scenic River status.

The East Fork is never wider than 20 feet. Wading is easy, requiring only hip waders or, in the warm summer months, shorts and an old pair of sneakers. Because the canyon is narrow and the rock walls plunge straight down into the stream, it is necessary to cross the stream many times while fishing upriver. In many areas, the banks are brush-covered, but rarely are there overhanging trees. Numerous small meadows flank the stream, often producing the best fishing. For the most part, the water is shallow and quick, and the riffles support healthy populations of stoneflies and caddis. Although the slow runs and pools are often shallow, the banks are grassy and hold many protected lies for trout.

Two kinds of trout are found in the East Fork: wild browns and stocked rainbows. Most of the hatchery fish stay near the road crossings of NM 4, where they are placed in the river. Away from the highway, you have a better chance of finding larger rainbows (14 inches or better) in the deeper pools, where they are eager to take nymphs. It is easy to tempt brown trout with a dry fly. Most browns are found in slack water near the faster currents—behind rocks, under fallen logs, and along the grassy banks. Most browns are in the 7–11-inch range, but skillful anglers can find fish up to 16 inches long. For the most part, the fish do not need a precise matching of naturals, although the larger browns require more care in pattern selection.

In the upper stretches, the East Fork flows near the boundary of the privately owned Baca Grant. In years past, the owners permitted the public to use their land, but because of many abuses to livestock and property, the Grant is now closed to the public. The boundary fence is well-marked and is regularly patrolled, and citations are frequently issued to trespassers. Please respect the rights of the property owner and keep off the Baca property.

Although half the length of the East Fork is on private land, access to the public water on the East Fork is excellent. There are four access points to the East Fork along NM 4 between Los Alamos and Jemez Springs.

Upstream from Las Conchas Campground (15 miles west of Los Alamos and 9 miles east of La Cueva) is a favorite section of the river. The tall cliffs force the informal trail that follows the riverbank to make many stream crossings. Clambering past VW-sized rocks and downed ponderosa pines discourages most fishermen from moving much beyond the campground. But the quality fishing begins about a quarter-mile in from the road and continues all the way to the Baca fence, about a mile from the road. On summer evenings, the many small riffles and pools in this section offer fine hatches of caddis and mayflies. The best trout are in the pools at the narrow meadows about a mile upstream from the road. Large boulders and undercut banks offer quality lies for the trout. The fish are very wary and must be approached with caution; it is often necessary to cast on your hands and knees.

A short half-mile west of Las Conchas is the second access point, a small parking area where NM 4 again crosses the river. For 2 miles downstream from here, the East Fork is lined with a long meadow. The area is popular with bait fishermen who tend to stay near the road. During the summer, much of this section is shallow and too warm for feeding trout at mid-day. A pleasant one-mile hike along the stream will take you to better water near the river's horseshoe bend. About 2 miles from the road, the canyon narrows dramatically and a small waterfall marks the eastern end of the East Fork Box. Because of waterfalls and deep pockets within the Box, wading beyond this point is impossible. A 300-foot climb up the south bank will lead into the rugged canyon. The Box is a different world, with steep cliffs towering above and often over the river and dozens of waterfalls, cascades, slides, and deep pools. Wading is often impossible in the Box, and moving along the stream often requires you to scramble around the 200-foot cliffs. A trip into the Box can net large wild browns, but the scenery is more rewarding than the fly-fishing.

NM 4 again crosses the East Fork near milepost 35, about 22 miles from Los Alamos and 4 miles east of La Cueva. Although the meadows in the first quarter-mile upstream are often crowded with picnickers and bait fishermen, the water beyond the trail's first stream crossing offers the best dry-fly-fishing on the river. Numerous shallow pools, each with fish in the 9–11-inch range, are located throughout the canyon. Larger trout lie in places where only a skillful cast and steady float will be successful. About a mile from the road, a steep trail leads over the hill at the Baca property fence and enters the west end of the East Fork Box, where wading is difficult and sometimes impossible.

At Battleship Rock, 6 miles north of Jemez Springs, the Rio San Antonio joins the East Fork to form the Jemez River. The elevation at the confluence is 6,800 feet, about 2,000 feet below the public water within the caldera, making this a great location for winter and early spring fishing. Upstream from the picnic area, the East Fork is fine pocket water with an abundance of deep holes holding large browns. Follow Trail 137 from the picnic area. As the trail diverges from the river, leave the main trail and follow the smaller paths along the stream. The farther from the road you hike, the better the fishing will be. Using streamers or nymphs, cast into the pools and the runs that are over 12 inches deep. Particularly effective are olive and black Woolly Buggers, Muddler Minnows, and Green Caddis Larva.

Caddis Larva

Each season creates its own fishing opportunities on the East Fork. The river is frozen over and snow-covered from early December to March. Near the east entrance to the Box, a small warm spring keeps a 200-yard stretch flowing free, and it can be fished throughout the winter. For those willing to snowshoe or cross-country ski to reach the open water, trout will take size 10 stonefly nymphs, such as a Brooks Stone.

As winter's ice melts in early March, runoff begins. Because of the large open area upstream of the canyon, runoff is a problem on the entire East Fork. When the snows of the Valle Grande melt, the stream is a torrent that takes on the color of hot chocolate and fishing is impossible. Runoff continues for 4–6 weeks, usually until mid-April.

When the water clears, nymph fishing produces the best results. With few insects hatching, only an occasional trout will rise to a dry fly. Small black stonefly patterns imitating *Capnia* will match the natural on the water but will seldom draw a rise. Much more effective are imitations of the *Rhyacophilia* (green) caddis larva fished in the riffles. Casting a size 12 or 14 Green Caddis Larva into all the feeding lanes of a riffle brings many strikes. Use a slightly weighted pattern, floating line, and a 6–8-foot leader. A piece of fluorescent fly line attached to the leader will help in detecting strikes. If the indicator hesitates or moves in an unusual way, pull back slightly to set the hook. In the spring, it is also worth trying the same technique using a size 10 brown stonefly pattern.

Hesperoperla and *Pteronarcys* stoneflies create exciting fishing in May and early June. The hatch is heaviest in the lower section of the river near Battleship Rock, where the nymphs begin crawling to the banks in mid-May. Fish stonefly nymphs dead-drift near the bottom and then allow the line to pull the fly across the current, imitating the migration of the nymph to shore. Brown Brooks Stones, sizes 8 or 10, are great for imitating nymphs, and size 8 Bird's Stonefly works well for the adults.

Dry-fly action begins in late May and early June. In May, morning fishing is slow until 11 a.m., when the water warms enough to get the fish active. Trout feed throughout the rest of the day into the evening. By June, however, mid-afternoon temperatures are high and mid-day fishing is slow. From June to September, the best times to be on the water are early in the morning and after 4 p.m.

Mid- to late summer hatches include a variety of small mayflies, mostly brown, red, and gray in color. From July to September, the dry-fly water below the East Fork Box produces nice hatches of Pale Morning Duns. A Light Cahill, size 16 or 18, dubbed with Pale Morning Dun poly material is a perfect pattern for this hatch. Among summer hatches, the *Trico* mayfly hatches are the most consistent, prolific, and difficult to fish. As tiny *Trico* mayflies swarm over the river on mid-summer mornings, quiet rises can cover entire pools and the fish become very selective. Tiny spinners (size 20 or less) with black bodies and white wings are best, but a Griffith's Gnat will do in a pinch. Hopper patterns take trout all summer long, particularly in the upper meadows. Terrestrials or attractor mayfly patterns fished tight along the grassy banks usually produce fish. Also effective in summer are caddis patterns, particularly in the late afternoon or evening. During late August and September, a *Siphlonurus* hatch drives the fish wild, and a size 12 Adams or Gray Wulff will do the trick. Small Blue-winged Olives (*Baetis* sp.) extend the dry-fly season through the fall.

Winter comes early in the high country; the upper East Fork starts to freeze by early November. At Battleship Rock, conditions are usually good through December. Fishing the lower river with caddis larva imitations in the deeper pockets can produce fair-sized fish even in mid-winter.

RIO SAN ANTONIO

Location: Jemez Mountains, Santa Fe National Forest
Altitude: 6,800 to 8,300 feet
Type of Water: shallow runs with grassy banks, pocket water
Best Times: April to June, September
Hatches: small stoneflies, Pale Morning Dun, Red Quill, caddisflies
Patterns: Kaufmann Stone, Adams, Red Quill, Light Cahill, Humpy, Green Caddis Larva
Localities Map Location: D5
USGS Quadrangle Maps: Seven Springs, Jemez Springs

DRAINING THE NORTHERN THIRD OF THE VALLES CALDERA IN THE JEMEZ Mountains, the Rio San Antonio heads on the private Baca Grant. Where the river crosses the Baca fence into the Santa Fe National Forest, the San Antonio flows through a wide, treeless, 3-mile meadow. On chilly late summer mornings, the place takes on an eerie feel as the mist rises and the sound of bugling elk echoes through the valley.

For beginning fly fishermen, the Jemez offers no better river than the upper San Antonio, where plenty of trout swim the water. The stream is small, and no casts greater than 20 feet are required. In the upper 2 miles, not a single tree grows within 100 yards of the stream, so casting is not only short but virtually snag-free. Grassy banks line much of the gently broken water, offering obvious trout lies over which to drift a fly where presentation is not critical. In-stream improvements provide slow water in which to practice more delicate casts. In the spring, the fish are not selective feeders, and easily seen patterns can be effectively used.

Ease of access is another attraction of this long meadow. From La Cueva at the junction of NM 4 and NM 126, travel west on the paved NM 126. After about 3 miles, as you climb the rim of the Jemez caldera, turn right onto Forest Road 376. Although bumpy, this gravel road is usually in good condition. About 5 miles from NM 126 the road drops down to the river. Because of its easy access, the upper San Antonio is heavily used. On weekends from May through October, a string of campers crowds the stream banks.

The upper San Antonio holds both rainbow and brown trout. Rainbows are stocked regularly throughout the summer. Most of the browns are stream-bred, but the New Mexico Department of Game and Fish occasionally stocks brown trout fry. The fish average 9 inches, and a 14-inch trout is considered a good fish in this section of river.

Spring is the perfect time to be on the upper meadows of the San Antonio. When FR 376 opens up in mid-April, the water is murky and visibility is limited to less than 2 feet, but the trout are hungry and fishing is excellent. Water temperatures are low, making it unnecessary to get to the river in the early morning; the fish usually wait until 2 p.m. to begin feeding. Thin hatches of small black stoneflies and Blue-winged Olive mayflies can tempt trout to the surface. Small green caddis hatches make Elk Hair Caddis (green body, size 18) effective when fished tight against the grassy banks. The most consistent fish-taker in spring is a Green Caddis Larva, size 14. This pattern imitates the *Rhyacophila* caddis larva, a species common in the riffles of all streams in the Jemez area. Try drifting the caddis larva through broken water and in the head of pools. Use a strike indicator to detect light hits from the fish, and gently set the hook whenever the indicator deviates from a normal float.

The San Antonio has few deep holes and no trees shade the water, conditions that create summer water temperatures that are too high for good trout fishing during mid-day. But summer also brings three dependable hatches that are worth trying. Little Red Quills (*Paraleptophlebia*) hatch throughout the day, but the fish are most interested in the hatch in the cool of the evening. Placing size 16 Red Quill patterns in the broken water will bring strikes. On early mornings in July, a Pale Morning Dun hatch breaks over the quiet water. During this hatch, delicate casts of a Light Cahill (size 16 or 18) can catch fish. *Trico* hatches are a regular mid-morning feature of summer fishing, but the trout are rarely active when the flies are on the water. In 1989, the Santa Fe National Forest added over 30 in-stream obstructions in the upper meadows. This effort may improve summer fishing on the river by providing more cold-water lies.

The uppermost 2 miles of public water are designated Special Trout Water. The boundaries of the area are clearly marked. In Special Trout Water, fishing is restricted to artificial flies or lures with single, barbless hooks. All trout under 12 inches must be returned to the water, and anglers are allowed to take a limit of two trout over 12 inches. As with all Special Trout Waters, anglers are encouraged to preserve the high quality of the fishery by releasing all trout.

At the south end of the long meadow, the San Antonio enters a deep wooded canyon that extends down to NM 126. Few fishermen take the time to hike into this section of river, so wild browns in this stretch rarely see a fly. The hike and the brushy stream banks make this a difficult place to fly-fish. Access is from the south, where Forest Road 132 turns from NM 126 at San Antonio Campground.

Between the village of La Cueva and the San Antonio's confluence with the East Fork, the river runs through a deep canyon, dropping a thousand feet in 3.5 miles. NM 4 parallels the stream for the entire stretch, and there are many parking areas along the road. Three major access points have names: Dark Canyon Rest Area, Hot Springs parking area, and Indian Head Picnic Area. In spite of the easy access, this fine stretch of pocket water rarely attracts fishermen. And once you are down along the river, even the busy road seems to disappear.

From Battleship Rock upstream for 2 miles, the San Antonio is a freestone stream with a lot of pocket water. It is common to find long pools that are 3 feet deep. The bottom alternates between sand and mud and large rocks. The river changes character at the Hot Springs parking area. From here to beyond Dark Canyon, a mile upstream, the pocket water is fast and furious. Four-foot waterfalls, deep plunge pools, and truck-sized boulders are everywhere. Fishing this stretch doesn't require wading; you have to boulder hop. Working upstream is not difficult, but you do need a lot of energy. Most of the rocks in the area are obsidian (volcanic glass) and extremely slippery, so wading this stretch of river requires caution. Although most of the stream is shallow, there are many deep holes and it is easy to slide into one. Felts are necessary, and chest waders are recommended to keep the water out of your waders during falls.

About a mile below the Hot Springs parking area, the river bends away from the road. The best stretch on the entire length of the San Antonio begins here and reaches upstream to just beyond Dark Canyon Rest Area. Park at Dark Canyon and walk down the road about a mile, then take any easy route down the steep hill to the river. If you fish that mile rigorously, it will take 4 hours to get back to your car.

The river is worth the effort. The head of every plunge pool holds a large brown trout, some up to 16 inches. The pools themselves protect wild browns in the 11–14-inch range, and plenty of smaller fish lie in the deeper runs between pools. A conservative estimate for the number of fish in the canyon is 400 fish per mile.

Although curious anglers can find a few mayfly nymphs clinging to the underside of rocks, the San Antonio in the canyon is a stonefly stream. Large *Pteronarcys* stoneflies hatch during May and June, and the smaller stones, such as Little Yellow (*Isoperla*) and *Malenka*, swarm above the water on summer evenings. Trout often leap out of the water in pursuit of these small insects.

Short-line nymphing is the best technique for fishing the pocket water. Keep as little line as possible on the water, drifting nymphs through the pockets; using a strike indicator will help detect any light hits. Large stonefly patterns are effective throughout the year. Brown Kaufmann or Brooks Stones on size 10 hooks work better than the more common patterns like Bitch Creek or Montana Stones. Tossing the nymph into the head of each plunge pool will let you catch some large trout. Smaller Hare's Ear nymphs are also effective, particularly in mid-summer and fall.

Dry flies can work very well in the pocket water. High-floating and easily seen patterns like Humpys and Elk Hair Caddis (size 14) are great choices in the plunge pools. In the evening, casting a fly into quiet water at the edge of the pool and allowing it to drift into the faster water will take the large trout. When black stoneflies are swarming just above the surface, a size 14 Adams will draw strikes on every cast into quiet water. Skittering the fly across the surface often draws a savage attack from a hungry fish.

When summer crowds make most of the rivers of the Jemez unappealing, try the canyon section of the San Antonio. The river will be all yours.

RIO CEBOLLA

Location: Jemez Mountains, Santa Fe National Forest
Altitude: 7,200 to 8,600 feet
Type of Water: deep pools, beaver ponds, small riffles
Best Times: mid-April to June, September
Hatches: caddisflies, small mayflies
Patterns: Elk Hair Caddis, Adams, Grizzly Wulff, Dave's Hopper
Localities Map Location: D5
USGS Quadrangle Maps: Seven Springs, San Miguel Mountain

THE RIO CEBOLLA IS PRIMARILY A MEADOW STREAM THAT MEANDERS south from the high peaks surrounding the west side of the Valles Caldera. The upper stretch of the river flows through a broad valley dotted with beaver ponds and then past the Seven Springs Fish Hatchery into Fenton Lake. Below the lake the river flows through another meadow, culminating in a mile of Special Trout Water. At the ghost town of Porter, the Cebolla joins the Rio de las Vacas to form the Rio Guadalupe.

For its entire length, the Rio Cebolla is a small stream, 3–10 feet wide. As the river flows quietly through the large meadows, anglers can find pools, runs, and a few riffles. About a mile above the Seven Springs Hatchery, a series of beaver dams create some still-water fishing. Throughout, the water is shallow and hip waders are all that you will need. Particularly in the upper section of the valley, casting is made difficult by willows growing in patches along the banks. The section of river from the crossing above Seven Springs Campground to Fenton Lake is very brushy.

The upper meadows of the Cebolla are just plain fun to fish. The trout are small wild browns, generally in the 7–10-inch range, and there are plenty of them. Hopper patterns work well, as do the traditional attractor patterns, such as Adams and Royal Wulff. Keep the imitations small, size 16 or less. On an autumn afternoon, almost every cast can produce a strike—that is, every cast that successfully lands on the water, because here the stream is only 2 or 3 feet wide. The narrow stream demands special techniques, and this is a fine place to practice some small-stream skills: downstream drifts, letting the fly float down on the current (without drag) under overhanging trees; tight roll casts that must be accurate to land on the water; and a cautious approach to the water, maintaining a low profile, casting while on your hands and knees.

The upper meadows of the Cebolla are reached by taking NM 126 from La Cueva. Head west on NM 126, following the signs to Fenton Lake and continuing as the road turns north at the lake. Fishing is permitted between Forest Road 378 and the boundary of private land at the town of Seven Springs. Private land borders the stream for 2.5 miles along NM 126 to the Seven Springs Hatchery. Just before the hatchery, turn right off of NM 126 onto Forest Road 314, and follow the signs to Seven Springs Campground. Public water begins just above the hatchery pond and continues to the headwaters of the Cebolla. Passenger cars can make the rough drive to the Cebolla crossing, about 2 miles above the hatchery.

The Cebolla between Fenton Lake and the upper meadows receives heavy fishing pressure. This section of the stream is overflowing with small stocked rainbows. Beaver ponds near the campground provide the best potential in this area, but be prepared to share the water. At the ponds, using still-water patterns to match the naturals often allows fly fishermen to land a trout while bait fishermen fail. Try parachute flies, damselfly nymphs, and small streamers.

Below Fenton Lake, the Special Trout Water is a part of the finest stretch of the Rio Cebolla and sees little fishing pressure. I was fooled at first by the small size of the stream. When I first glimpsed the narrow river hidden in the grasses of the spacious meadow, I thought it barely worthy of the name "creek" and dismissed the Cebolla as too small to hold any but the smallest trout. A third-hand report that the Cebolla trout were hungry coaxed me back one September afternoon, although I remained doubtful until I hit the water. The number of deep holes and undercut banks was amazing! In the corner of each frequent meander, the river has scoured a hole 3 or 4 feet deep, and each harbors a large trout. Lining the runs are protective undercut banks, hiding even more trout. In three hours of drifting dry flies over likely lies, I landed two 18-inch trout and four others over 14 inches. I was no longer a skeptic!

Hopper Splash

Most of the fish in the Special Trout Water are wild browns, but a few rainbows also inhabit this stretch. The browns lie in deep cuts in the river's numerous bends, and the rainbows swim in pools behind the small artificial dams. Fat trout found in the deep holes are larger than on any similar sized stream in New Mexico. Twelve-to-14-inch fish are common, and it is not unusual to find an 18-inch brown in the best lies.

Although hatches are thin and sporadic, this stretch of the Cebolla is premier dry-fly water. The trout are eager to leave the protection of the deep holes and snatch a fly from the surface. On sunny days, any dry attractor pattern will produce frequent strikes. Mayfly imitators work best: Adams, Royal Wulff, Grizzly Wulff, or a Cahill, sizes 14–18. Terrestrial patterns, especially grasshopper imitations, are also reliable from mid- to late summer until fall, but it is important to keep the hoppers small, size 14 or less. In the early or late season or on cloudy days, try the sub-surface patterns that do well on all the Jemez streams, Green Caddis Larva and small ties of the larger brown stoneflies like a Brooks Stone, size 10. Cast into the currents that run against the grassy banks in the river's numerous sharp bends.

The Special Trout Water stretches from the upper crossing of the Cebolla by Forest Road 376 to a point one mile downstream. The area is well-posted. All angling is restricted to the use of single hook, barbless flies or artificial lures. Limits are two trout 12 inches or longer per day or in possession. Anglers should be mindful that taking the larger fish will contribute to the decline of the average fish size on the Cebolla. To help maintain the high quality of the fishery on the Rio Cebolla, fly fishermen are encouraged to return all trout to the water.

The Special Trout Water can be reached from the north or south. From Los Alamos, go west on NM 4 to La Cueva, then turn right (west) on NM 126 toward Cuba. After 3 miles, turn left on Forest Road 376, a gravel road that is passable with a car except when it is wet. Continue on this road for about 5 miles until the road crosses the Cebolla. Traveling north on NM 4 from Albuquerque, turn left on NM 485 about a mile after you leave the Jemez Pueblo land and enter the Santa Fe National Forest. Continue on this road through the dramatic Guadalupe Box for about 11 miles to its junction with Forest Route 539. Turn right, staying on FR 376, and continue for about 3 miles, stopping at the large meadow.

RIO GUADALUPE

Location: Jemez Mountains, Santa Fe National Forest
Altitude: 5,600 to 7,200 feet
Type of Water: riffle and pool, pocket water
Best Times: late May to June, September
Hatches: *Pteronarcys* (stonefiles), caddis
Patterns: Bird's Stonefly, Kaufmann Stone Nymph, Humpy
Localities Map Location: D6
USGS Quadrangle Maps: Gilman, San Miguel Mountain

OF ALL THE SPECIES OF TROUT IN NEW MEXICO, MY DEEPEST ADMIRA-tion is for the brown trout, whose beauty and fight are so subtle. Browns are wary, skittish, wild, and eager to survive as the fittest. More than other trout, they are inclined to feed on the surface, and the way they slowly, deliberately take a fly is a thrill. When hooked, browns head upstream, stripping line from the reel, violently shaking their heads, and looking for anything in the water to entangle the leader. Catching a brown is not like a rainbow's flashy fight, but is a battle of strength and wits.

The Rio Guadalupe offers 10 miles of top-notch brown trout water. Created by the junction of the Rio Cebolla and the Rio de las Vacas, the Guadalupe flows through a conifer-covered canyon to meet the Jemez River at Cañones. Although paralleled by a gravel road for its entire length, most sections of the Guadalupe attract few fishermen.

The brown trout of the Rio Guadalupe are some of the most colorful and hard-fighting browns around. When hooked, their instincts immediately challenge an angler's skills by heading for the rocks. Landing half of the fish you hook is a worthy accomplishment. These stream-raised browns range from 7–20 inches; the average brown trout caught in the canyon during the spring and fall is 12 inches.

Access to the Rio Guadalupe is via NM 485 and Forest Road 376, one of the better gravel roads in the Jemez area. From either Los Alamos or Albuquerque, turn off NM 4 onto NM 485 8 miles south of Jemez Springs. NM 485 winds through the towns of Cañones and Gilman. In a few miles, the pavement turns to dirt, and the rugged Guadalupe Box looms as a formidable barrier. The road follows an old railroad bed through two tunnels blasted in the granite cliffs, the river tumbling and scouring out its own way beside the road. Beyond the Box, FR 376 follows the river for 6 miles.

The Guadalupe is quite a river. The current runs fast, broken by many rocks and small waterfalls. The width varies between 15 and 30 feet. Nearly every 50 yards is a nice rock-lined pool of slow water. Some holes are as deep as 10 feet but most are in the 4–6-foot range. The freestone and pool structure, along with the many in-stream rocks, creates rich trout water. There are literally thousands of likely places to cast in every mile of stream.

The river flows between heavily forested banks. Much of the river is shaded throughout the day by pines and steep walls. The channel is wide enough so that oaks and conifers growing along the shore rarely interfere with backcasts.

The Guadalupe offers many fine fishing locations. Large browns lurk in the deep pools throughout the Guadalupe Box above, near, and below the tunnels. Deer Creek Landing, a broad, flat area just above the tunnels, is a popular spot for campers and bait fishermen. The nice holes in this area are worth trying if no one else is in sight.

Up from Deer Creek Landing is a mile-long stretch of water in a wide, open canyon. Close to the road, angling pressure is heavy here. At the end of this section, FR 626 drops off to the river and the pleasant but often crowded camping spot known as Cebollita. The short road is rough, muddy, and often impassable except with a high clearance vehicle. North of Cebollita the river flows through 3 miles of deep canyon. Farther upstream, FR 376 crosses a bridge at the head of the Guadalupe. This is another popular and often crowded area with fine primitive camping and easy access to the upper river.

The canyon section, extending from FR 626 to just below the bridge at the head of the river, is the Guadalupe's premier water. Within the canyon the river seems endless, beckoning, and wild. To get to the river, hike upstream from FR 626 at Cebollita or park near any of the small dry canyons that drop to the river from FR 376. Your efforts will be greatly rewarded with fine fishing for large, wild trout, the exquisite scenery, and the noisy solitude.

There are no trails along the river in the canyon. The walls pinch in at many spots so that the stream fills the innermost gorge, and moving up or downstream requires wading rather than walking on the banks. Wading can be difficult on the round and slippery rocks, and it is easy to slide off the rocks into suddenly deep holes. But the water is not dangerous. Chest waders and felts are recommended in the early season, and wet wading is comfortable in July and August.

During the summer and fall when the water is moderate and low, it is possible to wade the entire river from Deer Creek Landing to the Junction of the Cebolla and the Rio de las Vacas, except for a small box with impassable cliffs located about a mile downstream from Porter. This second Guadalupe Box is about 200 yards long, with 50-foot cliffs dropping into a deep pool. Before continuing upstream, you must backtrack 100 yards, climb out of the inner canyon, then walk beyond the head of the box.

The Guadalupe supports the usual assortment of insects found in the Jemez. *Heptagenia* and *Ephemerella*, the most common mayflies, are the Pale Morning and Pale Evening Dun hatches that occur during early mornings and late evenings from mid- to late summer. When fishing these hatches in quiet water, use Light Cahills, size 16 or 18, or a variation of the Cahill with a body dubbed with yellow poly material. On July mornings, *Rhithrogenia* mayflies bring trout to the surface; this hatch is matched with a size 14 Red Quill. The tiny black and white *Tricorythodes* mayfly also hatches during mid-summer mornings. Evening caddis swarms can be dense from May through September, and gray or green Elk Hair Caddis sizes 14–18 work well, as do Goddard Caddis in the same sizes. In fall, late afternoon Blue Dun (*Baetis* sp.) hatches, size 16 or 18, bring trout to the surface. The fish can be selective feeders during this hatch, and a gray/blue parachute pattern fished carefully will bring more hooked fish than a traditional Blue-winged Olive pattern.

Although many smaller stoneflies—*Capnia, Isoperla, Hesperoperla*— are common in the Guadalupe, the year's most exciting fishing is the *Pteronarcys*, or Giant Stonefly hatch. When conditions are right, the Guadalupe provides excellent fishing throughout the late spring and early summer. The stonefly nymphs begin their migration to shore anywhere from the second week in May to the second week in June, depending on both winter snows and spring temperatures. Judging the timing of the hatch is tricky. Whatever the dates of the hatch, fishing large stonefly nymph patterns gets lots of attention from the trout throughout this month, and a good year can produce excellent fishing into July. Any large, dark nymph can be effective. Try patterns such as Montana Stone sizes 8 or 10, Brooks Stone sizes 6–10, and Bitch Creek sizes 8 or 10.

When the huge stonefly adults are clumsily thrashing around on the water, Sofa Pillows or Bird's Stonefly in sizes 8–12 can bring 15-inch trout to the surface. When fishing the stonefly adults, it is better to be a clumsy fly fisher. The naturals on the water hit the surface hard and then spend a lot of energy thrashing around; the disturbance attracts the trout to the insect. Overpower your casts of stonefly adults so the pattern hits the water with a splash. While the fly is on the water, frequently give the rod tip a twitch, creating a surface disturbance like that of the natural. Fishing the fly as a living insect can bring amazing results.

As important as the stonefly hatch is a sporadic occurrence of a black and gold cicada, the same insect that is found in the Jemez River. The cicadas are found on the water at about the same time as the stoneflies—from late May to early June—and follow the same patterns of abundance; both cicadas and stoneflies are abundant during the same years. The cicadas are not aquatic insects, but terrestrials that drop from the overhanging vegetation to float in the currents. Black stonefly nymphs are an effective imitation when they are fished dead-drift a few inches below the surface.

The Guadalupe watershed is the largest in the Jemez area, and runoff may be long and heavy. The high water usually begins in mid-March and lasts from 8–12 weeks. The water is highly turbid, with in-stream visibilities often less than one foot. These conditions can make fishing impossible. The excellent fishing of the large stonefly hatch makes the timing of runoff important. During years of low snow-pack and warm spring temperatures, runoff ends before the hatch and fishing is consistently excellent throughout May. A winter with heavy snow followed by cold spring temperatures creates runoff that extends through the hatch.

From July to September, the big browns seem to go into hiding. Except in the deeper pools in the canyon and in the rough water of the tunnel section near the Box, most fish taken by anglers are in the 6–9-inch range. In general, summer fishing is best in the morning, when mayfly hatches create some opportunities to catch fish with dry flies. High mid-day temperatures slow the action, but the trout in the deepest pools are always willing to try a streamer or nymph fished along the bottom. With the abundance of caddisflies, evening fishing can be good. Low flows in summer are an occasional problem, and thunderstorms often dramatically raise water levels and discolor the river for days.

Flows in the Guadalupe stabilize by September, and fishing can be excellent through the first cold spell in mid- to late October. In the fall, the trout are noticeably smaller than in spring. By December, the river as far down as the flats below the Box is usually frozen in for the winter.

While Deer Creek Landing and Porter receive regular plantings of rainbows, the New Mexico Department of Game and Fish manages most of the Guadalupe as a brown trout stream, and the river receives occasional plantings of brown trout fry. The river from the bridge at Porter downstream 1.3 miles to Llano Loco Spring is managed as Special Trout Water. Fishing is limited to the use of artificial flies and lures with single barbless hooks, and a two-trout limit is in effect. To maintain the high quality of the fishing experience on the Guadalupe, anglers are encouraged to treat the river as a no-kill area for brown trout.

RIO DE LAS VACAS

Location: Jemez Mountains, Santa Fe National Forest
Altitude: 7,200 to 9,000 feet
Type of Water: freestone, pools, stillwater
Best Times: May and September
Hatches: stoneflies, terrestrials
Patterns: parachutes, Letort Hoppers
Localities Map Location: D5
USGS Quadrangle Maps: San Miguel Mountain, Rancho del Chaparral

FISHING THE MEADOWS OF THE RIO DE LAS VACAS CAN BE A HUMBLING experience. The meadows are 7X-tippet country, where the fish demand perfect casts on the first attempt, absolutely drag-free drifts, and realistic flies. Here the stream is clear and shallow and filled with enough rocks and algae to foul any float. It is not fun fishing, but demanding and challenging.

At first glance, the Las Vacas does not look like much of a river. The road coming in on Forest Road 539 from the abandoned town of Porter appears to have more and deeper holes than the stream. During the low flows of summer, the river is less than a foot deep, the entire surface is broken with rocks, and the pools are few and far between.

Yet, as you walk or wade upstream, fish are continually darting for cover, some of them a healthy 11 inches long. In spite of its size and shallowness, the Las Vacas supports a fine population of trout.

Trout lies in the Las Vacas are often subtle. Some fish are in the shade under overhanging trees, but frequently they are hiding in a cave of algae, or under a rock that appears to be solidly based in the sand, or behind a tree root that didn't look as though it could be in water deep enough for fish. These less-than-obvious lies are usually discovered as you walk by them and spook the fish—and then it's too late!

Fishing the Las Vacas is never easy. To avoid spooking fish, long casts are required over a surface broken by many rocks. Each cast must be carefully planned: where to cast from, how far to throw the line, and between which rocks to let the cast fall. Once on the water, the line always wraps around a few rocks and retrieved flies are usually covered with algae. On those rare casts when everything goes just right, a sucker runs up to take the fly. Then, just as you move upstream and walk by the spot where you had been placing your fly, three nice trout dash for cover.

Aquatic insect life is sparse in the Las Vacas. Small populations of mayflies and stoneflies, including *Pteronarcys*, are found here. Pattern selection is not critical in the broken water; use high profile flies like Royal Wulffs or Brown Bivisibles, sizes 14–18. Terrestrials play an important part in the trout's diet in the meadows, where grasshopper and ant patterns are always a good choice.

The still-water bends in meadow sections of the Rio de las Vacas require special care. The water is 3–4 feet deep and very slow, with overhanging brush and submerged tree roots providing cover for the trout. Maintaining a low profile is important, and using a 7X-tippet is imperative. It is often necessary to use downstream casts that bring the fly to the fish before the leader. In such quiet water, no-hackle patterns are more effective. Parachute or Comparaduns are necessary to catch trout; bring a selection in gray and brown, sizes 16 or 18. Casts must be on target and land quietly on the water, an objective made difficult by overhanging trees. To catch a trout under these conditions is the mark of a fine fly fisherman.

Halfway between NM 126 and the ghost town of Porter, the Rancho del Chaparral Girl Scout Camp straddles the Rio de las Vacas. There is no public access here, so the camp divides the river into two sections. The upper section is reached from NM 126 about 10 miles west of Fenton Lake. Turn on Forest Road 539, which parallels the river for 3 miles to the Rancho del Chaparral boundary. This all-weather gravel road is in good condition when dry. There is private land in this area, so watch for posted land and respect the rights of the property owners.

The lower 4 miles of the Rio de las Vacas is reached from FR 376 at the confluence of the Las Vacas and the Cebolla, where the two streams join to form the Guadalupe. Travel on FR 539 can be difficult when the road is wet. Even when the road is dry, a high clearance vehicle is recommended, as two rough stream crossings are required to reach the meadows. Immediately above the confluence with the Cebolla, the water is very shallow. Drive beyond the second stream crossing, about 2.5 miles from FR 376, before getting out a rod.

Above Rancho del Chaparral, the meadows and canyon section of the Las Vacas hold both stocked rainbows and wild browns. The meadows just in from the turnoff from NM 126 provide fine fishing for rainbows, particularly in the early fall. Stream-bred browns are the quarry in the lower 4 miles of river.

The Rito Peñas Negras is the largest of the headwater creeks of the Rio de las Vacas. It is a quiet, still-water stream that flows for 10 miles through a long and lovely meadow. The little river sweeps wide and lazily meanders across the valley, creating an ample collection of river bends to fish. The Rito is narrow, from 2–4 feet across. The bottom is composed of mud-covered pebbles, and the banks are grasses and reeds. Attractive to trout, and thus also to the fly fishermen, are numerous undercut banks and deep holes. Rio Grande cutthroats, ranging from 7–12 inches, are well-hidden beneath the banks. The lower 2 miles of stream provide the best cover for the trout—deeper holes, more old beaver dams, more meanders—and offer the best fishing on the river.

As on the Rio de las Vacas, the stream is small, the water clear, and the fish spook easily. Fishing is tough. With such a narrow target, many casts land on the grass. Downstream fishing is difficult because of the muddy bottom and the clouds of silt that drift with the current as soon as you step into the water. Successful fishing on the Peñas Negras demands an ever-careful approach to the stream. Any shadow that crosses the water scares up a herd of suckers that quickly dart upstream, alerting the trout to the danger. To avoid shadows, try a cross-country cast to a likely trout lie from 10 or more feet back from the stream bank, allowing the line and part of the leader to rest on the grass as the fly falls on the water.

Mayfly nymphs, particularly *Baetis* and *Heptagenia*, and caddis larva are hidden under the rocks, but hatches are sparse. Terrestrials and dragonflies are important on the Peñas Negras. Fishing dragonfly nymph patterns through the riffles is an effective technique on summer mornings. Later in the day, try a Letort Hopper fished with an occasional twitch of the rod tip to give it some animation.

The lower stretch of the Rito Peñas Negras is reached by turning on Forest Road 103 from NM 126 about 12 miles west of Fenton Lake. You can find great meadows for camping just above the stream about a half mile up from its confluence with the Las Vacas. FR 103 is in good condition for a half mile, then turns rough but passable in dry weather. You reach the upper stretch of the river by taking the rough FR 117 about 9 miles from Fenton Lake or by traveling beyond FR 103 to FR 527 and turning east for 5 miles.

RIO FRIJOLES

Location: Jemez Mountains, Bandelier National Monument
Altitude: 6,800 to 8,000 feet
Type of Water: very small stream, pools
Best Times: April and May, September and October
Hatches: stoneflies, mayflies
Patterns: any attractor pattern
Localities Map Location: E5
USGS Quadrangle Maps: Frijoles, Bland

THE TINY RIO FRIJOLES HOLDS TWO ATTRACTIONS FOR FLY FISHERMEN: quiet solitude and brook trout. Fishing the Frijoles demands a hike of at least 3 miles and a 600-foot elevation change; the climb back out from the canyon floor is enough to discourage most anglers. Deep within the canyon, gullible brook trout will snatch anything that floats by. What the brookies lack in challenge they make up for in beauty: each fish is a trout palette of blended pastels.

Confined within a deep gorge for its entire length, the Rio Frijoles tumbles from its headwaters on the Cerro Grande to the Rio Grande. The geologically young canyon—it is less than a million years old— has completely carved its way through Bandelier Tuff, a rock made of fragments of volcanic ash that was spewed out during the eruption of the Valles Volcano. The result is a mountain in reverse. Cool and damp, the bottom of Frijoles canyon supports fir and spruce forest and a flowing stream; high above, the drier mesa tops are covered with junipers, piñons, and ponderosa pines. The Anasazi Indians used the lower Frijoles to irrigate their fields, and their homes were in the cliffs overlooking the river. The upper Frijoles has remained isolated and wild, protected by 600- to 800-foot canyon walls.

Reaching the stream requires no small effort. The trail upstream from the Bandelier Visitors Center, past the ruins of the ancient Tyuonyi Pueblo and beyond Ceremonial Cave, enters the wilderness area about 2 miles from the parking area. This route requires less walking and virtually no elevation gain, but few fish are found in the lower canyon and tourists often crowd the trail. A better trail begins at Ponderosa Campground, a quarter-mile east of the junction of NM 4 and NM 501 near Los Alamos. The Upper Crossing of the Frijoles is 2 miles from the trailhead and 600 feet below it. For strong hikers, another alternative is to begin at the Apache Springs trailhead. Leave one car at Ponderosa Campground and drive another to the trailhead located on the left side of NM 4 about a mile west from its junction with NM 501. Following the easy trail past the springs, you will reach the canyon edge in 3 miles. From here it is 800 feet straight down to the river. Fish downstream to Upper Crossing and hike out to Ponderosa Campground. It is 8 miles of walking, but the effort will bring you a fine wilderness angling experience.

The Rio Frijoles is never more than 3 feet wide, and it runs shallow with few deep holes. The entire stream is brush covered with willow, alder, elder, oak, locust, pine, spruce, and Douglas fir. Casting is impossible except for short roll casts in rare spots, and getting a fly on the water is always difficult. The clear, cold water supports a rich diversity of aquatic insects.

The Frijoles is loaded with brook trout, although rainbows and cutthroats are also found here. The small brookies are literally in every possible lie, and more. As you walk along the water, their shadows dart in all directions as they swim in desperate circles looking for escape. As they bolt for cover, they even bounce off your shoes. There are so many fish that a fish will be there to take any fly that floats on the water. It is almost impossible not to catch fish here.

When fishing the Frijoles, leave your waders at home. Wear shoes that will be comfortable during the hike into the canyon and assume they will get a little wet. With so much stream-side vegetation, an 8-foot rod is the maximum length advisable. For this kind of wilderness fishing, leave your vest behind and carry only a day pack with a rod, a box of flies, a spool of 5X tippet, an extra leader, and a pocket knife. Fly selection on the Frijoles is relatively unimportant. Royal Wulffs, Humpys, Adams, and Elk Hair Caddis in sizes 16 or 18 are sufficient.

The traditional upstream cast does not work well on a small stream like the Frijoles—too many "casts" end up in the trees. Downstream is the only way to go. Brook trout are much less wary than browns or rainbows, and an effective technique is to drop or swing a fly onto the water in front of you and let the current pull it downstream. Brookies will take a fly even when they can see the fisherman. The largest trout I have taken on the Frijoles, an 11-inch brookie, took a fly drifted to him while I was straddling the stream in full view. The line snagged on a low branch and the fly stopped 4 inches from the fish. I shook the line loose, the fly resumed its drift, and the trout still took it!

Royal Wulff

The section of stream between Upper Crossing and the trail down from Apache Springs offers the most solitude and the best fishing. An added attraction in this area is a series of old beaver ponds located near the descent from Apache Springs, about 2 miles upstream from Upper Crossing. Runoff is usually not a problem, and the Frijoles opens up in early April when other streams cannot be fished. The deep and shady canyon keeps the water cold throughout the summer, so fishing remains good through the fall. During holiday weekends, when other New Mexico rivers are crowded, try a quiet day on the Frijoles.

In early 1990, small quantities of pesticides were detected in the lower Frijoles. To avoid potential problems, the Park Service has closed the Frijoles to fishing from Ceremonial Cave to the Rio Grande; the stream above Ceremonial Cave remains open. Resolving the problem is likely to take several years. If you plan to fish the Frijoles, call Bandelier National Monument to find out the current status of the stream.

PERALTA CREEK

Location: Jemez Mountains, Santa Fe National Forest
Altitude: 7,500 to 8,500 feet
Type of Water: small freestone stream with pools
Best Times: September
Hatches: small stoneflies, mayflies
Patterns: Adams, Grizzly Wulff, Royal Wulff, Renegade
Localities Map Location: E6
USGS Quadrangle Maps: Redondo Peak

ON THE SOUTHEAST FLANK OF THE JEMEZ MOUNTAINS, PERALTA CREEK holds a B+ strain of Rio Grande cutthroats. This represents a relatively pure population (with A+ being the most pure) that shows few visible or genetic signs of hybridization with rainbows. The New Mexico Department of Game and Fish has evaluated the cutthroat population in Peralta Creek, and it appears to be both healthy and stable. A few years ago, Peralta Creek was managed as catch-and-release water; currently, there are no special regulations on the river.

Isolation has helped the cutthroats thrive in Peralta Creek. The single road into Peralta Canyon is rough, rutted, and long. Access is on Forest Road 280, off of NM 4 about 15 miles west of Los Alamos. The turnoff to the gravel road is well-marked. The first 2 miles of the road are deceptively easy. The last 4 miles are difficult, and a four-wheel drive vehicle or mountain bike is highly recommended. The rough section begins at a road junction at the top of the hill, about 2 miles from NM 4. Stay right on FR 280. About 6 miles in from NM 4, the road descends into a small ravine; beyond this point the road is impassable. Park at the ravine, and follow the signs down the hill a quarter-mile to Peralta Creek, where a trail follows the east bank of the river. It is possible to fish upstream for about a mile to a steep box canyon or downstream for 4 miles, where trout are limited by the ephemeral nature of the stream.

At most 4 feet wide, Peralta Creek is a small freestone stream that drops an average of 600 feet per mile. Pools are common, and the water is clear and cold all year long. The canyon bottom itself is wooded, and the stream is lined with brush and trees. But the vegetation is not very thick, and short casts are possible in most places along the creek.

The Rio Grande cutthroats who inhabit the small headwater creeks are small. Eleven inches is a great fish, and 14 inches is a monster. Light tackle is all that is required, and short rods (less than 8 feet) make casting easier under the trees. In spite of the stream's small size, it is often easiest to cast from the middle of the stream; hip waders or wet wading are recommended.

Although they are less vulnerable to a fly than brook trout, Rio Grande cutthroats are aggressive feeders who will strike at almost anything that drifts by with a natural-looking float. Thus, fly selection on Peralta Creek is not critical. An Adams, Grizzly Wulff, Elk Hair Caddis, Renegade, and Royal Wulff, sizes 14–18, are all effective when presented with a drag-free float. Casting into the heads of pools usually brings a strike. The best spots are the 2-foot-deep holes that are scattered along the entire creek near the undercut banks. Cast upstream above the hole, and allow the fly to drift on the fastest current over the deep water.

Peralta Creek drains a small watershed, and flows can be extremely variable. Runoff comes early, usually before the road into the creek is open. Adequate flows occur in late April and early May. By June, low flows make fishing difficult. Summer rains increase the flow volume again, but waiting until September guarantees a pleasant trip.

Fishing for Rio Grande cutthroats doesn't hold the challenge of casting to a wild brown trout; the attraction of this kind of fishing is quite different. When I land a cutthroat, admiring the red, yellow, and orange colors that quietly blend across the trout's belly and back, I can sense the wild past of the southern Rockies. This fish is the local native, the fish that trappers like Peg-leg Smith, William Wolfskill, and Kit Carson caught in the 1830s. The cutthroat is my link to the pristine wilderness that has vanished in northern New Mexico. So I treasure each fish for giving me this sense of past, a feeling that I want to share with my children and grandchildren. With each cutthroat I release, I hope that other anglers fishing Peralta Creek or any of the other cutthroat streams in New Mexico and Colorado will also help these fish maintain their tenuous hold on survival.

CHAPTER NINE

Small Rivers of the Taos Area

Taylor Streit

LITTLE RIO GRANDE WATERSHED

Location: Sangre de Cristo Mountains, Carson National Forest
Altitude: 7,000 to 10,000 feet
Type of Water: beaver ponds, small runs, freestone
Best Times: May to August
Hatches: midges, terrestrials
Patterns: Black Ant, Royal Wulff, Elk Hair Caddis, Green Drake
Localities Map Location: F4
USGS Quadrangle Maps: Ranchos de Taos, Shady Brook

THERE IS ONE PROBLEM WITH FLY-FISHING THE small rivers of the Little Rio Grande watershed—brush. The vegetation at streamside can be thick, and it usually is. In his book *If Mountains Die*, Taos author and fly fisherman John Nichols aptly describes the Little Rio Grande: "Even walking up the middle of the stream, . . . overhanging trees and brush make casting a fly nearly impossible. At its worst, the river is masochistic trout fishing at its best." Willows line the rivers' lower miles. Upstream, overhanging alder, oak, pine, fir,

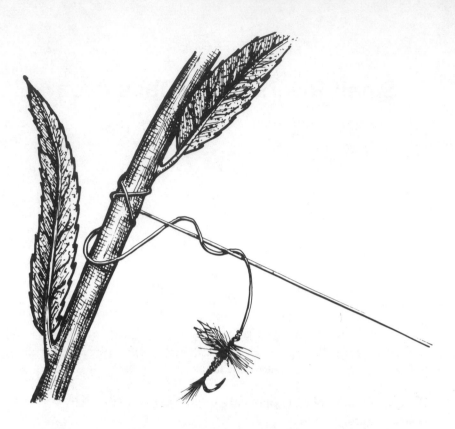

and spruce follow the rivers' every meander. In the rivers' uppermost reaches, meadows and beaver dams open up the banks, but casting a fly almost anywhere on these streams is difficult and sometimes impossible. A windy day in spring can quickly turn your casting into a nightmare of tangles.

The Little Rio Grande, also known as the Rio Grande del Rancho, is a small river that flows west from the Sangre de Cristo Mountains near Taos. With its tributary streams, the Rio Chiquito and Rito de la Olla (also known as Pot Creek), the Little Rio Grande offers cold, clear water that is perfect for trout. Sharing many characteristics, the three streams are like a matched set. Flowing through gently falling, steep-sided valleys, all three are found entirely in the Carson National Forest. From the headwaters at around 10,000 feet, the three streams join within a few miles of Taos at the 7,000-foot level. With plenty of trout, beaver ponds, and easy access on gravel roads, the Little Rio Grande watershed deserves fly fishermen's attention.

The Rio Chiquito, Rito de la Olla, and the Little Rio Grande are best described as freestone streams with many pools. The water is always cold and, by early summer, extremely clear. The streambeds are composed of small rounded rocks, with many stretches of silt and sand. All three streams remain small along their entire lengths, ranging from 5 to 15 feet across. The Little Rio Grande is the widest of the three, particularly in its lower stretch, where it swells to 20 feet across. Holes 3 to 4 feet deep are found along the streams, and only hip boots are needed for wading. Felts can be helpful in spots, but they are generally unnecessary.

Because of the watershed's relatively small size and its low elevation, these three streams have an early runoff. High water begins in March and usually subsides by early to mid-May. Runoff coincides with the windy season, creating nearly impossible conditions for fly-fishing from March through mid-May. From June through August, these streams are in their prime: summer flows are moderate, water temperatures are cold, and insects are plentiful. The low flows of September and October, combined with the wary nature of the brown trout, can make fall fishing very difficult. Consider these late spring and summer streams.

The Rio Chiquito is the smallest of the three rivers in the Little Rio Grande watershed, varying between 2 and 6 feet wide. The entire river from its confluence with the Little Rio Grande upstream to the 9,000-foot level is thickly covered with brush, making this the most difficult of the three rivers to fly-fish. The stream opens up in the high meadow about 12 miles from the paved road, and that is where Rio Grande cutthroats are found.

The Rito de la Olla also presents problems with thick brush and overhanging trees. A foot or two wider than the Rio Chiquito, this little river holds a few more open spots for casting, particularly above 8,000 feet. In such clear water, it is difficult to cast far enough so as not to be seen by the trout. Rito de la Olla is known for its beaver ponds. If you come in from NM 518 on FR 438, the first ponds you'll see are about a mile from the highway. The ponds are most numerous upstream from a point 5 miles in from NM 518. Old beaver dams create many-channeled flats; the active dams form clear, still-water ponds, with tree roots and brush providing excellent cover for trout.

The lower Little Rio Grande meanders through a wide valley. A mile east from the Carson National Forest boundary on NM 518 is a series of active beaver ponds that hold both rainbow and brown trout. The river upstream to the Tierra Azul Picnic Area is lined with willows, but there are few overhanging branches. Above the picnic area, the river flows through the Fort Burgwin Research Center, where it is closed to fishing. More public water is reached by way of Forest Road 439, just beyond the bridge on NM 518. For the first mile, the river flows through an open valley, and angling pressure is heavy here. Upstream, the valley narrows and the forest closes in on the stream. The brush is not so heavy as on the other two streams of the watershed, but there are many overhanging branches, tree falls, and log jams to frustrate presentations.

Wild brown trout are an angler's mainstay in the Little Rio Grande watershed. Although somewhat small, the browns are plentiful. Because of the small size of the streams and the clarity of the water, these trout are very wary and cautious approach is always appropriate. Hatchery rainbows, stocked from the highway crossings and the picnic area, are found in the stretch of the Little Rio Grande that parallels Highway 518. A nearly pure population of Rio Grande cutthroat is found in the upper meadows of the Rio Chiquito. Although this population is not protected by regulations, anglers on the Rio Chiquito are encouraged to release all cutthroats. Most fish in the watershed are small, averaging about 9 inches. Cutthroats in the Rio Chiquito have a maximum size of 11 inches; rainbows and browns in the beaver ponds can grow to 14 inches or more.

The cold, clear water of the Little Rio Grande watershed provides ideal habitat for a rich diversity of aquatic insects. Small populations of *Hesperoperla* and *Pteronarcella* stoneflies are found in the fast water. Large clinger mayflies (*Rhithrogena* and *Epeorus*) live on the underside of rocks at about 8,000 feet. Green Drakes (*Ephemerella*)

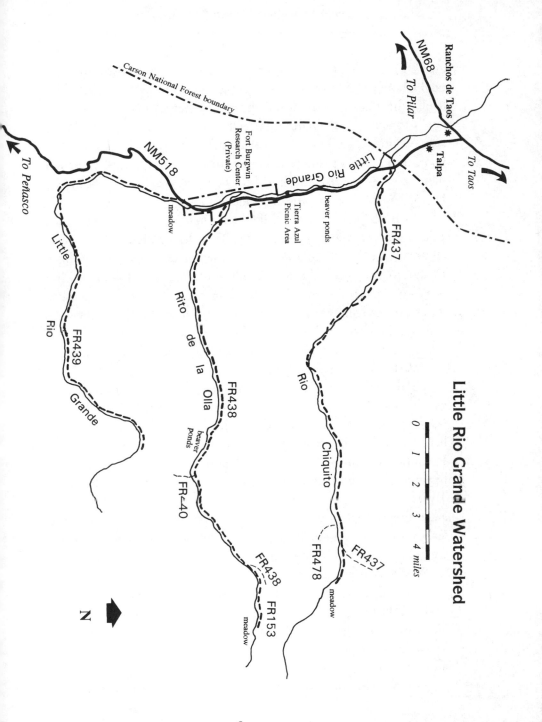

Little Rio Grande Watershed

To Pilar

NM68

Ranchos de Taos

To Taos

Talpa

Carson National Forest boundary

NM518

Fort Burgwin Research Center (Private)

Little Rio Grande

meadow

Tierra Azul Picnic Area

beaver ponds

FR437

To Peñasco

Little

Rio

FR439

Grande

Ritto de la Olla

FR438

beaver ponds

FR440

Rio

Chiquito

FR478

FR437

meadow

FR438

FR153

meadow

0 1 2 3 4 miles

N

are also common. Curiously, with the exception of midges, there are no big hatches. Throughout the spring and summer, terrestrials seem to play the major role in the diet of trout in these rivers.

Attractor mayfly patterns do well on these streams. Royal Wulffs, sizes 14 and 16, bring trout to the surface in the faster flowing sections, and a size 14 Adams may work in the beaver ponds. Parachute flies, size 14–18, tied in olive, brown, or gray, are most effective in fooling the fat little browns that hide among the tree roots in the still water behind the beaver dams. If Green Drakes are on the water, a size 12 or 14 Green Wulff is a perfect fly. Terrestrial patterns work best on all stretches of the three rivers. In summer, grasshopper patterns bring trout to the surface in the grassy areas, particularly on the lower Little Rio Grande. Try a Letort Hopper, sizes 12 or 14, fished as close to the grassy banks as possible. Pulling the fly off the bank onto the water will fool the larger brown trout in the meadow stretches. Probably because they imitate hoppers as well as caddis, Elk Hair Caddis in sizes 14 and 16 also catch a lot of fish.

Skillful fly fishermen can avoid some of the frustrating problems caused by the heavy brush. Start with the correct tackle: a small, lightweight 7-foot rod and short leaders of less than 7 feet. Always remember that stealth and patience are the primary rules on these streams, so practice roll and sidearm casting before you get to the river. Always be aware of the backcast, or your fly will end up in the hungry branches. Try fishing downstream with a long line, between 15 and 25 feet, and allow the current to pull a fly over a suspected trout lie. If all other techniques fail, you might try dapping: without really seeing what you are doing, lower the fly over the streamside brush to a suspected trout lie. It might just work!

Mosquitoes can be bothersome along these streams, especially near the beaver ponds on Rito de la Olla and the lower Little Rio Grande. Biting deer flies are an additional annoyance. Insect repellent is standard equipment in this area. Beware of rattlesnakes, which are common on all the streams below 7,500 feet.

All three of the rivers in the Little Rio Grande watershed are par-

alleled by roads that can be reached from Ranchos de Taos via NM
518. Forest Road 437 provides about 11 miles of access to the Rio
Chiquito. Turn off NM 518 at the well-marked junction just east of
the village of Talpa. Rito de la Olla enters the Little Rio Grande near
the Fort Burgwin Research Area, about 3.5 miles from the Carson
National Forest boundary. Turn at Forest Road 438, which follows
the valley of Rito de la Olla for about 9 miles. NM 518 follows the
Little Rio Grande from the Carson National Forest boundary to the
river crossing a few miles above the Fort Burgwin Research Center.
You can park at numerous pull-offs and at the Tierra Azul Picnic Area.
You can reach the upper river by turning east on Forest Road 439,
which intersects the highway about a half-mile beyond the bridge. The
three Forest Roads into the Little Rio Grande Watershed are well-
maintained. When they are dry, the roads are easy to travel in any
vehicle. During the spring and after summer rains, the roads become
muddy and may require four-wheel drive.

There are no developed campgrounds in the Little Rio Grande
watershed. Primitive camping is permitted in all areas, but good sites
are limited and usually found only in the lower stretches of each stream.

RIO HONDO

Location. Sangre de Cristo Mountains, Carson National Forest
Altitude: 6,400 to 10,000 feet
Type of Water: shallow runs, deep pools, freestone
Best Times: May, September to October
Hatches: caddis, stoneflies
Patterns: Royal Wulff, Humpy, Renegade, Elk Hair Caddis
Localities Map Location: F4
USGS Quadrangle Maps: Arroyo Seco, Wheeler Peak

THE RIO HONDO IS REALLY TWO RIVERS IN ONE. THE UPPER RIVER IS A
mountain stream that flows through a narrow, wooded canyon. The

lower river, from the town of Valdez to the Rio Grande, flows across the Taos Plateau and is usually hidden within a deep rocky canyon. Both stretches offer fine fly-fishing of totally different character.

The upper Rio Hondo flows within the Carson National Forest, with the headwaters at 11,000 feet in the high country to the north of Wheeler Peak. Above Twining, the upper forks hold a few cutthroats, but the water is generally too cold to hold many fish. The forks join near the Taos Ski Area, creating a stream about 15 feet across. Nine miles of public water begin below the ski area. Private land borders the Rio Hondo from just above Valdez to the Rio Grande, and anglers should stay out. Fortunately, permission is not required to fish the best water on the river, the lower mile near the John Dunn bridge.

The upper and lower Rio Hondo are easily reached from Taos. For the upper river, travel north from Taos on US 64, turn right on NM 150, and follow the signs to the Taos Ski Area. You can reach the lower river from the town of Arroyo Hondo, about 8 miles north of Taos on US 64/NM 522. Just past the bridge over the Rio Hondo, turn left on a gravel road and go west for about 3 miles to the John Dunn bridge.

Both stretches of the Rio Hondo hold plenty of trout—about 500 per mile on the upper river and perhaps 1,000 per mile on the lower. The richness of the stream may be explained by effluent from the Taos Ski Area, where the sewage treatment plant is permitted to release controlled amounts of effluent each day. The amount of added nutrient seems perfect for the stream, resulting in healthy algae growth that feeds and protects a large population of insects, which in turn support the great numbers of trout.

The Rio Hondo is clear but shallow and is never more than 30 feet wide. The upper river is a freestone stream with many riffles, with few pools above the forest boundary. It is not the easiest place to fly-fish. Banks are brush-covered, casting is difficult, and round, algae-coated boulders on the bottom make every foothold tenuous. The lower reaches of the river have more of a riffle-and-pool structure. The banks are open there, and casting presents few problems.

Both sections of the river can be fished in hip waders. Felt-soled boots make wading in the lower section easy, but they will not help much on the slippery rocks of the upper section. In the brushy areas of the upper river, a lightweight rod less than 8 feet long is helpful. The open, lower section allows a freer manipulation of line, and longer rods will make casting easier.

In the mountain section, the Rio Hondo is stocked with rainbows. Wild browns and some cutthroats inhabit the upper reaches of the river. A few rainbows drift down to the lower section, where they grow as long as 16 inches. The majority of trout in the lower river are wild browns, ranging from 9–14 inches; in deeper pools, an occasional fish reaches 18 inches.

To fish the upper Rio Hondo, look for the deeper pools. Search for spots with slow water and the least amount of brush. Avoid shallow runs where hungry trout have little protection, and concentrate on the deeper riffles and runs.

As with other high-altitude streams, runoff on the Rio Hondo begins late and extends into June. The water is high during runoff, but it remains clear. Temperatures are cold, the fish are sluggish, and fishing is slow. The best months on the upper Rio Hondo are July, August, and September. Even when valley temperatures rise into the 90s, water in the upper river remains cold.

The upper river produces no prolific insect hatches. On summer evenings, significant numbers of midges and small, sporadic hatches of mayflies are on the water. The best flies are attractor patterns that are easy to see in rough water, such as the Humpy, Royal Wulff, and Renegade, all in size 14. In slow-water pools, a more realistic pattern, such as an Adams or Cahill, may work the best. Although the best fishing is with dry flies, the larger browns can be caught by floating size 12 or 14 Hare's Ear Nymphs through the deeper pools.

At an elevation of nearly 6,000 feet, the season begins early on the lower Rio Hondo. By mid-May, the water is high but clear and is warm enough for the trout to become active. Fishing is good from May to October. During summer, the air can be hot and fishing slow unless it rains. Winter fishing is possible on warm afternoons, when air temperatures are in the upper 40s.

The best water is fished by starting at the confluence of the river with the Rio Grande and continuing upstream as far as you can. Numerous pools and riffles hold plenty of fish, and if you thoroughly cover the water you will take many fish. The best fishing is on summer evenings, when small mayfly and midge hatches give some action and the caddis hatches are often heavy. Elk Hair Caddis in sizes 14 and 16 are an excellent choice on July evenings.

Taos is a fine base of operations for fishing the Rio Hondo. Camping is not permitted on the private land surrounding the lower river, but a number of pleasant little Forest Service campgrounds along NM 150 are right on the upper river.

Unfortunately, the fine fishing currently found in the Rio Hondo may be short-lived. The Taos Ski Area has applied for a permit to allow increased discharge from the sewage plant, which could disrupt the river's delicate balance. Although the current level of waste disposal into the Rio Hondo seems to have improved the fishing, additional discharge levels could lead to a nutrient imbalance that could reduce or destroy the fishery.

RIO PUEBLO DE TAOS

> **Location:** Orilla Verde Recreation Area, formerly Rio Grande
>   Gorge State Park, Pueblo de Taos Indian Reservation,
>   some private land
> **Altitude:** 6,100 to 10,000 feet
> **Type of Water:** pocket water, riffles, flats
> **Best Times:** September and October
> **Hatches:** stoneflies, midges
> **Patterns:** Brooks Stone, Bitch Creek, Kaufmann Stone,
>   Midge Clusters
> **Localities Map Location:** F4
> **USGS Quadrangle Maps:** Taos SW

FLOWING FROM ITS HEADWATERS AT BLUE LAKE HIGH ABOVE THE VILLAGE
of Taos, the Rio Pueblo de Taos skirts the edges of its namesake to join
the Rio Grande 6 miles above Pilar. On days when the Rio Grande is
too muddy or too warm for fishing, the Rio Pueblo de Taos can save
the day. And in the fall, the river is excellent brown trout water.

Almost the entire Rio Pueblo de Taos is on private property. Above
the town of Taos the river is on the Taos Pueblo Reservation and is not
open to public fishing. Below Taos the river is on private land that is
not posted, giving anglers access to the stream.

Surrounded by high lava cliffs, the Rio Pueblo de Taos is fantastic freestone and pocket water that holds stocked rainbows and a fine
population of wild brown trout. The rainbows are in the 9–11-inch
range, and the browns range from 8–16 inches. The stream averages
15 feet in width, and depths range from 6-inch riffles to pools of 8 or
10 feet. Rocks from the lava cliffs have tumbled into the stream, damming the flow to form small waterfalls and plunge pools. It is a rugged
area filled with potential hazards. Caution is required when moving
up or downstream. Although the rocks are slippery and the holes are
deep, wading is easy. Hip waders are perfect for this water, and felt-
soled boots are a great help on the slick rocks. The banks are lined

with rocks and a few willows, and casting distances are short, with backcasts staying generally snag-free.

The easiest access to the river is just above its confluence with the Rio Grande. You can park in the Bureau of Land Management's Orilla Verde Recreation Area (formerly Rio Grande Gorge State Park) and at a few narrow pullouts along the gravel road that runs high above the river. You can fish the river by walking upstream along the rugged canyon trails. The farther upstream you go, the better the fishing will be. Begin fishing at least a quarter-mile above the Rio Grande.

You can also reach the river from NM 570, about 2 miles from its junction with NM 68. Turn right (north) and follow a dirt road toward a gravel pit. Stay on the east side of the gravel pit, and park at the end of the road. From here it is about one-quarter mile down a small side canyon to the river. From this point, you can fish the riffles and flats upstream or the pocket water downstream.

The Rio Pueblo de Taos is perfect habitat for large stoneflies, and fishing stonefly nymphs is the key to success on the river. Brooks Stones, sizes 8 or 10, tied in brown are effective fish-getters throughout the year; Bitch Creek and Kaufmann Stone patterns are also good choices. When searching for fish, you need only a few feet of line to drift the nymphs through the pockets. Keep leaders short. A strike indicator will help you make certain the fly is drifting drag-free and will help you detect hits. Once a fish is on, the battle is not over. Landing bigger fish is difficult in the river's small pools, while you maneuver the rocky terrain bordering the river.

Runoff on the Rio Pueblo de Taos is a problem throughout the spring, and summer storms often muddy the stream for days. Conditions improve as fall approaches, and from September into October or even November is the perfect time to be on the river. Fishing remains good as long as water temperatures remain above 42 degrees. Overcast, cold, and snowy days are often the best on the Rio Pueblo de Taos, when catching 10 or more fish an hour is not uncommon. In addition to nymphs, Midge Cluster patterns are a good choice on winter afternoons.

To reach the Rio Pueblo de Taos from Santa Fe, take NM 68 north from Española about 30 miles to NM 570 at Pilar. Turn left and continue north about 6 miles to just past the Taos Junction bridge. Then park along the road and drop down to the river at any convenient spot. From Taos, go south out of town on NM 68 for about 8 miles to NM 570. Turn right on NM 570. This road soon turns gravel and clings to the cliff as it parallels the river.

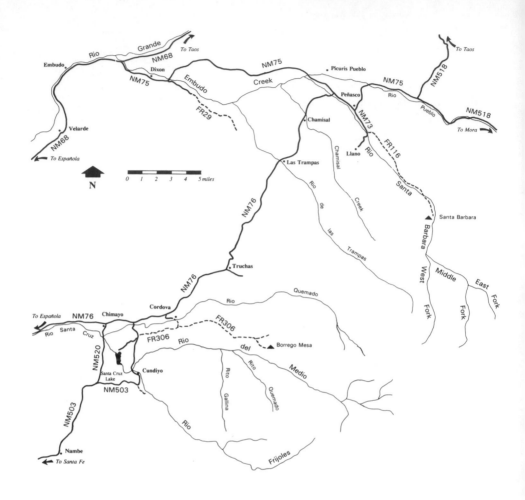

Embudo and Santa Cruz Watersheds

CHAPTER TEN

In the Middle: Rio del Medio and the Embudo Watershed

RIO DEL MEDIO
Craig Martin

Location: Sangre de Cristo Mountains, Santa Fe National Forest
Altitude: 6,800 to 11,000 feet
Type of Water: freestone stream with many pockets
Best Times: June to mid-September
Hatches: Red Quill, Green Drake, Little Yellow Mayfly,
    caddisflies, midges,
Patterns: Red Quill, Light Cahill, Elk Hair Caddis, Royal Wulff,
    Black Ant
Localities Map Location: F5
USGS Quadrangle Maps: Chimayo, Sierra Mosca, Truchas Peak

THE RIO DEL MEDIO (ALSO CALLED THE RIO Medio) flows from the sharp ridge between Pecos Baldy and the Truchas Peaks to the village of Cundiyo. Access to the river requires a long ride on gravel roads, then a steep, half-mile hike to the river. To reach the Rio del Medio from Santa Fe, go north on US 64-285 to Nambe, then turn right on NM 503. Travel east on NM 503 about 11 miles, passing the turnoff to Chimayo to the village of Cundiyo. In Cundiyo, NM 503 crosses the Rio Santa Cruz, where it is formed by the confluence of the Rio Frijoles and the Rio del Medio. Private land borders the rivers from the bridge upstream about 3 miles, so do not try to fish upstream from here. Instead, continue on NM 503 about 3 miles to just past NM 596 (the turnoff to Santa Cruz Lake). Turn right on FR 306. After the Santa Fe National Forest boundary, FR 436 takes off toward the river, but private land again bars access to fishing. Continue on FR 306 until it intersects with FR 435 about 9 miles from the paved road. A short ride up FR 435 will take you to Borrego Campground and the trailhead to the Rio del Medio. Park here, but be aware that the Forest Service cautions that vandalism is more common in this area than in more popular campgrounds.

At the trailhead, the river is still a half mile away and 500 feet below. The Rio Medio Trail (No. 155) drops to the river, then parallels the stream, climbing slowly over the next 7 miles to the ridge that divides the Pecos and Rio Grande watersheds. With the exception of the half-mile climb back from the river, it is an easy walk through narrow canyons and wide meadows. The entire river provides excellent summer fishing. Although the trail is popular for hiking and backpacking, few fishermen are found so far from the road.

A longer hike into the Rio del Medio is the Borrego Trail (No. 150). The trailhead is at the signpost on FR 306, about 7 miles from NM 503. From trailhead to river is about 2 miles, with the first 1.5 miles on the level mesa top and the last half-mile a 500-foot descent to the river. Solitude is guaranteed at Borrego Crossing. The Borrego Trail also provides access to the major tributaries to the Rio del Medio, the Rito Gallina, and the Rito Quemado.

The Rio del Medio is a typical Sangre de Cristo river, with cold, clear water and a rounded rock and pebble bottom. Near the campground, the river is 6–12 feet wide. As you hike upstream, the Rio del Medio quickly narrows as tributary streams join the river from the side canyons. The river is shallow with runs of less than 6 inches, but there is an abundance of deep holes and pockets and downed trees add to the number of trout lies. The banks are brushy, and the river often flows entirely beneath a canopy of tree branches. Casting is difficult in spots, but there is usually enough room for a roll cast. The river is easy to wade, but hip waders are necessary to protect against the cold water.

The New Mexico Department of Game and Fish stocks rainbow trout in Santa Cruz Lake, and fishermen catch a few rainbows in the lower miles of the Rio del Medio. Wild brown trout in the 8–11-inch range can be found throughout the river. Rio Grande cutthroats provide the most excitement on the upper Rio del Medio. The cutthroats are uncommonly strong fighters, making it difficult to land a fish in the smaller pockets. They are found in most places where the water is more than a foot deep. Nine-inch fish are common, with the deeper pools holding cutthroats as long as 14 inches.

The Rio del Medio supports aquatic insects that are typical on the west slope of the Sangre de Cristos. Large stoneflies (*Hesperoperla*) are found in the fast-flowing stretches, providing a sparse hatch in late May; smaller stoneflies are uncommon. A rich diversity of mayflies is found here: *Rhithrogena, Epeorus, Heptagenia, Baetis,* and, in the lower miles of the river, *Ephemerella grandis*. Morning Red Quill (*Rhithrogena*) hatches are sparse throughout the summer. In July and August, Little Yellow Mayfly (*Epeorus*) hatches provide good fishing at mid-morning. The best hatch on the river is the evening Western Green Drake hatches in August, but these large mayflies are found only in the lower 5 miles of the river, which are difficult to get to. Caddis are more common evening hatches to fish.

The trout of the Rio del Medio can be selective feeders. Size 14 Elk Hair Caddis and Yellow Humpy and sizes 12 or 14 Royal Wulff are good searching patterns, but they are often rejected by the fish. When a trout refuses an attractor, turn to a pattern that matches the naturals. Red Quills, size 14, match the *Rhithrogena* hatch, and Light Cahills and Grizzly Wulffs, sizes 16 or 18, match the *Epeorus*. If no hatch is in progress, terrestrials are the best choice. Black Ants, sizes 12–16, are consistent summer fish-getters on the Rio del Medio.

Spring runoff lasts from mid-April through late May and brings high but clear water to the Rio del Medio. In the upper canyon, cold water temperatures keep fishing slow until late June. *Epeorus*, caddis, and midge hatches stimulate the fish throughout mid-summer. In late July and throughout August, warm mid-day water temperatures slow the trout's feeding, but morning and evening are excellent times to be on the river.

Floating Ant

The Rio Frijoles is a sister stream to the Rio del Medio, flowing parallel about 5 miles to the south. The rivers share many characteristics, including their general nature, the timing of runoff, and the insects that live in the water. The Frijoles is smaller than the Rio del Medio, however, ranging from 3–8 feet wide. Like the Rio del Medio, the Rio Frijoles holds rainbows in the lower miles; browns and cutthroats share the water in the upper reaches. Fishing for these trout requires the same techniques and fly selection as on the Rio del Medio.

It is even more difficult to get to the Rio Frijoles than to the Rio del Medio. As a result, the Frijoles is a quiet stream that sees very little angling pressure. To reach the river from Nambe, head toward Cundiyo on NM 503. Two and a half miles beyond the intersection with the road to Chimayo, turn right on an unmarked dirt road (just beyond milepost 10). When dry, this road is passable with any vehicle. Continue about a mile to a "Road Closed" sign, and park here. Walk about a mile on the closed road past the private property to where the road drops to the river. From here, the Rio Frijoles Trail (No. 154) follows the river into the heart of the mountains. The first few miles are in a narrow canyon, but the stream opens into meadows about 6 miles from the trailhead. If you are looking for solitude and some great cutthroat fishing, try the Rio Frijoles.

The Rio Santa Cruz is formed when the Rio del Medio and the Rio Frijoles join at the NM 503 bridge in Cundiyo. The Santa Cruz runs through a narrow, rocky canyon for about a mile before emptying into the waters of Santa Cruz Lake. The mile-long stretch holds stocked rainbow and wild brown trout, alternating between freestone and pocket water. The rocky river is 10–15 feet wide, with shallow runs and many holes 4–10 feet deep. Both wading and casting are easy.

From the parking area at the bridge on NM 503, a trail leads down the canyon, in some places high above the water and in others leading through the willow thickets at stream-side. The trail crosses the stream many times but does not extend all the way to the lake. It is best to hike as far as you can and then fish upstream back to the bridge.

The Santa Cruz is heavily fished, and the trout are quite demanding. In the faster water, high floating dry flies can be effective during the morning and evening. Elk Hair Caddis perfectly matches the color of the granite rocks in the stream bottom and is nearly impossible to see on the water; instead, try Royal Wulffs and Humpys sizes 14 or 16. Grizzly Wulffs, sizes 14 or 16, are effective attractors during the summer because of the abundance of Little Yellow Mayflies in the river. During late summer evenings, there are sparse hatches of Western Green Drakes, and Green Wulffs or Green Paradrakes, sizes 10 or 12, will bring the fish to the surface. If dry flies are not working, try fishing nymphs deep through the pockets and holes. Muddler Minnows work well in the deepest places.

The Santa Cruz above the lake lies below 7,000 feet, making it a fine spot for winter fly-fishing. Runoff comes in April and May, and by mid-May conditions are perfect. By mid-June, the temperatures are too high for mid-day fishing. Summer also brings the possibility of flash floods, which can ruin fishing for weeks. The Santa Cruz is again perfect in the fall, and conditions can be good on the river through December.

RIO SANTA BARBARA
Taylor Streit

> **Location:** Sangre de Cristo Mountains, Carson National Forest
> **Altitude:** 8,600 to 11,000 feet
> **Type of Water:** freestone, pocket water, small pools
> **Best Times:** July to September
> **Hatches:** stoneflies, mayflies, caddisflies
> **Patterns:** Humpy, Royal Wulff, Elk Hair Caddis, Black Ant
> **Localities Map Location:** F5
> **USGS Quadrangle Maps:** Jicarita Peak, Pecos Falls

DURING THE EARLY NINETEENTH CENTURY, FUR TRAPPERS RANGED FROM their base in Taos into New Mexico's Sangre de Cristo Mountains searching for beaver. The mountains they explored were vast, untouched by signs of men, and rich in natural resources: timber, game, and beaver skins. The canyons were quiet and lonely. As the trappers worked their way up the icy streams, setting or checking their traps, they found trout: the Rio Grande cutthroat.

The Rio Santa Barbara watershed has not changed much since Kit Carson, Ewing Young, and Pegleg Smith worked in these mountains. This pristine watershed has rarely seen a logging truck, and it remains full of wildlife, tall trees, and crystal water that still holds native trout. The Rio Santa Barbara watershed lies within the Carson National Forest. Most is protected within the Pecos Wilderness, so it is likely to retain its pristine nature. By walking away from your car, you can still find solitude here. And the river offers some of the best cutthroat fishing in New Mexico.

Of all the river canyons in New Mexico, I think the Rio Santa Barbara is the wildest and the loveliest. The canyon is full of surprises, and the hike to the fishing water is as pleasant as the angling itself. The trail is cool and shady, always within earshot of the singing stream. From the upper meadows on the West Fork, the view of the high divide is astonishing. The silent basin is home to deer, elk, mountain lions, beaver dams, and a large variety of birds. Once while resting several miles upstream from the campground, a small junco flew out of nowhere and landed on my knee, to sit and share my rest for quite some time.

Three major forks drain the Rio Santa Barbara basin, each heading in the high divide that includes North Truchas and Chimayosos Peaks. From 12,000 feet, the forks of the Santa Barbara flow north through the wilderness, joining at 9,000 feet. Downstream, near the town of Peñasco, the Santa Barbara joins the Rio Pueblo to form the Rio Embudo.

Santa Barbara Campground is well situated for a base camp. You can reach the campground from NM 75 in Peñasco. About a mile east of the junction of NM 75 and NM 76, NM 75 turns sharply to the left. At this point, continue straight onto NM 73. In another 1.5 miles, watch for a turn to the left marked Forest Road 116, where there is usually a sign pointing to Santa Barbara Campground. This well-maintained, all-weather road deadends in about 4 miles at the campground.

Three miles of the Santa Barbara below the campground are open to fishing. This section parallels the road, and you get to the river at the bridges or by taking a short hike from the road. The lower stretch is brushy, so it is best to start fishing upstream from the first bridge. The river flows adjacent to the campground, where fishing pressure is heavy. Although this area is heavily fished, it still holds plenty of trout.

The upper Santa Barbara and both forks are accessible only by trail. Hiking along the river is difficult, but a well-maintained, easy-to-follow trail parallels the river to the forks. Beginning at the campground, Forest Trail No. 24 follows the river through conifer forest and meadow and into the Pecos Wilderness, climbing gently from 9,000 to 9,400 feet over the first 2 miles. The trail divides at the junction of the Middle and West forks of the river, with each trail branch following one of the forks. The Middle Fork trail follows the stream to its source near a high divide. The cutthroat fishing is exciting here, but the high stream gradient on the Middle Fork makes catching the fish difficult. The West Fork is a more gentle stream, often flowing through steep-sided meadows. Beaver ponds are common in the open areas, holding large browns and cutthroats. The summer combination of cut-throats, wildflowers, sunshine, and spectacular peaks makes the 4-mile hike to the West Fork well worth the effort.

The Rio Santa Barbara is crystal clear, and the water is always cold. The river averages 20 feet in width and about 18 inches in depth; the forks are about half the size of the main river. Because the water-shed has seen little disturbance from logging, the flow is quite stable, although heavy rains during the summer may swell the river for brief periods. All sections of the Santa Barbara system are freestone stream with some pocket water. The surface is churning almost everywhere. There are small pools on the lower stretches, and beaver ponds in the meadows of the West Fork offer welcome relief from the relentless fast water. The stream bottom is mostly round cobbles and rocks. Wading can be tough and felts are recommended, along with neoprene hip waders to protect against the cold water. The stream banks are forested, and vegetation hinders casting from the banks; it is best to cast from the middle of the stream.

Rainbow trout are stocked from the bridges and at the campground, and browns are found throughout the Santa Barbara. The river's great-est attraction is its cutthroats, and this is perhaps the best cutthroat stream in New Mexico. Although they are found in the entire river, cutthroats are more numerous in the upper reaches of the forks. Most wild fish are between 8 and 14 inches, and many reach 11 inches. The river holds perhaps 800 fish per mile.

As you might expect in a stream with such a large trout popula-tion, the Rio Santa Barbara is rich in insect life. The largest insects are Golden Stoneflies, *Hesperoperla*, which hatch in late May. Many species of mayflies are found on the stream: *Rhithrogena, Epeorus, Heptagenia*, and *Ephemerella*. Caddis hatches are reliable in the eve-ning during July and August. Ants and beetles are available to the trout under streamside vegetation. Hoppers are limited to meadow areas in the wilderness section of the river.

The Santa Barbara sometimes seems to be one long, choppy rif-fle. The water runs fast, and the surface is broken everywhere. Follow-ing a fly on the surface is difficult, and high-floating, easily seen dry flies work best. The fish have little time to inspect a fly, and most of the trout are not selective feeders. Three kinds of flies are sufficient for most dry-fly-fishing on the Santa Barbara: Royal Wulff, size 14; Elk Hair Caddis, size 14; and Humpy, sizes 12 or 14. For particularly tough fish, try a brown or black ant pattern. Nymphs fished in the deeper pools will also produce fish. Hare's Ear patterns in sizes 12 or 14 are the most consistent producers.

Most of the Santa Barbara watershed is above 9,000 feet. The streams drain predominantly north-facing slopes, creating not only con-sistently cold water but also a late runoff. Runoff begins as soon as the river opens up in April and continues through June and sometimes into July. The water remains clear during runoff, but high water on the already swift stream combined with the very low water tempera-tures makes fishing very difficult. The prime season for fishing the Santa Barbara is from July through September. In mid-summer, when other streams are warm and the trout seem uninterested in feeding, the Santa Barbara remains cold and the trout stay active. The abun-dance of insects adds to the excitement.

Humpy

Throughout the fishing season, the high elevation and cold wa-ter combine to make slow mornings on the Santa Barbara. This is an afternoon river, and the action generally picks up as the day wears on. Midges start to appear by afternoon. Mayfly hatches occur almost ex-clusively late in the day. Terrestrials may be active all day and are of-ten the best patterns to fish in the morning.

To fish the Santa Barbara, wade up the middle of the stream. Because of the broken surface, you won't see many fish, but they are there, hiding in the rocks. Cover the water thoroughly, casting to all likely lies. Don't be afraid to drift a fly over a good spot many times; the fish also have trouble seeing in this water and may miss the fly on the first passes. With such crystal-clear water, fishing upstream is necessary. Because the river flows north, anglers often have the sun in their eyes during summer afternoons; hats and sunglasses will help. Avoid low water situations during late September and October, since the fish spook easily in the clear water.

The Rio Santa Barbara is a special place. Don't spoil your experience here by fishing near the campground. Walk upstream along the trail, at least to the first bridge, before fishing. This narrow canyon section, from the bridge to the forks, is excellent water. Either the Middle Fork or the West Fork are worth your attention, and the beaver ponds on the West Fork about 4 miles from the trailhead are guaranteed to be exciting. Fishing the Santa Barbara is a total experience: leave your car behind, and discover some of the nineteenth century wilderness that remains in New Mexico.

EMBUDO CREEK
Craig Martin

Location: Bureau of Land Management
Altitude: 5,900 to 7,500 feet
Type of Water: pocket water, pools, riffles
Best Times: March to mid-April, September to November
Hatches: caddisflies, stoneflies
Patterns: Humpy, Elk Hair Caddis, Bitch Creek, Woolly Bugger
Localities Map Location: F5
USGS Quadrangle Maps: Trampas, Velarde

EMBUDO CREEK IS CREATED WHERE THE RIO PUEBLO JOINS THE RIO

Santa Barbara. The Embudo is a rugged and swift stream. For most of its length, it flows through a narrow granite canyon, churning and tumbling its short course to the Rio Grande. The river's name, which means funnel, comes from the shape of its canyon. For fly fishermen, the name might have been derived from the many narrow chutes of water created as the river is squeezed between two rocks.

The Santa Barbara and Rio Pueblo drain the Sangre de Cristo Range before joining just below Peñasco. In contrast, the Embudo flows amid flat-topped mesas, orange badlands, sagebrush, and dry arroyos, an unlikely place for a cold-water trout stream. Hidden at the bottom of a 400-foot canyon, the Embudo is quite a pleasant surprise.

Few fishermen know of the Embudo, and fewer are willing to take the time to get there. The lower Embudo, below the tunnel mouth, is private land. There is no access to the river below the canyon, nor is access permitted into the canyon from its mouth. The canyon itself is a mixture of BLM and private land. The private land is not posted, and access is permitted.

To reach the canyon of the Embudo from either Santa Fe or Taos, take the Dixon turnoff from NM 68 and travel east on NM 75. Go 3 miles east through Dixon, and turn right on an unmarked, unnamed paved road located just before the bridge crosses the Embudo. This road is paved for the first 2 miles and then becomes a graded dirt road that is easily passable in good weather. Continue past the end of the pavement for just under 2 miles, and look for a poor road heading to the left (north) and climbing a mesa. Pull off the main road onto the dirt track, and park before crossing the arroyo. Hike along the road, climbing about 300 feet to the mesa top. Then follow a faint dirt track that leads to a narrow slot in the granite wall. Walk through the gap and continue on the trail, which leads to the Embudo about 400 feet below.

At the bottom of the canyon, fly fishermen find a boiling, wild brown trout stream. The wild browns are mostly in the 8–11-inch range, with an uncommon fish reaching 18 inches. The stream is between 12 and 16 feet wide and from 6 inches to 6 feet deep. This is fast pocket water, with many stretches of current that are too swift for trout.

Where the gradient levels, short, shallow riffles and 12-inch-deep runs are the rule. The myriad deep pockets and slow water pools hold most of the Embudo's trout. Many pockets have too much white water for easy fishing, but the pools always hold trout in their depths. The water temperature in the Embudo is cold, even into mid-summer.

Embudo Creek is an easy stream to fish in terms of wading and casting. The banks are composed of rock, with scattered trees overhanging the stream and few willows to snag a backcast. Shallow water makes wading easy, and there are frequent places to cross the stream. The bottom is granite boulders, cobbles, and pebbles with occasional areas of deep silt. The granite boulders in the canyon are slick, the currents swift, and the holes deep, so hip boots and felts are recommended. Moving up or downstream requires boulder hopping, frequent stream crossings, and infrequent climbs away from the water, all of which can be quite tiring. Remember to save enough energy for the climb back to your vehicle. Because of the low elevation, remember to watch out for rattlesnakes in the area.

Because the watershed is large, runoff affects the Embudo for a long time. High water from the Rio Pueblo comes in mid-April, and runoff from the Santa Barbara continues to fill the Embudo until late June. The water is generally clear during runoff and sections of the stream can be fished, but wading conditions can be quite hazardous during the spring.

Because of the fast currents, the Embudo is a caddis and stonefly stream, although clinger mayflies, such as *Heptagenia* and *Epeorus*, are also found here. In such an isolated stream with little fishing pressure, the browns are not selective feeders. The keys to success in fishing the Embudo are getting the fly to the fish and making the fly float correctly.

Fishing the Embudo before runoff in March and early April is a perfect way to end the long winter. Fish during warm and clear days, waiting for afternoon temperatures to rise to stimulate feeding. Small stonefly nymphs and caddis larva patterns drifted through the pockets and pools will attract trout. If there are adults on the water, dry-fly-fishing with high floating attractors is possible. Cast size 12 or 14 Humpys, Irresistibles, or Elk Hair Caddis into the quieter water at the edges of pockets and current tongues.

Fall fishing with nymphs and streamers is excellent on the Embudo. In the fall, it is especially important to get the flies to the bottom of the pockets and pools where the fish are holding. Using weighted patterns may not be enough in such quick water, and a small split shot clamped on the leader about a foot from the fly will help sink the nymph to the bottom. Fish large stonefly nymphs, Pheasant Tails, or caddis larva deep along the rocks. Woolly Buggers fished with split shot and a slow twitch retrieve will bring many strikes in the deeper pools.

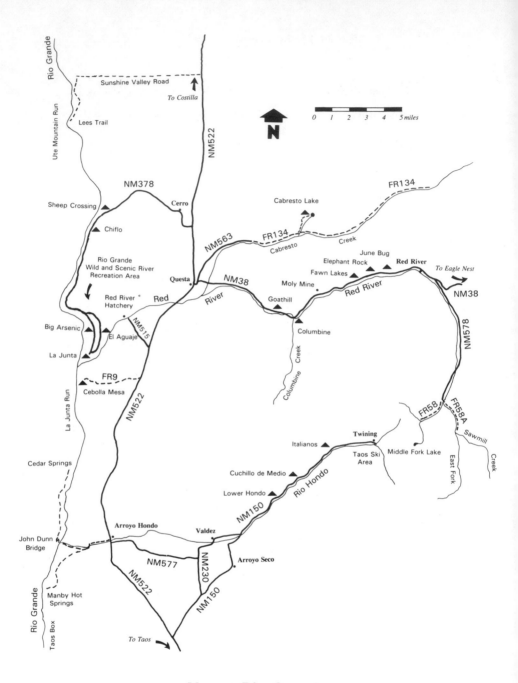

Upper Rio Grande

CHAPTER ELEVEN

The Great River: Rio Grande

RIO GRANDE GORGE
Van Beacham

Location: north-central New Mexico, Bureau of Land
      Management National Wild and Scenic River
Altitude: 6,200 to 7,400 feet
Type of Water: freestone, deep pockets, and holes to broad
      riffles and pools
Best Times: March to early May, September to October
Hatches: caddisflies, Blue-winged Olive, Ginger Dun, midges
Patterns: Elk Hair Caddis, blue, olive, and ginger Compara
      Duns, Griffith's Gnat, snowfly patterns,
      Peacock Nymph
Localities Map Location: F3, F4
Other Maps: Ute Mountain, Sunshine, Guadalupe Mountain,
      Arroyo Hondo, Los Cordovas, Taos SW

AFTER FLOWING FROM ITS HEADWATERS IN THE
San Juan Mountains of south-central Colorado, the
Rio Grande flows across the San Luis Valley to enter
the Rio Grande Gorge a dozen miles north of the New
Mexico-Colorado state line. The 70-mile Gorge is part of
the Rio Grande Rift, one of the largest tectonic cracks in the

world. The Rio Grande (or Great River) has carved out the majestic basalt canyon walls and has shaped the diverse ecology in the Gorge. When Congress passed the Wild and Scenic Rivers Act in 1968, the Rio Grande Gorge was named the country's first National Wild and Scenic River.

The history of the Rio Grande as a trout fishery has been one of change, and it is still constantly evolving. The river's future as a trout fishery remains uncertain as urban and agricultural interests increase their demand for water. Nevertheless, the Rio Grande remains New Mexico's wildest trout stream, with untold numbers of lunker browns, rainbows, and cutbows in a magnificent setting that is unique in the Rocky Mountain region.

Except during runoff, the river can be fished year-round. The best seasons in the Gorge are just before and after runoff, using nymphs and dry flies, and from September through November, using streamers, nymphs, and dries. During the winter, midges hatch daily and dry-fly-fishing is exciting and challenging. Northern New Mexico experiences a drought an average of one year in five, and fishing is superb during the prolific caddis hatches in May and June (when runoff should occur).

The Rio Grande is rarely crystal clear because of the geology of the area and the amount of its water that is irrigation return. The cloudiness deters many fishermen, even though trout can be seen rising when visibility is only 6 inches. The trout, like the river, are temperamental. A host of anglers, some with many years of experience, have tried to figure out the river, only to find the only rule here is constant change. The challenge is what keeps most fly fishermen going back time after time, even if they don't always catch fish. Sooner or later, they know they will hit the right place at the right time and have a tremendous day of fishing.

The Gorge is just the place for anglers who appreciate the finer aesthetics of fly-fishing and enjoy *trying* to catch trout almost as much as catching them. The Rio Grande Gorge is difficult to fish, but there are optimal times, places, and fly patterns that can enhance your opportunities for successful trips.

Anglers who fish the Rio Grande must meet the Gorge on its own terms. It is rough and potentially dangerous country, with rocky and steep terrain. In many places, the only access points require anglers to drop 800–1,000 feet to the river and then, when they are tired after the day's fishing, to climb back out. Thunderstorms, snowstorms, rattlesnakes, and uncertain footing are all potential hazards of a trip into the Gorge. Be sure to prepare carefully for any trip between the basalt walls.

The Gorge has been designated Special Trout Water from the Colorado state line to Taos Junction bridge, or the entire Gorge. Anglers on this stretch are limited to four trout, with no size limit. There are no restrictions on tackle. As in all Special Trout Waters, fly fishermen are encouraged to help preserve the high quality of the Rio Grande fishery by releasing all their catch.

The Gorge has four distinct sections, each with different characteristics: the Ute Mountain Run, the Wild and Scenic River Recreation Area, the La Junta Run, and the Taos Box.

Ute Mountain Run

From the beginning of the Gorge at Lobatos bridge in southern Colorado to Lees Crossing just north of Questa is a 35-mile stretch of water known as the Ute Mountain Run, named for the huge lava dome on the east rim of the river. Unlike most of the Gorge, this northernmost section is wide and not very deep. The banks of the river are lined with grass, willows, cedars, and an array of other riparian vegetation. The area is a sanctuary for wildlife, including bald and golden eagles, deer, elk, antelope, geese, ducks, and herons. The Ute Mountain Run is perfect for anglers who are willing to fish hard for a few big trout and who appreciate fishing in one of the wildest and most untouched stretches of river in the United States.

Within the Ute Mountain Run, the river is gentle with broad

riffles and pools, long flats, and boulder-strewn areas near the bends in the channel. In low water, when the fishing is best, wading is easy and hip waders are sufficient. Lug soles are best on the sand and silt, and you can walk in and out of the Gorge with them on.

The water quality and quantity of the Ute Mountain Run is not as good as the other sections of the Gorge, because most of the flow is irrigation return water from the farms in Colorado's San Luis Valley. The return water warms the river considerably, and on hot summer days it warms even more as it passes through the numerous shallow flats. The farther south you go, the cooler the water gets, as springs feed the river and as the steepening walls of the Gorge shade the water.

Although trout are present from the headwaters of the Rio Grande through the end of the Gorge, the San Luis Valley portion of the river is considered a warm water fishery by the U.S. Fish and Wildlife Service. Warm water species of fish are found throughout the Gorge, but their number decreases farther downstream.

The many flats on this section of the river reduce the protective cover available for trout, and most trout are near the boulder-strewn areas and the riffles at the heads of pools. There are fewer trout per mile here than in the other sections of river, but they are much larger, averaging 16–20 inches, with many browns weighing over 5 pounds. The trout are large for two reasons. First, although the habitat will not support a large number of trout, it is excellent for big trout in small numbers, with an unlimited supply of crayfish, minnows, suckers, chubs, carp, northern pike, and other trout. Second, this part of the river is hard to get to, with only a handful of primitive trails at the end of long, bumpy, and rocky roads. Many people have fished the river, but have failed to understand the fishery and ended up catching suckers and carp. This has given the Ute Mountain Run the reputation of having few or no trout.

Nevertheless, just before and after runoff and during the fall, fly-fishing the Ute Mountain Run is productive. In summer, water temperatures are too high and water quality and quantity are too low; in winter, water temperatures are too cold and access is very difficult. During spring, Peacock nymphs, large Hare's Ear, and Woolly Buggers fished deep in the riffles can be effective during the day, and caddis pupa or Elk Hair Caddis can produce nice fish in the evening. During the fall *Baetis* and midge hatches, look for large trout cruising the flats, sipping on the abundant, tiny flies, and use appropriate dry-fly patterns. When no hatch is in progress, actively strip a large, heavily weighted streamer through the heads of deep pools and along the side of boulders. But be ready! There are many browns up to 30 inches long in this section of river that, if you set the hook too hard, can even break 0X tippets. The lack of good spawning areas below the Ute Mountain Run induces many browns to move upstream during the fall to spawn in the many gravel bars, increasing the chances of catching some big browns.

Access to the Ute Mountain Run is from the Sunshine Valley Road north of Questa and the Jaroso Road in the town of Costilla. Both roads are long, about 8–10 miles, and rough. Once you reach the rim of the Gorge, you can follow the rim road north or south. Four-wheel drive is recommended because of the huge boulders, deep ruts, and slick mud when it rains. South of the Sunshine Valley Road, near Latir Canyon, is Lees Trail, the best trail into the Gorge and the easiest one to get to. North of Sunshine are a few primitive trails that are identified by only small pullouts and parking areas. The road and terrain get rougher near Ute Mountain, but the river has more boulders and bends there, creating more holding water. For more information on access, get in touch with the BLM Taos Resource Office or Los Rios Anglers in Taos.

When the water is high enough, it is possible to float the river, but be ready for a long and rugged trip. The only put-in is at Lobatos bridge in Colorado, and the only take-outs are south of Ute Mountain and at Lees Trail. Both take-outs require you to pack gear out of the Gorge. These trips can take from 3–10 days, depending on how much fishing you want to do. At least one commercial outfitter takes float fishing trips in this section. For information, get in touch with the BLM in Taos.

Rio Grande Wild and Scenic River National Recreation Area

From Lees Trail south to the Red River confluence is a 15-mile stretch known as the Rio Grande Wild and Scenic River National Recreation Area (NRA). This is the most developed section of the Gorge, and there are good roads, numerous trails, camping facilities, and a visitors center. The trails are well-marked and appear on most maps, and each is about one mile from rim to river with numerous switchbacks. La Junta, Little Arsenic, and Big Arsenic trails are interconnected at the bottom, and at the top of most trails are campsites with water and restrooms. Developed campsites with tables and shelters are found along the river, giving the angler over 4 miles of streamside access.

In the NRA, the Gorge is deep and narrow at the bottom, with basalt boulders all along the bank, some as big as small houses. Wading is difficult and dangerous, especially in the pocket water where the water can go from 1 foot to 10 feet deep in a single step. Use hip waders with lug soles to get around the edges. This stretch has a nice combination of riffles, pools, and boulder-strewn pocket water. Much of it cannot be run by anyone but the most experienced river rafters. Numerous springs enter the river here, cooling it and adding to the water's quality and quantity. The browns, rainbows, and cutbows are abundant and the boulders provide plenty of cover.

Except during spring runoff, the NRA can be fished year-round. Springs keep the river cool in the summer and warm in the winter. Just before and after runoff, caddis hatches provide excellent opportunities for nymph, wet-fly, and dry-fly fishing for trout 12–20 inches. The most popular and productive pattern during this time is a Double Hackle Peacock, fished on the bottom or wet just under the surface. Additional hatches include Pale Morning Duns in June and July, Ginger Duns in July and early August, Blue-winged Olives in early spring and fall, and enormous midge hatches in the winter, when fishing near the springs can be especially good.

The best fishing for large browns is during the fall. Use Blue-winged Olives during the *Baetis* hatch and hopper patterns and streamers the rest of the time. Because of the numerous boulders, streamers are the best way to cover the water. On good days, the excitement is constant as browns lash out for your streamer from behind every rock.

To get to the NRA from Taos, go north on US 64 and continue straight on NM 522 when US 64 turns west to the High Bridge. North of Questa, take NM 378 and follow the signs to the visitor center.

La Junta Run

The La Junta Run is 10 miles of the Rio Grande from its confluence with the Red River downstream to the John Dunn bridge. It is a remote stretch of river with limited access. Because of its many insect-producing riffles, La Junta was once considered the best fly-fishing stretch on the river. During the late 1970s and early 1980s, several pipeline breaks spilled raw tailings from the molybdenum mine near Red River into the river, severely damaging insect populations. During the second half of the 1980s, the river made a remarkable comeback and is now producing good hatches and sometimes excellent fishing for trout that average 16 inches or more.

The best fishing is usually just before and after runoff, during the famous caddis hatches. Double Hackle Peacocks work best during the day, and emergers and Elk Hair Caddis work well in the late afternoon. Evening dry fly fishing remains good throughout the summer, especially when skittering a caddis pattern along the edges of the river.

In August and September, hoppers drifted along the bank work well, particularly a little known pattern, the Desert Hopper (black body with a red underwing). As in most of the Gorge, streamers are effective just about any time, particularly during the fall brown trout and winter cutbow spawning runs. During the winter, midges are abundant and Griffith's Gnats drifted downstream into the tails of long pools can produce excellent results.

Wading in La Junta is easy, but basalt boulders line much of the banks, making it difficult to get around with felt soles. Hip waders with lug soles are best, and anglers can wear them to hike in to the river.

Three locations provide access to La Junta. The top end of the run is at the river's confluence with the Red River. From Taos, go north on US 64 and NM 522. Turn left (west) at FR 9, south of Questa, to Cebolla Mesa Campground, where a 1.5 mile trail descends to the river. To reach the south end of the run, take NM 522 and turn left on a gravel road at Arroyo Hondo, just after crossing the Rio Hondo. Drive 3 miles on this road to the John Dunn bridge, the only place where you can drive to the river in the interior of the Gorge.

The best fly-fishing on this stretch is at Cedar Springs, located in the middle of the run where there are numerous long riffles with good populations of trout. Access to Cedar Springs is across the John Dunn bridge and up the west side to the rim. Follow the rim road north for 3.5 miles, staying on the best road until it ends at the Cedar Springs trailhead.

The La Junta Run can be floated year-round, but you must pack in your gear at Cebolla Mesa. Also, several commercial outfitters float this section. Get in touch with the BLM in Taos for permits and information.

The Taos Box

From John Dunn bridge to Taos Junction bridge is 18 miles of river called the Taos Box. Known for its tremendous whitewater during runoff, this section of the Gorge sees heavy use by rafters. Consisting of riffles, pools, deep holes, and pocket water, the variety of this stretch is limitless, but access for anglers is not. Experienced guides use several over-the-boulder trails, but there are only three easy access points. One is at John Dunn bridge at the north end of the Box. You can reach the south end where NM 570 crosses the river in the BLM's Orilla Verde Recreation Area. The wild middle section of the Box is reached 2 miles south of the John Dunn Bridge on the old Stage Coach Road at Manby Hot Springs. Take the gravel road west of Arroyo Hondo for about 1.5 miles, and then turn south on another gravel road, traveling about 2 miles to the rim, where a steep trail leads down to the river.

Like other sections of the Rio Grande, fishing is best before and after runoff using caddis imitations and in the fall using streamers or a Blue-winged Olive during hatches. In the winter, midge fishing at John Dunn bridge and Manby Springs can be excellent, particularly after the sun drops behind the rim.

The Taos Box is best floated by experienced rafters only. If the water level is less than 500 cfs at John Dunn bridge, rafting is not advised. Several commercial outfitters float this stretch, and 4 days are required to fish the stretch effectively. Get in touch with the BLM in Taos for permits and information.

The Rio Grande Gorge is one of the nation's wildest and most unfished rivers, offering year-round fly-fishing in unmatched scenery. Winter, spring, summer, or fall—pockets, riffles, or holes—the Rio Grande Gorge offers something for every fly fisherman.

RIO GRANDE NEAR PILAR
Barrie Bush

Location: Rio Grande Wild and Scenic River (BLM)
Altitude: 5,700 to 7,500 feet
Type of Water: pocket water, riffle-run-pool
Best Times: October and November, January and February
Hatches: Little Brown Stoneflies, caddisflies, Blue-winged
        Olives, midges
Patterns: Little Brown Stonefly Nymph, Brown Hackle Peacock
        Nymph, Green Caddis Larva, Elk Hair Caddis,
        Blue Dun, Midge Clusters
Localities Map Location: F3, F4, F5
USGS Quadrangle Maps: Ute Mountain, Sunshine, Guadalupe
                       Mountain, Arroyo Hondo, Los
                       Cordovas, Taos SW

Although the Rio Grande Box offers spectacular fall fishing for large trout, getting to the river can present a problem. The Rio Grande Gorge near Pilar, however, gives fly fishermen easier access to fishing the Great River. This section of river, formerly the Rio Grande Gorge State Park, is managed by the Bureau of Land Management and is now called the Orilla Verde Recreation Area. The area is located just off of NM 68 between Española and Taos. Coming from the south, turn on NM 570 at the village of Pilar, about 20 miles south of Taos. From Taos, turn west on NM 570 about 6 miles south of Ranchos de Taos. This road becomes gravel and narrows as it follows the gorge of the Rio Pueblo de Taos to the Rio Grande. Currently, there are no fees for day users in the area. Plenty of streamside parking is available, and there are developed campsites within the Gorge.

Near Pilar, the Rio Grande flows in a deep gorge carved through the black basalt of ancient lava flows. NM 570 parallels the river for 6 miles, eliminating the need to hike from the top of the mesa 1,000 feet down to the river. The river is 50–75 feet wide and from less than one to 10 feet deep. The ideal conditions for trout fishing are at depths of 18 inches to 6 feet and at low flow rates of 300 to 600 cfs. Throughout the Gorge, classic trout stream conditions prevail in a series of riffle-run-pool sequences. A small section of pocket water below the junction with the Rio Pueblo de Taos adds still more diversity to the river.

This section of the Rio Grande has easy access. Wading is easy on the gravel and small cobble bottom, although deep silt accumulates where currents are slow. Caution is advised throughout, particularly in sections with rocky banks, steep drop-offs into deep water, and swift currents. Hip boots are acceptable, but chest waders allow access to more of the river. During the cold winter months, chest waders are necessary to protect against frigid water lapping into waders. Felts are an asset on the slippery gravels, but cleats are unnecessary. Casting clearance is excellent throughout. Banks vary from rocky with overhanging willows to grassy areas with willows. In most places, it is possible to wade the shallows away from potential snags. Many gravel bars allow fishermen to wade across the entire river.

The entire Rio Grande holds fantastic numbers of trout. Most of the fish in this area are stocked rainbows running in the 8–20-inch range, and 12–14-inch fish are not uncommon. Brown trout are found here, too, ranging from 6–18 inches, with an occasional lunker caught in the fall. The browns are mostly wild fish, but brown fingerlings are occasionally planted in the river. The cutthroat-rainbow hybrids that are sometimes caught can exceed 20 inches.

The Rio Grande gives its resident trout a diversity of insects. Caddis larva and stonefly nymphs are abundant in the riffles throughout the year, and caddis and stonefly adults are important at specific times during the year. Mayflies and midges are generally found in the quieter water. Each insect group assumes prominence for a few weeks during the year, and these famous hatches provide the year's best fishing.

As the water begins to warm in mid-March and early April, stoneflies living in the riffles become more active, producing a nice hatch of small brown stoneflies of the family Capniidae, the winter stoneflies. Fishing size 10 or 12 dark brown stonefly nymphs along the bottom of riffles is the most effective way to fish this hatch, both when adults are seen on the water or vegetation and before the hatch is underway. Use a small brown Brooks Stone or a Rosborough Little Brown Stonefly to imitate the naturals.

The spring caddis hatch provides exciting fishing in late March and April, usually reaching its peak around the third week of April. Then the afternoon air is thick with millions of insects, with the rocks and streamside vegetation covered with millions more. The hatch moves upstream from day to day, covering the distance from near Velarde to the Rio Grande Box in about two weeks. In all types of water, from pocket to pools, the size 16 or 18 caddis bring large trout to the surface. An angler's favorite caddis pattern will be perfect for fishing the hatch, with Elk Hair Caddis patterns seen more often than others. This hatch is so stimulating to the trout that they will often take dry flies even if the water is muddy from snowmelt.

The Blue-wing Olives (*Baetis* sp.) present the most significant mayfly hatch on the Rio Grande. These small mayflies are on the water during both the spring and fall, with peak emergences throughout April and from late September to mid-November. The hatch begins each day at around 1 p.m. and continues sporadically until the sun retreats behind the canyon walls. Match this hatch with a size 16–20 Blue-winged Olive or Blue Dun. Emerger patterns are often more effective than dry flies. Casting to rising fish will increase your chance of success.

Surprisingly, mid-winter is the best time for dry-fly-fishing on this section of the Rio Grande. January and February afternoons bring the river's most famous hatch: snowflies. The snowflies are small midges with black bodies and gray wings that cover the surface in the millions. The late afternoon midge hatches mean excellent dry-fly-fishing for anglers who know a few basic rules for catching winter trout. Using midge clusters is the first key to success; fishing traditional midge patterns will not always work.

Fore-and-Aft Midge Cluster

Midge cluster patterns are relatively new. Two simple patterns require only black thread and grizzly hackle on a size 12 or 14 hook. For the Fore-and-Aft Midge Cluster, simply take several turns of a grizzly hackle around the aft end of the hook shank, wrap the shank with black thread, then repeat with another grizzly hackle at the front. For a Parachute Midge Cluster, wrap the hook with black thread, tie on a small hank of white calf tail as an upright wing in the center of the shank, and wrap a grizzly hackle around the wing parachute-style. Clip the calf tail wing short, leaving just enough to help make the fly more visible on the water.

The second key to successful winter fishing on the Rio Grande is timing. Although it runs counter to logic, the best times to fish the river are when the sun is off the water and the air is cold. Water temperatures reach their daily peak at about 4 p.m., about the time the sun is disappearing behind the walls of the Gorge. This is when the fish begin to take midges on the surface; fishing before the sun is off the water is often futile. Winter fishing on the Rio is also good on overcast days and when it is snowing.

When fishing midge clusters, cast only to rising fish. Be sure to look for rises at the tail end of pools and in the slicks immediately above the riffles. Float the fly in the current seams and in the eddies where the naturals accumulate. Fish can often be found in shallow water and close to the shore. A cautious approach to these shallow areas will prevent scattering the spooky trout. Look for places to cross the river, and fish tight against the west bank. A downstream drift is most effective. Watch carefully for a rise, as the take is often subtle.

Some patterns used on the Rio Grande are effective all year long. When searching for trout in riffles, stonefly nymph patterns, sizes 10 or 12, are always a good choice. Another fine choice for fishing riffles is a Green Caddis Larva in sizes 12–18. A local favorite searching pattern that does not imitate a specific insect is the Brown or Gray Hackle Peacock, sizes 10–16. The fly is simply a 2X-long hook wrapped with a peacock herl body and either brown or grizzly hackle wound at both ends, sometimes tied with a red tail.

Nymph patterns should be fished deep in the riffles, runs, and pocket water. Currents on the Rio Grande are swift, and it is often necessary to add a small split shot to the leader—about a foot up from the fly—to sink flies quickly. Patterns dragging along the bottom are more likely to attract trout than those drifting at mid-depths. Fish the riffles thoroughly, covering all the water, making many casts before moving upstream.

Nymphs imitating mayfly species should be fished in the river's runs and pools. A collection of searching nymphs should include Hare's Ears and Pheasant Tails, sizes 14–20. These patterns are most effective when fished with a floating line and strike indicator in water between

18 and 36 inches deep. For best results, dead-drift the nymph as close to the bottom as possible.

Many anglers on the Rio Grande use streamers only in the fall, but they can be effective throughout the year. Woolly Buggers, leech patterns, and Muddler Minnows, sizes 6–10, can excite the larger trout. Fish streamers in shallow gravel areas near quiet water and around in-stream boulders. When using streamers, be sure to fish the complete cast; a trout will often take the streamer as it is hauled upstream.

As the snows of Colorado's San Juan Mountains melt in late April and May, runoff occurs on the Rio Grande in New Mexico. The high, muddy water usually begins around the first of May and continues through early July. Fishing throughout this period is poor. In summer, the river is muddied again by frequent rainstorms, and conditions remain marginal to poor throughout the warm months. Water temperatures often rise above 70 degrees in July and August, creating poor fishing conditions. For the best results in summer, fish during the early mornings and evenings and only when the water is clear.

Throughout the Orilla Verde Recreation Area, numerous spots hold plenty of trout. Try the short section of excellent pocket water above the Taos Junction bridge, the fine riffle-run-pool sequence above the stream gauge, and the narrow but deep channels around the small islands below the stream gauge. Also worthwhile is a slow drive on the road that parallels the river, keeping an eye on the stream and watching for rising fish.

The Rio Grande is an extremely moody river that can give even the best fly fishermen totally frustrating days. But the Rio can offer great rewards to those who can accept the poor days along with the good ones and who are willing to go often enough to hit the river when it is on. Especially during the winter, when dry-fly-fishing is at its peak, the river experiences surprisingly little fishing pressure. The Rio is an excellent quick getaway from anywhere in north-central New Mexico, providing welcome relief to the slow winter season. When the river is in a good mood, catching 10 fish per hour is not unusual. Rio Grande trout are very spunky, particularly the browns, which are strong fighters. For an afternoon of great fun, head to the river with a 3–5-weight outfit and use light tippets (5X–6X). If you keep in mind the simple rules for success and if the river is good to you, you will have a memorable day.

FLY-FISHING FOR NORTHERN PIKE ON THE RIO GRANDE
Jerral Derryberry

NORTHERN PIKE ARE NOT NATIVE TO THE SOUTHWEST BUT WERE INTRO-duced to the Rio Grande watershed by the state of Colorado. Successive generations of these fish spread downstream through the irrigation canals of the San Luis Valley to establish themselves in New Mexico from the Rio Grande Gorge to Cochiti Lake near Santa Fe. The result is one of the finest fast-water pike fisheries possible.

Pike grow fast and large. They average 22–30 inches, but in prime habitats they commonly reach 4 feet in length. One reason for the pike's rapid growth is their aggressive feeding style. The pike is a killing machine, whose nickname "waterwolf" is most appropriate. One 30-inch pike, for example, was found with a 20-inch fish in its stomach. Not only are pike cannibalistic, but they also eat chubs, carp, rainbow trout, brown trout, rodents, ducks, and almost anything else unlucky enough to float by.

Northern pike are primarily daylight feeders, attacking their prey from mid-morning until 11 a.m. and then from 1:30 p.m. until 4 p.m. Their favorite meal time seems to be 3 p.m. Most of the day the fish lie on the bottom of deep pools, looking like logs, waiting for a dawdling fish to wander by. If the water is clear, they will charge with incredible ferocity from the bottom to snatch a fish on the surface. Unlike most fast-water species, a pike will sometimes stalk its prey, following its meal to the surface or a vertical barrier before taking it. In

the evening, pike will move from deep pools into the shallows to inter-
cept trout that have gone there to feed.

Pike are seldom seen in the Gorge during the summer and fall.
In December, pike begin to appear in their spawning areas. The females are the first to arrive in the Gorge, with the axe-handle males
beginning to appear as March approaches. Toward the middle of March,
both males and females become ravenous and the fishing becomes
exciting.

The pike's predatory nature demands that fly fishermen use large
streamers that imitate forage fish. The streamers should be 6–8 inches
long, tied on 4X–6X long shank hooks, and heavily weighted to get
them deep into the pools. Barbs should be depressed so the hook will
penetrate the pike's tough cartilage mouth. Pike flies require plenty of
dyed bucktail and feather on top to keep them vertical and in appropriate color combinations to match the intended bait. (A sample pike
pattern can be found at the end of this chapter.)

Fishing for Rio Grande pike requires some heavy equipment. A
9-foot, 7 or 8 weight fly rod is recommended. Use weight-forward floating line, 100 yards of 20-pound backing, and about 10 feet of 0X leader.
A good pair of long-nose hook removers and a large net are necessary
to avoid the sharp teeth of a hooked fish.

The Taos Junction Bridge Pool and the other pools in the trout
waters of the old Rio Grande Gorge State Park are good places to look
for pike in the Rio Grande. Particularly promising are areas where the
deep water runs next to the bank. An effective technique for fishing
these pools from the bank is to stand on the deep side at the head of
the pool. Cast slightly up and across the current, mending the line so
that the streamer has the chance to drop deep into the water. As the
streamer swings across the pool, it will rise slightly in the current and
fall in the back swirl. Use a slow retrieve to imitate a wandering forage
fish. At the end of the retrieve, as the streamer approaches the surface
and nears the bank, be prepared to see what resembles a German Shep-
herd's face with a snake's body following the fly. The pike will wait just
long enough for your heart to get into your throat; then, as you choke

on your pulse, it will slam the fly. Now wait for what seems an eternity (really only about 2 seconds) before setting the hook. If you wait too long, you risk pulling the fly right out of the fish's mouth, as the pike will stop and open its mouth to take the victim head-first.

If a pike does not follow your streamer in or attack it on the swing, then lengthen the line by about 2 feet or take a step downstream and cast again. When a Northern Pike finally decides to have your streamer for lunch, well . . . enough said!

A RIO GRANDE PIKE STREAMER
Little Rainbow Trout

Hook: Mustad 79580, Size 2
Tail: 4 long, white streamer feathers and pearl crystal flash
Weight: Heavy lead on shank from directly above the point of hook to 1/4" from the eye of the hook; a second layer of lead from halfway forward to 6 turns from the front of the bottom layer
Body: White wool yarn well-picked out and wrapped to the end of the top layer of lead and held in check
Vail: A single lime-colored hackle on each side
Secondary wing: Brown bucktail set low (continue wrapping the body forward to the head)
Throat: Sparse white bucktail to point of hook
Under wing: Brown bucktail and peacock crystal flash
Main wing: Brown streamer feathers
Sides: Raspberry-colored streamer feathers
Notes: Sometimes full quill feathers, fluff and all, are used to keep the streamer vertical. To complete the assembly, attach a 25-pound test shock tippet using a Randle or similar knot at the eye and a surgeon's loop on the other end.

CHAPTER TWELVE

Red River Country

Van Beacham

Location: Carson National Forest, BLM Wild and Scenic River
Altitude: 7,000 to 12,000 feet
Type of Water: freestone, spring creek character
Best Times: mid-June to July, September to March
Hatches: Golden Stoneflies, Little Brown Stoneflies,
        Blue-winged Olive, caddisflies, midges
Patterns: Peacock Nymph, Sofa Pillow, Blue Dun, Elk Hair
        Caddis, Woolly Buggers, Griffith's Gnat
Localities Map Location: F3
USGS Quadrangle Maps: Wheeler Peak, Red River, Questa,
        Guadalupe Mountain

THE RED RIVER ORIGINATES IN NEW MEXICO'S highest country, beneath the 13,161-foot Wheeler Peak. The river ends its varied journey when it joins the Rio Grande deep within the Gorge. Like other rivers that head high in the mountains and flow across the basalt flows of the Taos Plateau, the Red River has two dramatically different characters. In the mountains of the Carson National Forest, the Red is a classic freestone stream flowing across wide meadows and through narrow canyons. As it nears the Rio Grande, the Red has carved a deep canyon in the black rock, and it flows as boulder-choked pocket water, much like the Rio Grande itself. In both sections, the Red River offers fly fishermen the opportunity to take large trout.

The headwaters of the Red River consist of four small creeks, three of which are on public land: Sawmill Creek, East Fork Creek, and Middle Fork. The three creeks are similar, with stretches of heavy forest, open meadows, and beaver ponds. These are small streams that are never over 5 feet wide except in the beaver ponds concentrated near their confluence. The native Rio Grande cutthroats, brook trout, and cutbows in these small headwaters are opportunistic feeders. Some hatches occur—notably tiny brown stoneflies and midges—but they are not consistent. In July and August, brown or tan caddis imitations in sizes 16 and 18 work well, and Griffith's Gnat in sizes 16–20 work in the beaver ponds, especially in the evenings. Small Woolly Buggers are also effective in the beaver ponds during the brook trout pre-spawning season in September and October.

The headwater creeks converge south of the town of Red River near the end of NM 578. To reach the East Fork and Sawmill Creek, turn right on FR 58A as soon as the pavement ends. To get to the Middle Fork, turn right on FR 58 about 100 yards before the turnoff to the East Fork and Sawmill Creek.

Downstream from the confluence are 3 miles of open meadows with beaver ponds, riffles, deep pools, and undercut banks. The fish average between 8 and 14 inches. Rainbows are stocked here, and some large rainbows that the Chamber of Commerce stocks at the townsite migrate up to this stretch and take hold. Diligent anglers will find brown trout up to 16 inches. Because this section is on private land, it is necessary to ask permission of the landowner before fishing here.

The next 3 miles the Red runs through a narrow, heavily forested canyon with limited access. The river is about 15–20 feet wide, with lots of structure and some deep pools. Truly wild trout, including Rio Grande cutthroats up to 16 inches long, are found in the canyon. This is perhaps the best section of the river for dry flies. Caddisflies hatch from June through August, when a size 14 or 16 Elk Hair Caddis will bring plenty of trout to the surface.

Once out of the canyon, the river runs through the tourist town of Red River. Within the town limits, the river seems more like a city park than a mountain trout stream. Here you will find bait fishermen (sometimes shoulder to shoulder), kids throwing rocks in the water, and 9-inch stocked rainbows by the thousands. If this isn't enough insult to the river, almost every tree and willow along the banks has been cut down, the flows have been channelized, and pesticides are used on the banks each summer. Despite all of this, during September and October, after the tourists go home, there is good dry-fly-fishing in town. Brown trout move in from downstream and feed on midges hatching from the dredged gravel bottom. Griffith's Gnats are an excellent choice of pattern at this time. And be prepared for a fight if you find a leftover lunker rainbow stocked by the Chamber of Commerce.

Four miles downstream from the town of Red River, the river runs through a tight, steep canyon. Fishing is fair for stocked rainbows and a few browns. There are only a few pools and lots of pressure from bait fishermen. Several good campgrounds are located next to the river, and two artificial impoundments, the Fawn Lakes, hold some nice rainbows.

For fishermen the river is dead from the Molycorp Molybdenum Mine downstream 10 miles to the Red River Hatchery near the town of Questa. Mining activities over the last 20 years have disrupted the ecological balance of the river. The river has been clouded by hundreds of raw tailings spills; thoughtless construction practices along the river have caused severe erosion; and aluminization of sediment, a concreting of gravel and rocks, has given the water an aqua-blue color. These practices have decimated insect populations and have made it impossible for trout to spawn. With its beautiful riffles and pools, cottonwoods, willows, and excellent hatches of caddis, mayflies, and stoneflies, this once was the best section of river for dry-fly-fishing. Now it is a lifeless zone of sediment and eroded stream banks.

One shining spot along this tarnished stretch is Cabresto Creek, a small tributary that joins the Red River in Questa. The Cabresto offers about 12 miles of excellent fly-fishing for browns, rainbows, cut-throats, and brook trout using standard patterns. To reach Cabresto Creek from Questa, turn east from NM 522 onto NM 38, heading toward the town of Red River. After a quarter-mile, take a sharp left at an intersection marked for Cabresto. Travel up a small hill and through a housing area onto FR 134. This well-maintained gravel road parallels Cabresto Creek for over 10 miles.

As with many of New Mexico's small creeks, Cabresto is brushy and fishing it is difficult for all but the most experienced and patient anglers. It is a different and demanding type of fly-fishing, where stalking the fish is the challenge, not a long, pretty cast. Having the proper equipment can increase your chance for success: use a 7-foot rod and a 5X or 6X leader no more than 8 feet long. Stealth is important on such a small stream. Creep upstream with a low profile, hiding behind bushes, trees, and clumps of grass; in open areas, it is often necessary to crawl on your belly. All of this effort will get you as close to the fish as possible, perhaps only a rod-length away. To get the fly to the fish, use roll casts, bow casts, or dabbling the fly, with leader only, upstream of the fish. These techniques prevent spooking the fish and insure a good drift by keeping excess line off the water.

The 4 miles from the Red River Hatchery downstream to the confluence of the river with the Rio Grande, the Red River Canyon is part of the Rio Grande Wild and Scenic River and takes on the characteristics of the Rio Grande Gorge. Numerous springs enter the river in this section, tripling the volume of flow and helping carve out the magnificent basalt canyon walls that surround it.

The springs endow the river with special qualities. During the summer, water temperatures stay cool, usually less than 65 degrees; winter water temperatures remain high, at 48 degrees or more, making the Red one of the only natural winter trout fisheries in northern New Mexico. The lower Red is also the main spawning tributary of the Rio Grande for brown trout (in the fall) and cutbows (in the winter and spring).

Although it is not widely known, the lower Red River, along with the Rio Grande Gorge, was once considered one of the top fisheries in the United States for large brown trout. As upstream mining activities increased, however, the quality of the fishery declined. Fortunately, the effects of mining on water quality are diluted by the increase in flow from the springs along the lower river. While the resident population of browns has dropped, fish from the Rio Grande come back year after year to spawn. The molybdenum mine closed in 1986, and the river had some time to recover. By 1989, many spawning browns and cutbows were remaining in the Red, and their offspring are now re-populating the river. Spawning populations have increased, and insect hatches are improving.

The mine reopened in 1989. Molycorp is currently seeking new property for tailings ponds. Unfortunately, the land sought by the mining company sits on top of the aquifer feeding the springs that empty into the Red River. Lawsuits have been filed, and there is reason to be optimistic that the permits will be denied. Even more fortuitous for the river is the falling price of molybdenum, which may force the mine to close indefinitely.

You can get to the lower Red River from the Red River Hatchery. From Taos, go north on US 64, and continue straight on NM 522 when US 64 turns west. About three miles south of Questa, turn left (west) on NM 515 toward the hatchery. From the parking area, follow the primitive trail downstream along the river to the Red's confluence with the Rio Grande.

Two developed trails lead to the river from the north rim of the canyon in the Rio Grande Wild and Scenic Recreation Area north of Questa. Take NM 522 north from Questa. After about 3 miles, turn left (west) onto NM 378. Follow the road for about 10 miles to the trailheads at La Junta and El Aguaje campgrounds. Both trails are about a mile from rim to river, each dropping 800 feet. The El Aguaje Trail is usually in better condition and is an easier walk.

In its lower stretch, the Red is classic boulder-strewn pocket water filled with big browns and cutbows. It flows through a rugged canyon, with breathtaking scenery, and the fishing is almost always exciting.

From September through November, big spawning browns that move in from the Rio Grande eagerly gobble caddis larvae, brown stonefly nymphs, mayfly nymphs, and small minnows. In September, fishing is best with nymphs; streamers are more effective as November approaches.

About the time the browns start moving back to the Rio Grande, the big cutbows and rainbows begin moving in to spawn in the clear 50-degree water. Throughout March, the aggressive cutbows and resident browns take peacock nymphs, Hare's Ear nymphs, and, on warm days, a caddis pattern fished on the surface. When nothing seems to work, an egg pattern is often effective. Runoff occurs from April to mid-June. In June and July, there is good nymph and dry-fly-fishing using Golden Stones and olive caddis.

Soft Hackle

The lower Red River has been designated Special Trout Water with the same regulations which are in effect throughout the Rio Grande Gorge. The boundaries of the Special Trout Water are one-half mile below the Red River Hatchery and the confluence with the Rio Grande. Anglers are limited to four trout in possession, with no size limits. There are no restrictions on tackle.

The Red River is perhaps the most crucial tributary of the Rio Grande. Because of the long-term effects of molybdenum mining, most fly fishermen do not realize its importance or its potential. If the mine closes and remains so for a long period of time, then the river will undoubtedly continue to improve. Then perhaps the Red will return to the high-quality fishery for which it was once famous.

CHAPTER THIRTEEN

To The Mississippi:
Cimarron River

Van Beacham

Location: Sangre de Cristo Mountains, Colin Neblett Wildlife
    Area, Cimarron Canyon State Park
Altitude: 8,000 to 8,500 feet
Type of Water: small tailwater, riffles, pools, beaver ponds
Best Times: June through September
Hatches: Golden Stoneflies, March Browns, Blue-winged Olives,
    Pale Morning Duns, Little Yellow Stones, caddisflies,
    midges
Patterns: Bird's Stone, Stimulator, Ginger Dun, Blue-winged
    Olive, Elk Hair Caddis, Griffith's Gnat, Dave's
    Hopper, Black Ant
Localities Map Location: G4
USGS Quadrangle Maps: Eagle Nest, Ute Peak

SPRINGING OUT FROM THE BOTTOM OF EAGLE
Nest Lake, the Cimarron River winds its way through
the narrow, densely forested Cimarron Canyon. The
course of the Cimarron begins like many other northern New Mexico trout streams; it is its destination that makes
this river different. Ninety percent of the trout waters in the

region are part of the Rio Grande watershed, flowing south through the state to the Gulf of Mexico. The Cimarron is part of the Mississippi River system, flowing east, then south through the Canadian and Arkansas rivers, and finally to the Mississippi itself.

The Cimarron is among the richest rivers in the state and, for its size, holds the most fish per mile. In 1982, the New Mexico Department of Game and Fish electroshocked the river and found over 16,000 fish per mile, about 3,500 of which were catchable-sized trout.

The first half-mile of the Cimarron below Eagle Nest Dam is private and posted by the C.S. Cattle Company, and fishing is by permit only. Below the mouth of Tolby Creek is the Colin Neblett Wildlife Area, managed by the New Mexico Department of Game and Fish. This is among the finest stretches of fly water in the state, boasting phenomenal insect activity. Below the wildlife area are 8 more miles of excellent water on private property, most of which runs through the heavily posted Philmont Boy Scout Ranch.

The Cimarron River is a medium-sized stream, averaging between 10 and 20 feet wide and with flows in the 30 cfs range. The river has a unique combination of riffles, pools, and beaver ponds, and numerous submerged logs, cliffs, undercut banks, overhanging willows, cottonwoods, alders, and other vegetation provide an abundance of cover and holding water for the enormous trout population. Many gravel bars provide excellent habitat for spawning trout and insect populations.

The river is easily waded with hip boots during average or low water flows. Water depths are about 2 feet, with some deeper pools and beaver ponds. When the demand from downstream irrigators increases, more water is released from the dam and wading can be difficult. The bottom is mostly gravel with small boulders, except in the beaver ponds, which are usually silty.

Short, lightweight rods, 2–4 weight and 7–8-feet long, are ideal for the Cimarron. Keep leaders short, under 8 feet, and use light tippets in the 4X–6X range.

While the Cimarron is a model fly fishery, it is not recommended for beginners because of the heavy brush along the river that makes

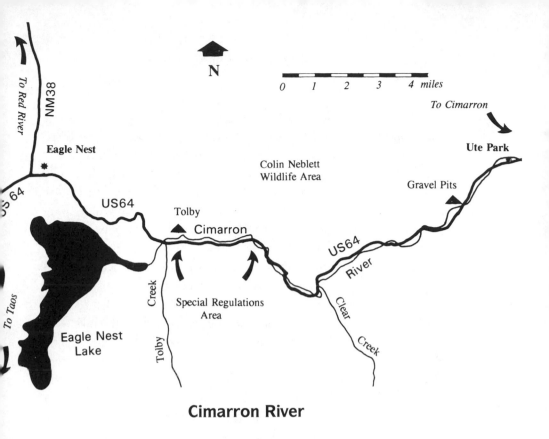

Cimarron River

casting very difficult. The most effective way to fish this little jewel is to wade right up the middle, making short roll, flip, or bow casts into the heads of pools, under brush, and along the edge of undercut banks. When making longer casts into long, shallow pools, it usually necessary to keep your backcast in the middle of the river to avoid hanging up on streamside vegetation.

Drift is very important on the Cimarron; the closer you can get to the fish and the shorter your cast, the easier it is to control the float of your fly. A common mistake is to try to make a beautiful long cast, which results in a long drift full of drag and spooks every brown in a pool. Many of the fish taken on the river are less than a rod-length away. Short lines also make it easier to land hooked fish, since there is no extra line on the water to become tangled or wrapped under a log or around a root.

The Cimarron can be fished by early April, but water releases from Eagle Nest Lake don't usually begin until mid-May. April's low water conditions make fishing tough, and the fish are very spooky. Stalking individual fish is the best technique early in the season. Spot several trout in a deep pool or beaver pond before casting, and then carefully pull out the required amount of line and, avoiding too much false casting, place the fly just above the largest fish. You rarely have more than one chance, so it is important to make the first cast count.

A *Baetis* mayfly hatch, which is quite heavy at times, occurs early during the season, and a Blue-winged Olive Dun, size 18, is a good match. There is good midge activity in the beaver ponds, particularly in the evenings. Nymphs also work well when they are fished deep with a short line in the seams of riffles and along undercut banks.

By mid-May, when flow volume is adequate and the water is fairly clear, the famous gold and orange stoneflies (*Pteronarcys*) begin to hatch. Emergence starts in the lower end of the river on private land and works its way upstream to the dam, ending in late July. To imitate the stoneflies, use a Bird's Stonefly or a Kaufmann Stimulator, sizes 10–14, in gold and orange. Fish them dry or wet just under the surface. Casting downstream to a feeding fish and skittering the fly right over it will often produce a vicious strike. The best stonefly action is during mid-day from 10 a.m. to 3 p.m.

On early summer afternoons, look for heavy hatches of brown and ginger mayflies of the genus *Rhithrogena*. Match this hatch with Ginger Duns or March Browns, sizes 14–18. Fish the heads of riffles and the main current. In the evenings, all hell can break loose with multiple caddis hatches and mayfly spinners blanketing the water and freely feeding browns everywhere. In the beaver ponds, you can test your skill on fat browns that are lazily sipping emerging midge pupa. On such days, good anglers can catch and release up to 100 browns in the 8–14-inch range, with a few up to 20 inches. On an average day, you will catch at least a dozen fish, mostly wild browns. Seldom does a fly fisherman get a rainbow here, but when he does they are fat and quick.

Matching the hatch is the most successful way to fish the Cimarron, but it is not a requirement because of the smorgasbord of food on the water. Olive Elk Hair Caddis, size 14, or an Adams Irresistible, size 16, is always a good choice. In the beaver ponds, try a midge pupa or Griffith's Gnat, sizes 18 or 20.

August hatches are not prolific, but caddis, Little Yellow Stones, and Pale Morning and Evening Duns are abundant on the river, as are the midges in the beaver ponds. Ants, beetles, and hoppers are also productive, particularly when hatches are sparse. Fish terrestrials close to the bank, letting them drift under overhanging brush, trees, and grass. From September through October, Blue-winged Olives hatch throughout mid-day. The water is usually lower in the fall, and a *Baetis* No-Hackle or Compara-Dun is usually required to fool the trout.

By mid-October, the flow to the river has been shut off at the dam to store water for irrigation. Fishing is all but impossible from late October through the winter.

Low flows in the fall force the brown trout to spawn in very little water (3–10 cfs). Appropriate in-stream flow legislation, recognizing the nondiversionary use of water for fish, wildlife, and a healthy stream ecosystem, would greatly help the Cimarron's population of wild trout. Such a law would allow negotiations with the owners of the water, resulting in more flow volume during the brown trout's critical spawning and incubation period. While such legislation is introduced in each session of the New Mexico legislature, it has little support among its members. Fly fishermen need to work with local fishing clubs to help make in-stream flow legislation an important debate in the state capitol.

In 1989, as a result of public recommendation, New Mexico Game

Dave's Hopper

and Fish placed special regulations on the first 1.5 miles of the Colin Neblett Wildlife Area. In the Special Trout Water, angling is limited to the use of artificial flies and lures with a single, barbless hook. The river is fast becoming popular, and additional regulations may be needed to protect the high quality of the fishery. As in all Special Trout Waters, anglers are encouraged to release all wild brown trout caught in the area.

To get to the Cimarron, take US 64 east out of Taos, past Angel Fire to the town of Eagle Nest (about 24 miles). One mile east of Eagle Nest, the road drops down into Cimarron Canyon and the Colin Neblett Wildlife Area. Campgrounds along US 64 in Cimarron Canyon are operated by the State Parks and Recreation Division.

The Cimarron is a dream stream. Even the finest spring creeks in Montana and Idaho fail to produce more or larger fish than this river. For its size, it is one of the best rivers in the West, particularly if you like brown trout on dry flies. Try it on a warm June day, and you will become a believer!

CHAPTER FOURTEEN

High and Lonesome: Valle Vidal

Richard Wilder

IT IS UNUSUAL TO THINK KINDLY OF THE INTERNAL Revenue Service at any time, let alone while fishing. But it is the IRS we have to thank when angling in the spectacular 100,000-acre Valle Vidal Unit of the Carson National Forest. Let me explain.

In 1842, Carlos Beaubien and Guadalupe Miranda received a land grant from Mexican Governor Manuel Armijo. Encompassing almost two million acres, the grant was the largest ever given in what would become the state of New Mexico. Many years and several owners later, this huge tract of land, known as the Maxwell Land Grant, became a famous private hunting and fishing ranch. The Penzoil Company bought the ranch in 1973. In 1982, the federal government had the foresight to accept some of the ranch lands in settlement for taxes due and opened the once private area to public use.

The property was added to the Carson National Forest as the Valle Vidal Unit, named for a small, stunning valley in the area. The entire tract is beautiful and unspoiled, full of breathtaking scenery and abundant wildlife. The U.S. Forest Service and the New Mexico Department of Game and Fish are committed to keeping it that way. Both agencies recognize the special nature of the Valle Vidal Unit and manage the area in unique ways. The Forest Service manages the area with a special emphasis on wildlife, and Game and Fish has implemented special regulations on hunting and fishing.

The Valle Vidal Unit is closed to fishing from January 1 to June 30 each year in order to protect the native cutthroats during their spawning season. The Rio Grande cutthroats are further protected by a catch-and-release designation for all waters within Valle Vidal. Only flies and artificial lures with single, barbless hooks are permitted, and all fish must be immediately released.

COSTILLA CREEK
Craig Martin

Location: Sangre de Cristo Mountains, Carson National Forest, New Mexico Game and Fish, some private
Altitude: 8,500 to 9,900 feet
Type of Water: freestone, pools, pocket water
Best Times: July to late September
Hatches: caddisflies, mayflies
Patterns: Elk Hair Caddis, Adams, Rio Grande King, Letort Hopper
Localities Map Location: F3, G3
USGS Quadrangle Maps: Latir Peak, Comanche Point

COSTILLA CREEK IS A MEDIUM-SIZED RIVER THAT HEADS IN COLORADO'S Culebra Range, flows south into New Mexico and the Valle Vidal Unit of the Carson National Forest, and runs east for 20 miles before turning north again to flow into the Rio Grande just above the Colorado state line. The Costilla is a diverse stream that offers high mountain, broad meadow, and steep canyon fishing. Management of the Costilla is under the Vermejo Park Ranch, the U.S. Forest Service, New Mexico Game and Fish, and the private Rio Costilla Cooperative Live-

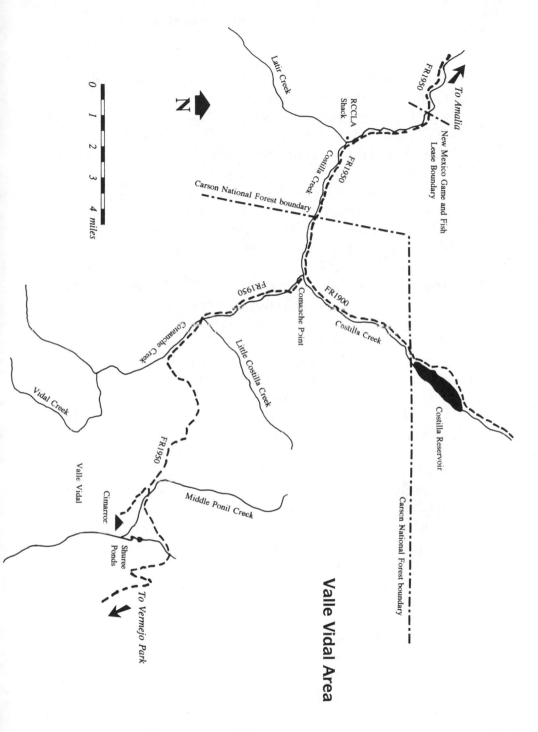

Valle Vidal Area

137

stock Association (RCCLA). In spite of its many managers, the entire Costilla is an excellent fishing river.

The two forks of the headwaters of Costilla Creek are on private land, with excellent fishing available for a fee from Vermejo Park Ranch. Water from the two forks is impounded in Costilla Reservoir, a private lake that is also part of the Vermejo Park Ranch.

Below the reservoir, the Costilla enters the Valle Vidal area, where it flows through broad meadows to the Carson National Forest boundary. Meadow fishing, with quiet water and long pools, continues in the Special Trout Water section of the New Mexico Game and Fish lease, which ends at Latir Creek. Here the river enters a narrow canyon, and the gradient becomes much higher. Freestone and pocket water dominate the canyon section with rocks, cliffs, overhanging trees, and deep holes offering protection to trout. The canyon continues to the end of the New Mexico Game and Fish lease property. Downstream, the Costilla flows through private land, but you can fish this water with a permit from the RCCLA. Permits are included with camping or may be purchased separately.

Along this 20-mile section of river, the fishing regulations change four times. On Costilla Reservoir and the streams above, Vermejo Park Ranch regulations apply and fishing is by permit only. Below the reservoir, in the Carson National Forest, Valle Vidal rules apply: catch-and-release fishing with single, barbless hooks, season running from July 1 to December 31. On the Game and Fish lease, from the Valle Vidal boundary downstream to Latir Creek, there is no closed season but otherwise regulations are identical with those in Valle Vidal. The remaining Game and Fish lease downstream from Latir Creek has no special regulations, as does the RCCLA property. Each area is well-marked.

Flows on Costilla Creek, and consequently the quality of fishing, depend on water releases from Costilla Reservoir. In general, the high flows necessary for irrigation are released from the dam from Sunday night through Thursday night. Flows during weekends are generally lower and more suitable for fishing. This pattern also ensures good flows throughout summer months: in mid-summer, when other New Mexico streams can be too low and warm for fishing, the Costilla is at its peak. The best time to be on the Costilla is from July through late September. Irrigation needs drop in October, and flows in the Costilla slow to a trickle.

The Costilla is an easy river to fly-fish. Almost the entire river is shallow and slow enough for easy wading in hip boots. The meadows and most of the canyon section have little brush, so casting is almost snag free. Picking a prime location to fish is not difficult, since there are plenty of trout in the river.

Not too many years ago, the Costilla was considered the best cut-throat stream in New Mexico. But hybridization with rainbows, graz-ing patterns, erosion, and changes in dam operations at Costilla Reservoir have diminished the river's quality. If management practices change to favor the cutthroats, if grazing becomes better regulated, and if dam reconstruction causes no long-term damage, the river's future as a cutthroat stream could be bright.

Rainbows are stocked in Costilla Creek on the Game and Fish lease below Latir Creek. The upper portions of the river are consid-ered a cutthroat fishery and are not stocked. Most of the "cutthroats" are actually cutthroat-rainbow hybrids, but some fish show few signs of genetic mixing and can be considered true Rio Grande cutthroats. Rainbows are in the 9–16-inch range; hybrids and cutthroats are a bit smaller, from 7–14 inches. Anglers are encouraged to release all na-tive Rio Grande cutthroats.

The Costilla holds abundant insect populations. Although there are no detailed studies on the aquatic insect populations, anglers will find hatches of mayflies and caddisflies throughout the warmer months. In the spring, stoneflies are found in the fast currents of the canyon section. Ample populations of grasshoppers are found in the meadows in late summer and fall.

All types of flies are successfully used on Costilla Creek. Stonefly nymphs are popular in the riffles and pocket water of the canyon sec-tion below Latir Creek. Dry flies that match the color and size of naturals are effective with the cutthroats in the meadow sections of the river. A grey-bodied mayfly, for example, matched with a parachute or Compara dun pattern dubbed with a muskrat fur body in size 14 or 16, hatches on July afternoons. If there is no hatch, try Rio Grande Kings sizes 12 or 14, Elk Hair Caddis, sizes 14 or 16, and Grizzly or Gray Wulffs sizes 14 or 18. Letort Hoppers, sizes 12 or 14, will take fish throughout the summer in the quiet water of the meadows. This fly is particularly effective when it is pulled off the bank onto the water just above a suspected trout lie, or when plopped hard onto the surface and drifted with an occasional twitch. Basic nymph patterns, such as the Pheasant Tail and Gold-Ribbed Hare's Ear, are effective on the entire river.

To get to the Costilla, travel north on US 64 from Taos. When US 64 turns west to cross the Rio Grande, continue north on NM 522 through Questa. About 40 miles from Taos, at the town of Costilla, turn right on NM 196 toward Amalia, Ski Rio, and Valle Vidal. This paved road turns to all-weather gravel just past the turnoff to Ski Rio. Public water on the Game and Fish lease begins about 4 miles past Ski Rio. Camping is available in campgrounds on RCCLA property with an RCCLA permit and within Valle Vidal at Cimarron or McCrystal campgrounds.

To fish the upper forks of the Costilla and the Costilla Reservoir, you will need a permit from the Vermejo Park Ranch. Rates are $250 per day and up and include lodging. Call the ranch (505-445-3097) for the latest rates and information. You will also need a permit from RCCLA if you want to fish the Costilla on Rio Costilla Park. Permits for fishing and camping are available at the RCCLA office in the town of Costilla, at the shack at the mouth of Latir Creek (which is often closed), or by mail (RCCLA, P.O. Box 111, Costilla, NM 87524). The fee in 1990 was $5 per day per person. If you have questions, call RCCLA at (505) 586-0542.

Fishing the Costilla and exploring Valle Vidal make for fantastic summer weekends in the high country. It is best to head to the Costilla after July 1 in order to enjoy fishing farther into Valle Vidal on Comanche Creek and at Shuree Ponds. But whenever you take the trip, the red peaks, soft valleys, herds of elk, and great fishing will make the journey memorable.

COMANCHE CREEK
Richard Wilder

> **Location:** Carson National Forest, Valle Vidal Unit
> **Altitude:** 9,000 to 10,200 feet
> **Type of Water:** spring creek, pools, flats
> **Best Times:** July to September
> **Hatches:** terrestrials, grasshoppers, caddisflies
> **Patterns:** Elk Hair Caddis, Letort Hopper, Royal Wulff
> **Localities Map Location:** G3
> **USGS Quadrangle Maps:** Comanche Point, Red River Pass

COSTILLA CREEK IS FED BY ONE MAIN TRIBUTARY IN VALLE VIDAL. IT is a fine, small stream—and I do mean small! Almost every time I have fished there, someone has called down from the road, a sense of disbelief apparent in his voice, to ask, "Any fish in that thing?" I don't blame anyone for being skeptical, for in many places Comanche Creek is small enough to cross in a single step. I harbored the same doubts myself the first time I fished it. I approached the stream very casually, only to find myself standing dumbfounded as I watched numerous cut-throats racing for cover. I quickly learned that both approach and presentation are critical in the clear, shallow, open water of Comanche Creek.

The setting for Comanche Creek is reminiscent of the northern Rockies. It flows through a small valley flanked by meadows and granite outcrops, winding toward a backdrop of high peaks above timberline. Stands of aspen, spruce, and fir grow in patches on the surrounding hillsides. The stream itself remains small, seldom wider than 3 feet. It consists of slow and quiet water where pools and shallow flats are the rule. The bottom is lined with small pebbles, cobbles, and sand. The entire valley is open meadow, and there are very few trees within 50 yards of the stream.

Comanche Creek joins Costilla Creek at Comanche Point, about 2 miles from the Carson National Forest Boundary on FR 1950. This graded gravel road parallels Comanche Creek for about 4 miles; consequently, this section of creek is most heavily fished. As the main road turns away from the stream and continues toward Shuree Ponds, a small spur road leads to a parking area. From here, there are 3 miles of hike-in water upstream.

Although it is a small stream, Comanche Creek does have many undercut banks and some relatively deep holes. This cover and holding water enables the stream to support a large number of beautiful Rio Grande cutthroats. Anglers who brave the often windy conditions of the open meadows, and who have the patience for the commando-type approach combined with delicate presentation that the stream requires, will be in for some really fun fishing.

Comanche Creek is part of Valle Vidal, so is only open for fishing from July 1 to December 31. Early season fly patterns are not important on this stream. By the time the season begins, mayfly and caddis hatches are regular occurrences. Terrestrials, especially grasshoppers, are very important through much of the season. Also successful are attractor patterns, from size 14 early in the season to size 18 or even 20 late in the year. A Royal Coachman, tied trude style, is a particularly favorite pattern.

Comanche Creek is great dry-fly water, and anglers seldom fish anything below the surface. Fishing is not difficult, for casting is unobstructed and the fish are numerous and willing. If you can approach the trout and present the fly without spooking them, you are in for a good day's fishing. You can catch and release a bunch of fish in a day, but don't expect to see any big fish. Most cutthroats are in the 7–11-inch range.

Remember that Comanche Creek is managed as catch-and-release water and that angling is restricted to flies and lures with single, barbless hooks. All fish must be immediately released.

For those who want to wander, other small streams in Valle Vidal are also worth exploring. I have a very difficult time driving alongside Costilla and Comanche creeks without eventually giving in to the urge to stop at a stretch that looks too good to pass by. When you visit Valle Vidal, you'll see what I mean!

SHUREE PONDS
Martha Noss

Location: Carson National Forest, Valle Vidal Unit
Altitude: 9,000 feet
Size: 15 acres
Best Times: July to September
Hatches: midges, caddisflies
Patterns: Elk Hair Caddis, Black Woolly Bugger
Localities Map Location: G3
USGS Quadrangle Maps: Ash Mountain

IF YOU ARE IN VALLE VIDAL AND GET AN URGE TO HOOK INTO SOMETHING bigger than the cutthroats in Comanche Creek, drive up the road to Shuree Ponds. Here you will find oversized rainbows and hybrid Rio Grande cutthroats and the chance for a fish of 20 inches or better. And at dawn and dusk, you will be rewarded with the sight of huge herds of elk grazing on the grassy hillsides.

Five ponds are on the property of the Old Shuree Lodge, but only three hold trout. Most of the angling is done in the largest pond, closest to the parking area. The second largest pond can be just as good and is sometimes a little less crowded. The third is reserved for children under 12, making this a perfect destination for a family outing. There are picnic and restroom facilities at the parking lots, and the largest lake is equipped for handicap access. No camping is permitted around the lakes, but Cimarron Campground is just a mile away.

The larger two lakes are just the right size for float tubing or canoeing, although many anglers simply fish from shore. Casting black or olive Woolly Buggers, sizes 8–12, is effective for fish holding deep, or try a dragonfly or damselfly nymph. One afternoon in early October, my fishing partner and I picked up a good number of big fish with black and olive Woolly Buggers using a varied, start-and-stop retrieve. As we fished from our float tubes, we watched a small herd of deer as they meandered through a hillside meadow, casually feeding and staring down at the pond, no doubt wondering at the strange animals floating on the water.

If you avoid hot and dry spells, summer and autumn fishing are excellent. Dry-fly action includes caddis, midges, and a flying ant fall. As soon as the sun dips below the Culebra Range and the lake calms, the trout begin rising to midges and caddis, and the surface boils with one rise after another. Any small fly will bring a strike, but Elk Hair Caddis and midge imitations work best. Cast to a spot 20–30 feet from shore and allow the fly to sit, or locate a rising trout and quickly cast your fly into the rings of the last rise. When an 18-inch rainbow takes your size 18 Elk Hair Caddis, be ready for a fight.

Like all waters within Valle Vidal, the Shuree Ponds are managed as Special Trout Water. The season opens on July 1 and runs through December 31, and only single-hook flies and artificial lures are permitted. The daily bag and possession is two fish over 15 inches.

To reach Shuree Ponds, follow the directions to Valle Vidal found earlier in this chapter. From the Valle Vidal boundary, signs will direct you to Shuree, about 10 miles into the area on FR 1950. Access to Shuree, as well as to the other waters of Valle Vidal, is also available on FR 1950 from east of Cimarron.

CHAPTER FIFTEEN

Hidden Gems: Rio de Los Piños and Rio Vallecitos

RIO DE LOS PIÑOS
Bob Widgren

Location: Carson National Forest, New Mexico Game and Fish
Altitude: 7,600 to 11,600 feet
Type of Water: freestone, riffle, and pool
Best Times: late June, early July, September to November
Hatches: Golden Stoneflies, mystery hatch, Pale Morning Duns, caddisflies, midges
Patterns: Golden Stonefly Nymph, Brooks Stone, Peacock Simulator, Bird's Stonefly, Brown Wulff, Adams, Light Hendrickson, Elk Hair Caddis, Griffith's Gnat, Green Caddis Larva
Localities Map Location: E2, E3
USGS Quadrangle Maps: Cumbres (Colorado), Toltec Mesa, Bighorn Peak, Los Pinos

HIDDEN AMONG MOUNTAINS, MESAS, AND THE state line, the Rio de Los Piños is a river almost unknown to New Mexicans. After heading high above Trujillo Meadows in Colorado's San Juan Mountains, the Los Piños flows south into New Mexico. Paralleling the Colorado state line and never flowing more than 3 miles from it, the Los Piños travels 20 miles through New Mexico before turning north once again to Colorado. The easiest access to the river is through Colorado.

The Rio de Los Piños is a small to moderate-sized, extremely rich trout stream with all the characteristics and beauty that only the high western mountains can provide. The uppermost meadows in Colorado give fly fishermen open country fishing amid dramatic mountain scenery; in the border region, where access is difficult, backcountry anglers will find ample streamside solitude; and the lower section provides a moderate-sized stream teeming with hefty trout. Whether fishing in the meadows or the gorge, anglers have a dramatic backdrop to their sport.

In the area of Toltec Gorge, the Los Piños is a small stream ranging from 10–15 feet wide. The lower section of the river is considerably larger, varying from 25–40 feet in width. Depths range from less than one to 4 feet with pools of up to 10 feet. Except in the uppermost meadows in Colorado, the river is a classic freestone stream with frequent riffling and moderate pooling. When looking for trout, runs between 18 and 36 inches deep are best. It is easy to find a variety of cover for trout—overhanging cliffs, fast currents along trailing branches, downed trees straddling the water, and slow backwaters.

Wading in all sections of the Rio de los Piños is easy. During the warm months, wet wading is popular, and hip boots are acceptable any time of the year. Felt-soled wading shoes are recommended due to the slippery bottom of cobbles and slickrock. Willows and grasses grow along the banks, but the stream is wide enough to permit easy casts. Casting distances are usually less than 20 feet.

The Los Piños is loaded with all kinds of trout. In the upper stretch in the area of Toltec Gorge, there are many small wild brown and brook trout. The lower section is stocked throughout the summer with hundreds of rainbows, most in the 9–14-inch range. Over-wintering rainbows can reach 16–18 inches. Wild browns are also found in the lower section, with most fish between 8 and 12 inches. Even in heavily fished areas, wild-jumping 18-inch browns are caught in deep runs.

Especially in the deeper pools, the Rio de los Piños normally stays open from December to March, but the access road to the stream is often closed due to snow and mud. If the road is open, nymph fishing is the rule. Because of the stream's rich aquatic populations, almost any kind of nymph pattern can be successful. Use searching patterns, such as the Peacock Nymph, Pheasant Tail, stonefly nymphs, and Hare's Ear, all tied in sizes 10–18. Nymphing is particularly good in the deeper pools. Use heavily weighted patterns or split shot on the leader to sink the fly quickly to the fish on the stream bottom.

Runoff comes early to a river with such a large watershed. Depending on the snowpack in the San Juan Mountains, high water usually begins in late March and continues through the end of May. During runoff the water is high, swift, and brown. Still, short-line nymphing techniques can be effective. Use large, shiny patterns, and patiently and thoroughly fish the water. *Pteronarcys californica* (Giant Stoneflies) are active during runoff. It is best to fish this hatch with nymph patterns such as a Peacock Simulator, a Peacock Nymph, or a brown Brooks Stone. A warm spring can create an early runoff that may close the access road due to water and mud.

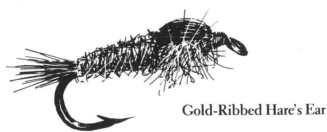

Gold-Ribbed Hare's Ear

By late April, Winter Stoneflies *(Capnia)*, caddis, and mayflies are on the water, signaling the beginning of the dry-fly season. Late May and early June brings the Golden Stonefly *(Hesperoperla pacifica)* hatch. Even with high and cloudy water, fishing this hatch can be exciting, as large trout feed hungrily on these 2-inch-long insects. As the nymphs migrate to shore, climbing on rocks and vegetation to emerge, most of the action is below the surface. Use patterns such as the Golden Stone Nymph, a Brooks Yellow Stone, or even a Bitch Creek Nymph, all tied on size 6–10 long shank hooks. Imitate the migration of the nymphs by fishing the pattern along the bottom, first drifting downstream and then swinging the fly across the current to the bank with a tight line. If the water is clear, large fish come to the surface to take dry patterns, such as the Golden Adult Stonefly or the Bird's Stonefly tied on size 8 or 10 hooks. Fish the dry patterns by plopping them noisily on the water and imparting action to the fly by skimming it across the surface for short distances.

Although the Los Piños offers fine fly-fishing throughout the year, early summer, especially late June and early July, is the best time to be on the river. During this period, water levels are perfect and temperature changes are not severe. Early summer also brings heavy hatches of mayflies, stoneflies, and caddis.

The most prolific early summer insects are the thousands of caddisflies that skim the water in the evening and lie thick on the streamside vegetation. The insects are large, with dark bodies and wings. An Elk Hair Caddis in sizes 12 or 14 is an adequate match. From any spot on the river, anglers can find a half-dozen rising trout to cast a fly to. Both rainbows and browns eagerly rise to this hatch, and a catch of 8–10 fish an hour is not unusual.

Caddis Adult

Another important early summer hatch is the huge, juicy mayfly, probably the largest member of this order in New Mexico. The identity of this insect is currently in question; some anglers believe it is a *Rhithrogena*, and others find it closer to a *Hexagenia* species. Whatever its scientific classification, it is a fantastic hatch. The mayflies have gray-brown bodies that are almost an inch long, with yellowish ribbing and gray wings. They can be imitated with a Brown Wulff or an Adams on size 10 or 12 hooks. The mayflies hatch from mid-morning until noon, with a sporadic spinner fall lasting throughout the day. Fish the imitation dead drift in all types of water, paying special attention to runs over 18 inches deep. Fishing this hatch has produced many trout 16 inches or better.

A number of lesser but still important hatches occur in late June and early July. Small green and yellow stoneflies *(Sweltsa* and *Isoperla)* are on the water from noon to evening. The trout are not selective feeders to these insects, but using size 16 or 18 green or pheasant tail Soft Hackle patterns fished dead-drift will bring strikes from trout feeding on nymphs. A mid-morning hatch of Western Blue Quills *(Paraleptophlebia)* in quiet water finds a few trout selectively feeding on the small duns. Cast Red Quills or Blue Quills, sizes 16 or 18, to rising trout in the pools and runs. More important is a little yellow mayfly *(Heptagenia)* hatch that comes off fast water from late morning to just after noon. Trout often feed selectively on this insect, and having a pattern to match the hatch is necessary for success. In pockets of quiet water, a size 16 or 18 Light Cahill is an excellent choice, but the duns often float in swift and choppy water where a Cahill will easily sink. In this situation, small Grizzly Wulffs offer superior floating qualities that make it the better choice for fishing the *Heptagenia* hatch. Drift the patterns over rising fish or use it as a searching pattern.

Midges are important on the Los Piños throughout the summer, and some areas have them in extraordinary numbers. When the air is thick with these tiny insects, tie some 7X tippet on the end of your leader and float a size 20 Griffith's Gnat. If the dry fly is consistently refused or simply isn't working, the fish may be feeding on emerging midge pupa just under the surface. In this situation, try size 18–22 midge pupa fished just under the surface using the greased leader technique. Use fly floatant to grease your leader from the end of the fly line to about 6 inches from the fly. This will keep the pupa pattern suspended a short distance below the surface in the zone where the trout are feeding.

As summer progresses and the days grow warmer, water temperatures in the Los Piños rise to levels that are uncomfortable for trout, so July and August can be slow months on the river. Many small mayflies hatch during this period, but the fish feed most regularly in the morning and evening. An exception is during late July, when a large tan mayfly hatch occurs between 10:30 a.m. and noon. The insects, probably an *Ephemerella* species, are matched with a size 12 Light Hendrickson fished over the runs and light riffles. The fish are very selective at this time, and the pattern must match the naturals and the float must be perfect to get a take. Once this hatch is over for the day, fishing slows until evening.

When there are no hatches on the water, try fishing attractors or terrestrials. Proven patterns on the Los Piños include Royal Coachman, Adams, and Stimulators, all tied in sizes 12–18. Size 10–14 Woolly Worms in brown, black, and olive are excellent searching wet flies. Often a size 14–18 Black or Cinnamon Ant will tempt a quiet trout. On windy summer days, any hopper pattern is a good choice.

Caddis larva are another fine mid-summer avenue for fooling trout. An abundance of *Rhyacophilia, Hydropsyche,* and *Brachycentrus* caddis larva live on the stream bottom. Throughout the year, caddis larva patterns fished deep will lure trout. Try a Green Caddis Larva, Cased Caddis, or soft hackle patterns, in sizes 12–16.

As on most New Mexico streams, fishing picks up on the Los Piños in mid-September and continues to be good through winter's first cold spell. Attractors, terrestrials, and nymphs are the best patterns to select for fall and winter fishing. Try casting attractors to rising fish. When using nymphs, it is important to get the fly to the bottom of the deepest pools where the trout lie during the colder weather. Sinking line, weighted flies, and split shot on the leader will all help late season angling.

The Los Piños is a mosaic of public and private waters, with the private waters well-marked and usually fenced off. The upper portions of the river in Colorado are in the Rio Grande National Forest, and the Toltec Gorge area in New Mexico is in the Carson National Forest. The lower portion of the Los Piños is managed by the New Mexico Department of Game and Fish as the Rio de los Piños Wildlife and Fishing Area. About 3 miles above the Game and Fish property, the river again flows through a small part of the National Forest. Campgrounds are available at Trujillo Meadows and in the Wildlife and Fishing Area, and fine primitive camping sites are scattered throughout the National Forest areas.

You can reach the upper meadows of the Rio de los Piños by way of CO 17 from either Chama, New Mexico, or Antonito, Colorado. Near the summit of Cumbres Pass, turn north on FR 118 following the signs to Trujillo Meadows Reservoir and campground. From the reservoir area, four-wheel drive roads lead to the Los Piños above and below the impoundment.

Two approaches are possible when fishing the Toltec Canyon area. You can take FR 103 off of CO 17 about 11 miles west of Antonito. This is a long, rough dirt road that twists its way for about 18 miles to the town of Osier and the Los Piños. Four-wheel drive is recommended. Another approach is to ride the Cumbres and Toltec Scenic Railroad to Osier. The railroad is flexible (for a price), and arrangements can be made to be dropped off and picked up later the same day or a few days later. Get in touch with the railroad in Chama (505-756- 2151) for details.

The lower section of river is reached from Antonito, Colorado. Immediately south of the intersection of US 285 and CO 17 and the railroad crossing on US 285, turn west on a paved road. Follow the road through the small town of San Antonio. Look for an intersection where the paved road turns left toward the town of Ortiz and a gravel road heads straight. Take the gravel road 5 miles to the Game and Fish public water. Beyond the western boundary of the Wildlife and Fishing Area is a 3-mile stretch of private land. The road continues to parallel the stream in the Carson National Forest, but becomes rough 2 miles beyond the forest boundary and requires a high clearance vehicle to continue to the next fence.

The Los Piños offers fantastic fishing experiences both in the number and size of the fish to be caught. Beginning fly fishermen will find plenty of rising trout to cast to, trout that are not only eager for a meal but are also smart enough to present a challenge. The river's moderate size allows for easy casting and yet offers a variety of trout lies to practice on. For experienced anglers, early summer days can provide almost continuous action.

RIO VALLECITOS
Craig Martin

Location: Tusas Mountains, Carson National Forest,
    some private
Altitude: 6,500 to 9,800 feet
Type of Water: medium-sized freestone stream with pockets
    and pools
Best Times: June to mid-July, September
Hatches: Golden Stoneflies, mystery hatch, Red Quill, caddisflies
Patterns: Adams, Brown Wulff, Humpy, Red Quill,
    Elk Hair Caddis
Localities Map Location: E4
USGS Quadrangle Maps: La Madera, Cañon Plaza, Burned
    Mountain

TUCKED FAR AWAY IN A QUIET CORNER OF RIO ARRIBA COUNTY IS A sparkling little trout stream, the Rio Vallecitos. The river is a quiet haven that normally sees light angling pressure. Loaded with eagerly rising wild brown trout, this gem of a stream makes it easy to catch and release a dozen fish in the course of a lazy afternoon.

The Rio Vallecitos flows southeast from its headwaters in the Tusas

Mountains to join Ojo Caliente Creek, a tributary of the Rio Chama. Its course is determined by a zone of faults that have brought Precambrian rocks—some of the oldest rocks in New Mexico—to the surface. The granites are very resistant to erosion, and the river is often confined in narrow, rocky canyons. As a result, the Vallecitos flows through a pattern of alternating broad valleys and narrow gorges. Within the canyons, the hard rock gives the stream a freestone nature, mixed with pocket water and numerous deep holes, perfect habitat for brown trout and fly fishermen.

The Vallecitos is a medium-sized stream ranging in width from 15–30 feet. Depths during an average flow are from 6–18 inches, with holes of up to 6 feet deep. This is a free-stone stream with an excellent mix of runs, riffles, pockets, and pools. In-stream boulders are common. Unlike similar streams in the state, the Vallecitos offers frequent stretches of quiet water. The stream bottom is composed of rounded granite and gneiss boulders, cobbles, and pebbles, all covered with algae, making them slippery. Wading the slow, shallow water presents no problem, but the slick bottom requires anglers to wear felt-soled boots. Casting on the river is easy: the banks are lined with willows, alders, and grass, but there are few overhanging branches and the stream is wide enough to permit snag-free backcasts. Casting distances are less than 25 feet.

Two forks comprise the headwaters of the Vallecitos. Placer Creek, the stream that is dammed to form Hopewell Lake, heads below Jawbone Mountain. Above the lake, Placer Creek can be fished in the spring for spawning brook trout, but the small stream dries up during the summer. Below Hopewell, the creek holds plenty of brown trout as it flows through a small canyon about 2 miles long before joining the main Vallecitos. The main fork heads on the private Tierra Amarilla Land Grant before flowing into the Carson National Forest. It can be fished for wild browns upstream for about 3 miles from the junction with Placer Creek.

To reach the headwaters of the Vallecitos, take US 64 to Hopewell Lake, about 16 miles west of Tres Piedras or 20 miles east of Tierra

Amarilla. Follow Placer Creek from the dam at Hopewell; the junction with the Vallecitos is about 2 miles below the lake.

The lower river is reached through a number of small mountain communities in central Rio Arriba County. From Española, take US 84 west to the junction with US 285, about 6 miles north of town. Turn right and follow US 285 north through Ojo Caliente to the junction with NM 111 (about 22 miles from US 84). Turn left (west) and follow NM 111 past the junction with NM 554 through the town of La Madera. A short stretch of public water begins about 4 miles above La Madera from about milepost 9 to milepost 11. The river swings away from the road in the lower canyon, flowing between high, rugged walls, and then returns to parallel the road for a mile. This stretch is mostly pocket water with a few very deep holes; it is excellent water for fishing with nymphs.

To reach the main canyon section, continue on NM 111 through the villages of Vallecitos and Cañon Plaza. Just beyond Cañon Plaza, about 20 miles from US 285, turn west on FR 274. This gravel road is easily passable in any vehicle during dry weather. Private land borders the river for 3 miles, up to the bridge over the river. Public water begins upstream from the bridge and continues for about 3.5 miles to the junction of Jarosa Creek. This section is the most productive on the river, with many runs and deep pools to harbor trout.

Cañada Escondida, another access point, is reached by continuing on FR 274. Past the bridge, FR 274 is rough and a high clearance vehicle is recommended. Travel on FR 274 for 2 miles and park at a dirt track leading downhill to a grassy meadow. (If you go to the cattle guard and private property, you have gone too far.) Walk down the dirt track, then follow a trail to the dry bottom of Cañada Escondida. The valley leads to the Vallecitos, which is about a half-mile from the parking area.

The Vallecitos holds mostly stream-bred brown trout, although catching a stocked rainbow is not unusual. The browns are small, averaging 9 inches, and their number is amazing. In the deeper holes of the lower section near La Madera and in the upper miles of the main canyon above Cañon Plaza, the average size of fish increases to 12 inches, with an occasional fish at 15 inches or more. These wild browns are strong fighters and are more likely to jump than most brown trout in New Mexico.

To effectively fish the Vallecitos, cover the water thoroughly. When possible, cast from the middle of the stream, hitting all the pockets and along the banks. Pay particular attention to runs or pockets that are over 12 inches deep, the front side of in-stream boulders, and the tails of runs and pools. The largest fish are often in fast and broken water close to the banks.

Runoff on the Vallecitos begins in mid-April and continues to late May. By early June, the river is in perfect condition—clear water, moderate flows, and cool temperatures—and fantastic insect activity covers the water. During June, it is not unusual to find multiple hatches of 8–10 insects.

The action begins around 10 a.m. with two important mayfly hatches. The largest mayfly is the same species that hatches 2 weeks later on the Rio de los Piños. While the identity of the insect is in doubt, there is no question that the one-inch long insects, with gray-brown bodies and gray wings, are attractive to trout. They can be imitated with an Adams or a Brown Wulff in sizes 10 or 12. Fish the pattern to rising trout or use it as an attractor, covering all the likely holding lies. This hatch continues until noon, with small numbers of insects remaining on the water throughout the day.

Occurring at about the same time is a hatch of smaller but more numerous mayflies of the genus *Paraleptophlebia*. These insects have reddish-brown bodies and gray wings; effective imitations are Red Quills and Brown Wulffs in sizes 14 or 16. In quiet water, a brown/gray parachute or Compara-Dun pattern may be required to fool the larger trout.

Lesser mayfly hatches and at least four stonefly hatches (including Little Yellow Stones and a *Malenka* species) overlap the two large mayfly hatches to produce some fantastic fishing. In the evening, caddis hatches, including a gray-winged size 10 species, add to the parade of insects available to the trout. Although some of the fish are selec-

157

tive feeders, most of the trout are willing to take any pattern. In pocket water within the main canyon, high floating patterns like Humpys and Royal Wulffs are as effective as more closely matched flies.

Depending on summer temperatures, a small hatch of Golden Stoneflies occurs from mid-June to early July. These large insects migrate from areas of fast currents to shore, where they emerge on rocks or vegetation. When nymphal shucks are observed on the rocks or adults are seen flying over the stream, fishing with any large, light-colored stonefly nymph pattern can attract large fish. Fish the pattern dead-drift through riffles, then swing it toward the bank to imitate the insect's migration to shore. Adult stonefly patterns, such as the Sofa Pillow, are also effective during this hatch.

Excellent fishing on the Vallecitos continues through early July. Mid-summer hatches include *Ephemerella* and *Heptagenia* mayflies, midges, and numerous caddis species. The most important caddis is a dark, size 10 caddis that swarms over the water in the late afternoon and on overcast days. Most attractor patterns are effective in the riffles and pocket water, and Elk Hair Caddis is the most consistent fish attractor in July.

By late July, water temperatures on the Vallecitos climb into the upper 60s while flow volume is low. Fishing is tough, as the temperature makes the fish lethargic and the low water makes them spooky. Difficult conditions remain through August into mid-September, when cooling temperatures stimulate feeding. Sporadic Blue-winged Olives hatch in the fall, but fishing any attractor pattern is usually effective. By November, cold temperatures have put an end to the fishing.

The near-perfect stream structure of the Vallecitos has created a very special brown trout fishery. This wild population of trout maintains high numbers, but there are some indications that the fishery is on the decline. As more anglers discover the Vallecitos, it is important to consider the river's future. Fly fishermen should consider releasing all brown trout taken from this gem of a stream.

Tierra Amarilla:
Rio Chama and Rio Brazos

WHEN THE LAST OF THE GREAT SEAS THAT COV-
ered northern New Mexico receded about seventy
million years ago, it left behind thick accumulations
of sand, silt, and mud that were slowly compressed and
turned to rock. The thickest of these many layers—the soft,
tan stratum known as Mancos Shale—is exposed in much of
western Rio Arriba County, giving the earth a distinct yellow tinge. This
extensive area is drained by two important rivers, the Rio Chama and
its tributary, the Rio Brazos.

The Rio Chama is a long and diverse river and is the major tributary of the Rio Grande in northern New Mexico. Flowing from headwaters in Colorado's San Juan Mountains, the Chama enters New
Mexico as a small and tumbling cold-water trout stream. Gathering
momentum and volume from numerous small tributaries, the river
carves out a deep canyon before its impoundment in El Vado Reservoir. Below El Vado Dam is another deep canyon section, where the
Chama acquires Wild and Scenic River status. Impounded again in
Abiquiu Lake, the Chama takes on the character of a warm-water fishery, only to support trout again in the tailwaters of Abiquiu Dam. Along
this disparate journey, the river is a patchwork of public and private

land. Fortunately, most of the finest fishing water is accessible to the fisherman. The Chama is best known for its tailwater fisheries below the two dams that were built to provide water for downstream irrigation interests.

The Rio Brazos feeds the Chama just north of the town of Tierra Amarilla. After heading in high meadows, the Brazos becomes a rough and tumbling mountain stream, carving out the impressive gorge known as the Brazos Box. In contrast to the Chama, most of the finest water on the Brazos is on private land. Fine summer hatches on the Brazos make it a favorite river for many local fly fishermen.

UPPER RIO CHAMA
Dirk Kortz

Location: Edward Sargent Wildlife Area, Rio Chama Wildlife Area, some private
Altitude: 7,200 to 10,000 feet
Type of Water: freestone, riffle and pool, pocket water
Best Times: late spring through early fall
Hatches: caddisflies, stoneflies, mayflies
Patterns: Brooks Stone, Humpy, Renegade, Woolly Worm, Muddler Minnow
Localities Map Location: E3
USGS Quadrangle Maps: Chama, Heron Reservoir

THE UPPER RIO CHAMA EXTENDS FROM BENEATH CHAMA PEAK IN Colorado, through the town of Chama, New Mexico, to the Rio Chama Wildlife Area managed by the New Mexico Department of Game and Fish. This 50-mile stretch of water is a mosaic of public and private land, but plenty of locations provide access to fine fishing.

The headwaters of the Chama are in Colorado's Rio Grande National Forest. Here the river flows through meadows and canyons as a

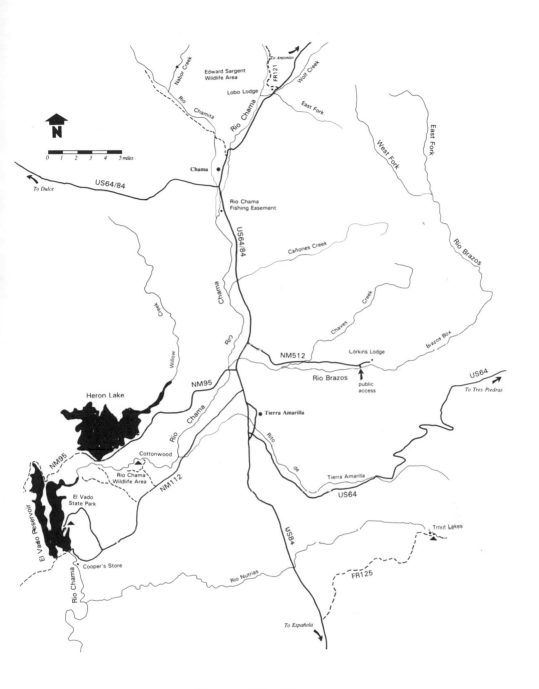

Upper Rio Chama

small freestone stream with many beaver ponds. At nearly 10,000 feet, these upper meadows see a short fishing season that lasts from late June through September. Few anglers make the trip into this section, and the rainbows and wild browns are not selective. On fast-moving water, attractor patterns, Humpys, and stonefly nymphs are effective. On the beaver ponds, a cautious approach and more realistic flies, such as parachute patterns and Comparaduns, are required.

Below the National Forest boundary is about 10 miles of private water controlled by the Lobo Lodge. For the price of a night's lodging, you can fish the Chama for wild browns and some stocked rainbows, or try a small tributary, Wolf Creek, for cutthroats. The nature of the stream is much the same as in the public section above, and the same patterns and techniques are effective.

This uppermost section of the Chama is subject to periods of turbid flow, which make the river unfishable for days. The source of the problem is frequent landslides on the unstable soils of the upper basin. Heavy rains or snowmelt can cause slides of up to 30 acres, which deposit tons of silt on the Chama's floodplain. After a slide, any rainfall can turn the river cloudy as the deposited silt is washed into the stream. Because of these conditions, it is best to fish the upper basin during dry periods.

To reach either the National Forest section or the Lobo Lodge water, drive about 5 miles north of the town of Chama, New Mexico, on NM 17. Turn left (north) on FR 121. Lobo Lodge is a short distance up the road. The Rio Grande National Forest boundary is another 8 miles north.

Downstream from the Lobo Lodge property, the next access point to the Chama is through the Edward Sargent Wildlife Area, a 20,000-acre tract managed by the New Mexico Department of Game and Fish. The Chama forms the area's southeastern boundary, giving anglers who are willing to hike access to about 3 miles of river. To get to the river in the Sargent Area, turn west off NM 17 onto First Street in the town of Chama. Go two blocks, then turn north on Pine Street, continuing to the Edward Sargent boundary where there is a small parking area. It is a half-mile hike along the trail to the river. Camping is permitted in the designated area near the entrance.

At this point, the Chama is a medium-sized freestone stream. The river is wide enough for easy casting and shallow enough for safe wading with felt-soled boots and hip waders. In the river, anglers will find wild brown trout and stocked rainbows, in the 9–15-inch range. Fishing is best from late June to late September.

The river is home to fine populations of mayflies, caddisflies, and stoneflies, and the trout are not selective in their feeding habits. Large, dry attractor flies, sizes 12 or 14, are effective during the morning and evening hours. Try the old reliables: Elk Hair Caddis, Adams, Humpys, and any of the Wulffs. Throughout the year, nymphs are an excellent choice at any time of day. Brooks Stone and similar stonefly patterns in sizes 8–12 should be fished along the bottom. Pheasant Tail Nymphs, sizes 12–16, will imitate the many mayfly nymphs in the river. Forage fish and leech patterns are also important here. Try black or olive Woolly Buggers, Little Brown Trout Streamers, or Muddler Minnows in sizes 8 or 10.

Muddler

This portion of the Chama is managed as Special Trout Water, and a two-trout possession limit is in effect. When you have kept two trout, you must stop fishing. Only flies and artificial lures with single, barbless hooks may be used.

Below the town of Chama, the river flows through many miles of private land. The New Mexico Department of Game and Fish maintains two river tracts, known jointly as the Chama River Fishing Easement, which provide access to about 4 miles of river. This heavily used area is located west of US 64/84 about 2 miles south of the town of Chama. Watch for signs along the highway.

Large numbers of rainbows are stocked here on a regular basis, and, if you can escape the crowds, fishing is often excellent. The river is a moderate-sized freestone stream with good riffles, runs, and pools. Stream-bred browns are also present, and, provided there has been adequate summer rainfall, fishing for them improves greatly during their autumn spawning. Wading is not difficult, but felt-soled wading shoes are recommended. Hip boots are usually adequate, although chest waders are better in the early season. Wet wading is popular in the summer. Late spring and early summer are the best times to be on this section of river. Flows can be low in late summer and autumn, and the river is iced over during the winter. Favorite patterns here are Woolly Worms in black, brown, and olive; Bitch Creek Nymphs; Renegades; and small mayfly nymph imitations like the Gold-ribbed Hare's Ear. Dry-fly-fishing is sporadic though it is wise to carry a few dependables like the Adams, Elk Hair Caddis, and Griffith's Gnat.

For the next 10 miles, the Chama flows through private land. It is possible to fish the river at the NM 95 bridge, but the conditions are much better downstream in the Rio Chama Wildlife Area, managed by the New Mexico Department of Game and Fish. Access is from NM 112 (El Vado Dam Road), which is off US 64/84 one mile north of Tierra Amarilla. A little less than 6 miles from the turnoff is a large Game and Fish sign on the right at the entrance to the Wildlife Area. Turn here and follow the dirt road for about a mile down to the river at the eastern boundary of the property. A second entrance, a mile farther down NM 112, will take you to Cottonwood Campground, an excellent base for fishing this section of the Chama. A third entrance off NM 112 leads to the river farther downstream, but without a topographic map it is easy to get lost in the maze of dirt roads. All of these dirt roads in the Wildlife Area are impassable after heavy rains.

At the Wildlife Area, the Chama remains a moderate-sized freestone river. Casting and wading are easy, and the rainbows and browns are eager to feed and readily take both dry flies and nymphs. Patterns such as stonefly nymphs, caddis larva, Gold-ribbed Hare's Ears, and

Pheasant Tails in sizes 12–16 are the best bets for subsurface fishing; size 12 or 14 attractor dry flies produce the best results on top.

Fishing improves with a short hike up or downstream from the camping areas. The river from Cottonwood Campground upstream to the eastern boundary of the Game and Fish property is managed as Special Trout Water. Fishing is restricted to the use of flies and artificial lures with a single, barbless hook, and only two trout over 12 inches may be in possession.

TAILWATER FISHERIES OF THE RIO CHAMA
Dirk Kortz

Location: Bureau of Land Management, New Mexico
        Game and Fish
Altitude: 6,000 to 7,800 feet
Type of Water: freestone, riffle and pool
Best Times: late June, July, late September to December
Hatches: Golden Stoneflies, caddisflies, mayflies
Patterns: Peacock Nymph, Woolly Worm, Hare's Ear Nymph,
        Renegade, Bitch Creek Nymph, Little Brown Trout
        Streamer, Adams, Light Cahill, Elk Hair Caddis,
        Griffith's Gnat
Localities Map Location: D3, E4, E5
USGS Quadrangle Maps: Chama, Heron Reservoir, El Vado,
        Cañones, Abiquiu

THERE ARE TWO DAMS ON THE RIO CHAMA THAT ARE OPERATED BY the Army Corps of Engineers and the Bureau of Land Management, and a third dam nearby also affects the river and the fishing. Abiquiu Dam is about 32 miles upstream from the confluence of the Rio Grande and the Chama, and El Vado Dam is approximately 45 miles above Abiquiu Dam. The mainstem of the upper Chama above El Vado

165

Reservoir is undammed; but Heron Dam, located just a little above El Vado Reservoir, is on Willow Creek, a small tributary of the Chama.

The areas below El Vado and Abiquiu dams (and sometimes below Heron Dam, which occasionally releases water to the Rio Chama) are tailwater fisheries in which the volume of water may fluctuate greatly. Water release rates depend on a variety of factors, including agricultural needs, flood control, and the water demands from the city of Albuquerque. Releases are also made from El Vado to accommodate whitewater rafters. The dates and times of rafting releases below El Vado can be obtained from a recorded message from the Bureau of Land Management Taos Resource Office (505-758-8148). It is advisable to call about the flows and stream conditions before setting out.

Rio Chama Below Heron Dam

The Rio Chama flows around Heron Lake, passing just below Heron Dam. (Most of the water in Heron comes from the San Juan watershed via a trans-mountain pipeline.) The Chama is not a true tailwater fishery here, even though you are downriver from a dam. Water from the lake is rarely released, so anglers can generally expect low flows during the late summer and plenty of ice during the winter. Late spring and early summer are usually the best times for fishing, but autumn can also be very good depending on summer rainfall. In a very dry year, the upper Chama may run as low as 25 cfs in the late fall and, unless water is released from Heron Lake, that doesn't leave much room for the fish.

There is a little over a mile of free-running river below the dam before the slack water backed up by El Vado Reservoir. It is possible to fish this quiet water by wading the edges and casting Woolly Buggers, but it is a lot of work. It is much easier to fish the moving water of this section, a freestone stream 40–60 feet wide with moderate to large boulders. There are good-sized riffles, runs, and pools (some quite deep) and high canyon walls on both sides. There is also some very good water upriver from the dam. The lower boundary of the Special Regulations Water at Cottonwood Campground is about 4 miles upriver from Heron Dam.

A large population of stocked and holdover rainbows are found here, running from 8–14 inches, as well as a lesser number of slightly smaller self-sustaining browns. There is also an occasional lunker up from El Vado Reservoir.

Wading is relatively easy once the runoff is over in late spring, and the river is wide enough for easy casting. Wet wading is possible by mid-June *if* the sun is out. Hip boots are adequate, but chest waders are better, and felt-soled wading shoes are highly recommended.

Many different subsurface patterns work well here: Woolly Worms, Bitch Creeks, most streamers, Renegades, beetles, Black Ants, Gold-ribbed Hare's Ear, and Pheasant Tails. Dry-fly-fishing is sporadic, although it is worth carrying Adams and Griffith's Gnats in small sizes, along with some size 14 Elk Hair Caddis.

Access to this stretch of the Chama is off US 84. Two miles above Tierra Amarilla, take NM 95 and go about 10 miles to Heron Lake. Stop at the Visitor Center about midway along this road to get a parking permit, which currently is not available at the dam. Just before you reach the dam is a gravel road on the left that leads to a parking area and trailhead. The stairway leading down to the river will put you a quarter-mile upriver from Heron Dam. Walking along the river involves some scrambling over boulders, particularly downriver, and the stairway is noticeably longer on the return trip.

For information on releases from Heron Dam, call the Army Corps of Engineers in Albuquerque at (505) 766-1744.

Rio Chama Below El Vado Dam

To fish the Chama below El Vado you must begin at El Vado Ranch, the only access point on this stretch. El Vado Ranch is run by David Cooper and his family, who charge a small fee for parking and also run a small campground. For something more comfortable than a plot beneath the piñons, the Coopers also rent cabins at reasonable rates, but then you'd miss some enchanting wildlife experiences. (I could relate several interesting skunk anecdotes if space permitted, but I'll only offer one small piece of advice: when you go to sleep, don't leave the cap off your whiskey bottle.)

There is some excellent water in the mile upstream from the ranch to the dam. You can find classic riffles, runs, and pools and a lot of nice pocket water, all in a picturesque canyon that is populated with local wildlife. During the spring and summer, the area is also populated with fishermen. Even though you are not likely to get the river all to yourself, there is some very good fishing here.

Heavy stocking of rainbows (mostly 8–13 inches, but some larger ones as well) occurs from April through September. Some browns are occasionally stocked, but there is a healthy population of wild browns as well as plenty of good-sized holdover rainbows, so fishing the off-season can also be rewarding. Fall can be especially good when the browns move up to spawn. There is also a late autumn Kokanee salmon run. When water temperatures dip down to the high 30s, from about the beginning of December until spring, the fishing slacks off and on a good day you can take two or three fish.

For those willing to walk, the Chama downriver from the ranch offers as much solitude as any river reach in New Mexico. The river is wider here, with lots of riffle water. There are still plenty of runs, pools, boulders, and pockets as well as some undercut banks. Besides being less crowded than the upstream area, the fishing is better. You can catch more wild browns as you move downriver, and they are generally larger the farther downriver you go. The state record brown trout came out of this part of the Rio Chama in 1946 (20 lbs., 4 oz.), and Carl Cooper took a 14-pounder in 1963. Trout of that size are not caught very often, but 18–20-inch browns are not uncommon.

Wading in hip boots will somewhat restrict mobility unless the flows are below 100 cfs and, even at low flows, there will inevitably be places where you might wish your boots were one inch higher. Chest waders are much better, both up and downriver. Wet wading is enjoyable during warm days, but remember that the water temperature coming out of the dam is never much above the mid-50s. Although wading in sneakers is possible, felt-soled wading shoes are recommended to negotiate the mossy bottom.

Because in-stream flows vary so widely, wading ranges from easy (with the right shoes) to dangerous, no matter what you wear on your feet. At 100 cfs you can cross just about anywhere, but at 200 cfs your choices begin to narrow considerably. Above 350 cfs you would be well-advised to use the footbridge located at the ranch, unless you feel in need of a bath. Fly-fishing is best at flows of around 90–150 cfs, and success diminishes as the flows increase. If you like flinging a Woolly Bugger with a quarter-pound of lead, you can fish when the river is running 600 cfs and higher.

In 1989, this section of the Rio Chama was officially designated a Wild and Scenic River, largely due to the efforts of rafting interests. In the spring, the rafters have quite a bit of control over the flows. But water levels that are attractive to rafters are not so attractive to wading fly fishermen, and it is strongly recommended that you telephone the Taos BLM Office to check flow rates before leaving home for the Chama.

Wherever there are large brown trout there are going to be large things for them to eat. Downriver from Cooper's, you will occasionally catch big browns on tiny dry flies or nymphs, but not very often. There is a good stock of forage fish here, so bucktails and streamers are effective. Imitations of dace, chub, and suckers are all useful and, trout being the cannibals that they are, a properly presented Little Brown Trout streamer is almost a sure thing. In fact, any streamers with yellow in them should work, for example, a yellow and brown Woolly Bugger. Black, brown, or olive Woolly Worms, Woolly Buggers, Peacock Nymphs, and attractor flies, all in large sizes, are effective. Plenty of rainbows live downriver, too, and they will also go for the big patterns, but usually in slightly smaller sizes. Include a size 14 Gold-ribbed Hare's Ear or similar pattern for the rainbows. Very late in the year, you should be prepared for midge hatches and a Blue-wing Olive *(Baetis)* hatch. Upstream from the ranch, where rainbows predominate for most of the year, an excellent first choice is a size 14 or 16 Gold-ribbed Hare's Ear nymph. Woolly Worms and Renegades are also popular.

To get to El Vado Ranch from US 84, turn west onto NM 112 (El Vado Dam Road) about one mile north of Tierra Amarilla. Drive about 13 miles to El Vado Ranch Road, which is marked with a big sign. Follow this road for three-quarters of a mile and you will be at the ranch and on the river.

For information on fishing conditions and releases from El Vado Dam, call the Cooper family at El Vado Ranch 505-588-7354.

Rio Chama Below Abiquiu Dam

The Rio Chama below Abiquiu Dam is classified as a marginal cold-water/warm-water fishery. Due to wildly fluctuating flows, heavy siltation, and almost continual muddiness, this area is not considered good habitat for trout. Due to these conditions, the amount of stocking presently done by the New Mexico Department of Game and Fish is negligible. This may be fortunate, as stocked fish do not intrude on the durable but sometimes marginal population of wild browns that live here.

This part of the Rio Chama has sustained staggering abuse and neglect, and even seemingly outright contempt. The river badly needs to be re-evaluated and protected if it is ever going to become the quality fishery that it has the potential to be. As of this writing, surveys are underway to accumulate data on the river's potential, but surveys are by no means a guarantee that anything will be done about the problems. The long-range goals should be habitat improvement, regulated flows, and stronger protective kill limits than those enacted in 1990. A longer-range wish is that at some point the bottom level outflow of Abiquiu Reservoir will be replaced with an adjustable system that will not pass tons of sediment through the reservoir at the expense of the downriver environment. All of this requires a lot of effort by concerned fly fishermen.

There is also a growing danger that increased fishing pressure could cause the New Mexico Department of Game and Fish to increase stocking. This would be a step in the wrong direction, only adding to the woes of the already beleaguered resident browns. What is needed is not more stocked trout but a dramatic improvement in the management of the river itself, so that a valuable resource (not only for fishermen) is enhanced.

A step in the right direction was taken recently when the Chama below Abiquiu Dam was designated Special Trout Water. A two-trout limit is in effect from Abiquiu Dam downstream to the US 84 bridge just north of the town of Abiquiu. No tackle restrictions are in effect.

Considering the continuing damage to insect populations and trout spawning beds, combined with the high mortality and slow growth rate of the fish, it is remarkable how good the fishing can be when flows are stable and the water clears. If you choose to fish here and are fortunate enough to visit when conditions are right, please remember

that these fish have enough problems surviving and consider return-
ing the browns you catch to the water.

Except for the first half-mile or so below the dam, where the sides
of the Chama are steep and rocky, the river has a moderate-to-wide
freestone bed with some soft, deeply silted areas. It is not difficult to
wade with sneakers, but felt-soled wading shoes give you an advantage
at higher flows, especially when the river has been flowing at the same
level for a while and moss has had time to accumulate. Casting is
virtually unobstructed, except in a few places.

The river can be fished year-round as long as flow and visibility
permit. Optimum flows are 200–350 cfs. Fishing is not bad at flows
from 100–500 cfs, but at lower flows the fish tend to hide and wait for
better times; at higher flows, discoloration increases and wading is limited. Flow rates and visibility play a larger part than time of year in
determining when you fish here. Even with seemingly perfect conditions the fish can be extremely unpredictable; but, considering the
unpredictability of their environment, this is not surprising.

As on the upper sections of the Rio Chama, these fish do most of
their feeding deep, and wet flies are much more important than dry
flies. Caddis larva and mayfly nymphs exist in the faster moving water,
where siltation is least prevalent. There are sporadic emergences of
caddis, when you will find a few widely scattered rising fish.

If you are on the river during the first half of July and the water is
fishable, you will want to carry some size 12 and 16 Light Cahills or
Pale Yellow Comparaduns. These flies approximate the two different
sized but similarly colored mayflies that hatch during this period. The
trout do not seem to mind if your imitation is less than perfect. You
may find nymphing these hatches to be more productive.

Midges are abundant. The hatches that bring up consistent risers
occur late in the year and right near the dam. A size 22 Griffith's Gnat
should be close enough to get results, as long as it is presented carefully. These fish aren't terribly selective, but they are wild and they
don't tolerate much line splashing when they are feeding on the surface.

There are forage fish like chub, dace, and suckers, and streamers are a good choice of pattern. Because this is a reproducing population, small brown trout can be imitated with a variety of streamers, not the least of which is the Little Brown Trout Streamer. Woolly Worms, Woolly Buggers, Gold-ribbed Hare's Ear, and any nymph with peacock on it should also work.

To reach Abiquiu Dam, take US 84 for approximately 27 miles north of Española. Turn left on the Dam Road, NM 96, and in 2 miles you will be at the dam. The road leading down to the river is on the left just before the dam. Drive past the perpetual construction site, and you will find a parking lot on your left a half-mile downriver. You can drive farther downstream and park along the road, but be advised that this road can get sloppy in wet weather and even when dry there are places where it is tough on a low-slung vehicle. About 1.5 miles downriver, there is a second parking area near a large irrigation dam. From here you can fish either back up toward Abiquiu Dam or downriver until you hit private property.

The Army Corps of Engineers has a toll-free message with information on releases from Abiquiu Dam (800-843-3029). This message is geared to downstream agricultural water users, and you have to wait until the end of the message to see whether or not it will tell you what you need to know about fishing. If you are not satisfied with what you hear, call the ACOE project office at Abiquiu Dam at 505-685-4371.

RIO BRAZOS
Craig Martin

Location: Brazos Ridge, private land, with some public access
Altitude: 7,600 to 10,700 feet
Type of Water: freestone, pocket water, riffle, and pool
Best Times: May to mid-June, September and October
Hatches: Giant Stonefly, caddisflies
Patterns: Brooks Stone, Bird's Stonefly, Humpy, Elk Hair
          Caddis, Woolly Worm
Localities Map Location: E3
USGS Quadrangle Maps: Tierra Amarilla, Penasco Amarillo,
                          Lagunitas Creek, West Fork
                          Rio Brazos

THE RIO BRAZOS IS A LONG, WILD STREAM IN NORTHERN NEW MEXICO that is famous for its wild brown trout. Heading in the high mountains east of Chama near the Colorado state line, the two main forks of the Brazos join to flow south through the Brazos Meadows and the dramatic granite cliffs of the Brazos Box. For its last miles, the river is confined to a shallow canyon before opening up to a broad valley where it meets the Rio Chama.

The rugged landscape combined with private land makes much of the Brazos inaccessible to anglers. The entire river flows through private property. Fortunately, most landowners who wish to keep out anglers carefully mark their property. Other landowners do not mind granting permission to considerate anglers who want to fish the river. If the land is posted, stay off; after gaining permission, use unposted land appropriately. The river above Corkins Lodge is reserved for lodge guests only, closing off the Box and Brazos Meadows to public fishing.

The New Mexico Department of Game and Fish has negotiated an easement to provide public access to the Brazos at a point 8 miles up NM 512 from the US 64 turnoff. There is a small parking area here, and anglers can fish downstream for a short stretch or upstream to the Corkins Lodge boundary, over a mile of fine water.

The Brazos is a moderate-sized stream, never wider than 30 feet. The headwater forks are creek-sized, and the stream acquires its full dimensions in the meadows. The river is freestone in nature, with plenty of pocket water in its canyons. In the lower section, the river acquires some riffle-run-pool structure. In all areas, the currents run fast and wading is difficult. Large, slippery, algae-covered boulders on the bottom increase the problems. Hip waders are recommended, felt-soled boots are a must, and cleats can make wading much easier. The stream is brush-lined almost everywhere, making each cast a challenge. The trout are most often found in difficult locations, under fallen trees and hidden beneath overhanging branches.

The entire Brazos from the Chaves Creek Bridge upstream is perfect water for trout. In summer, however, water diversion for irrigation limits flows and makes fishing impossible from a mile below the Game and Fish public access all the way to the Chama.

Rainbows are found near the public access water below Corkins; they are stocked at that location by both Game and Fish and the lodge. The rainbows are in the 9–12-inch range, with a few fish up to 15 inches. Like their wild counterparts, the stocked trout are very sporting to catch.

Brown trout are found throughout the river and range between 9 and 14 inches. Large browns up to 18 inches are common, but they are very wary and are seldom caught. Look for them holding in places that are difficult to reach—under overhanging branches, beneath large rocks, in the quieter currents at the edge of plunge pools, and under fallen logs parallel to the current. The brown trout fishery continues upstream through the Box into Brazos Meadows, where the river forks. Browns are found in the West Fork, and the East Fork holds a population of Rio Grande cutthroats. Fishing the section of the Brazos controlled by Corkins Lodge can be exciting. This section of river is especially fine for wild browns and oversized stocked rainbows. Call the lodge (505-588-7261) for information and current prices.

The Brazos runs low and clear for almost the entire year, except after summer thunderstorms in its headwaters. Runoff is short, coming around the first of April and ending in early May. Spring fishing is good before runoff, and sometimes right through runoff, and is excellent after the high water recedes. Conditions remain perfect until early July, when increasing water temperatures in the lower sections of the river slow the action. Irrigation drawdown and debris entering the river are additional summer problems on the lower Brazos. September brings the return of low, clear, and cool water, conditions that last until the cold weather arrives in late October.

The year's first important hatch on the Rio Brazos is Giant Stoneflies *(Pteronarcys)*. The hatch begins in early May and continues through early June. In most years, runoff is over by this time and fishing can be excellent using stonefly nymphs (Brooks Stone or Bitch Creek, sizes 6–10) or adult patterns (Bird's Stonefly or Sofa Pillow, sizes 8 or 10). A significant caddis hatch begins in early July and lasts through August. Nymph fishing works well with caddis pupa patterns or a size 12 or 14 Hare's Ear Nymph. If the water is not too low, dry caddis patterns are effective in July and August. Tan Elk Hair Caddis in sizes 14 or 16 are a sure bet.

Elk Hair Caddis

Fishing the numerous mayfly hatches requires careful pattern selection in slow water. Where the water is fast, a selection of Humpys and Irresistibles in sizes 12–18 is important. When all else fails, consider using Woolly Worms, in size 8 or 10, with black or brown bodies, grizzly hackle, and a red tail. Drift them along the banks and under the trees.

CHAPTER SEVENTEEN

Trophy Water: Quality Water of the San Juan River

Mark and Jan Gruber

Location: northwest New Mexico below Navajo Dam
Altitude: 5,710 feet at outflow of Navajo Dam
Type of Water: tailwater with riffles, deep pools and runs,
           wide flats with many holding areas throughout
Best Times: year-round
Hatches: midges, Blue-winged Olive, Pale Morning Duns,
        caddisflies
Patterns: midge larva, pupa, emerger and adult, Griffith's Gnat,
        Comparaduns, Adams, Light Cahill, Pale Morning
        Dun, Pheasant Tail and Gold-ribbed Hare's Ear
        Nymphs, Elk Hair Caddis, San Juan worms,
        Woolly Buggers, egg and leech patterns
Localities Map Location: B3, C3
USGS Quadrangle Maps: Navajo Dam, Archuleta

THE SAN JUAN RIVER RANKS WITH OTHER NOTABLE North American tailwaters—the Bighorn, Green, Colorado, White, and Bow. The San Juan offers a wide array of fishing experiences for all anglers, from novices to experts. With proper instruction, even anglers who have never cast a fly before stand a good chance of hooking and

177

landing a prize rainbow trout. At the same time, experienced fly fishermen can find endless challenges fishing tiny dry flies to extremely selective large trout. In addition to excellent fishing, the river also provides a haven for wildlife, including deer, coyotes, beaver, muskrats, geese, ducks, eagles, ospreys, and numerous songbirds.

When we talk of fishing the San Juan, we are concerned only with that portion between Navajo Dam and Abe's (NM 173) bridge, the first bridge downstream from the dam. Although trout do live in the river below that point, the number of fish and the quality of water are not in the same class as the water above. The best part of the river is the stretch that runs 3.75 miles immediately downstream from the dam—the Quality Water section of the San Juan.

You can easily reach the San Juan by following major highways: NM 44 via Cuba to Bloomfield to NM 511; from Aztec on NM 173 to NM 511; from Ignacio, Colorado, on CO/NM 511; and from Chama via Dulce on US 64 to NM 539 to NM 511. The Quality Water parallels NM 511 north of the highway between Abe's bridge and the dam. The river is on public land. The New Mexico Parks and Recreation Department and the U.S. Bureau of Reclamation have provided many public parking areas so anglers can easily get to the river.

The New Mexico Parks and Recreation Department operates two campgrounds, Cottonwood Campground and Navajo Lake State Park. Cottonwood Campground is located on the north side of the river just downstream of the Quality Water section. The campground, off of NM 173 just west of Abe's bridge, has limited camping facilities and restrooms. Navajo Lake State Park is located off NM 511 above the lake, northeast of the Quality Water. It has a large number of camping facilities along with restrooms, showers, and a boat ramp for the lake. There is a fee for camping in the campgrounds and for parking along the river, and self-service pay stations are located at the campgrounds and major parking areas. Carry some dollar bills with you so you can leave the correct amount in the pay envelopes. Lodging and restaurant facilities are adjacent to the intersection of NM 173 and NM 511; complete facilities are located in Bloomfield, Aztec, and Farmington.

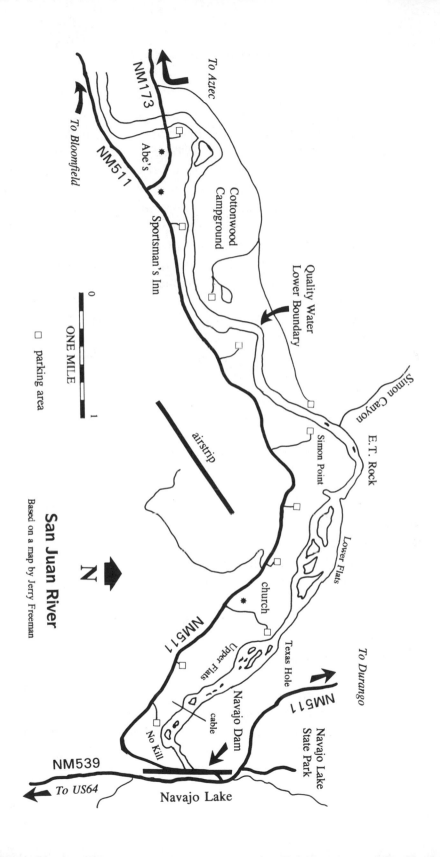

San Juan River

Based on a map by Jerry Freeman

N

☐ parking area

ONE MILE

0   1

To Bloomfield

NM511

NM173

To Aztec

Abe's

Sportsman's Inn

Cottonwood Campground

Quality Water
Lower Boundary

airstrip

Simon Canyon

Simon Point

E.T. Rock

Lower Flats

church

Upper Flats

Texas Hole

Navajo Dam

cable

No Kill

NM511

To Durango

Navajo Lake
State Park

NM511

NM539

To US64

Navajo Lake

The nature of the San Juan dictates that anglers always think about wading safety. Prolific algal growth makes footing very slippery in many areas, and eroded slots and deep pools can fool even the most practiced wader. It is essential that you wear felt-soled wading shoes to reduce the chances of dunking. When using chest waders, always wear a wading belt to prevent your waders from filling up in case you fall in the water. A number of anglers have drowned on the river, so please be careful the next time you chase that big rainbow downstream.

For comfort and safety, synthetic underwear under your wading gear is always recommended. The temperature of the water, even in mid-summer, is only in the mid-40s, and hypothermia can be a concern especially during the late season. Neoprene waders are a real asset on the San Juan.

Long rods, 9 feet or longer, are a distinct advantage in mending line and playing large fish. Line weights 3–5 are best for dry-fly-fishing. Heavier rods, with line weights 5 and 6, are adequate for fishing heavier flies. In almost all cases, floating lines are recommended. Single-action fly reels with smooth drags allow anglers to play large fish on fine tippets. Leaders should be matched to the fishing situation. A 7½-foot leader with a 4X tippet is fine for larger nymphs. More delicate fishing methods may require 12 feet or more of leader with a 6X or 7X tippet. When fishing with nymphs, strike indicators help detect subtle takes. When fishing minute pupae or dries, use tiny indicators or small, visible dry flies placed several feet up the tippet.

Other important equipment on the San Juan is polarized sunglasses, sunscreen, a wide-brimmed hat, a water canteen, and some food. Warm, fleece clothing is excellent on this 40-degree water because it is lightweight, will not absorb water, and dries quickly. Fingerless gloves can be a real comfort in cold weather, and extra clothing is a good idea if you fish early or late in the day.

In the Quality Water section, the San Juan flows through a wide, shallow sandstone canyon. Scattered cottonwoods and dense willow and tamarisk thickets fill the valley floor. Piñon and juniper cover the canyon walls and the mesa top. Although the weather in the canyon runs the gamut from searing heat to intense cold, the river runs a stable 43–45 degrees. The constant water temperature is a significant factor in the river's productivity, as it supports a continuous growth of aquatic food organisms and fish. Flow rates vary depending on regional winter snow pack and irrigators' needs. Outflows range from 500 to over 5,000 cfs, averaging 600–1,200 cfs. The San Juan is not known for the dangerous rapid rises in water level that are so common on other tailwater fisheries.

The San Juan River was impounded by Navajo Dam in June 1962. Prior to damming, the river was turbid, warm, and unsuitable for trout. The Navajo Reservoir now acts as a settling basin to remove the river's burden of silt, and the reservoir's great volume (1.7 million acre-feet) moderates the water temperature in the fishery below. The water is withdrawn from the reservoir at a depth of 203 feet below the maximum water elevation, ensuring a constant optimum temperature.

Beyond the biological reasons for a healthy fish population, special regulations are the other important factor in maintaining the quality of the fishery. Since 1966, the New Mexico Department of Game and Fish has placed special regulations on this section of river, gradually increasing minimum size limits and decreasing bag limits. On the San Juan, anglers are limited to keeping one fish over 20 inches; they must use single, barbless hooks, and no bait fishing is allowed. These restrictions allow for an exceptional nondestructive use of this valuable fish resource. If a "legal" fish is killed, then the angler must stop fishing or fish only in the catch-and-release water. A one-quarter-mile stretch adjacent to the dam is further protected as a catch-and-release (no-kill) area.

The San Juan is primarily a rainbow trout fishery, where rainbows are stocked mostly as fingerlings. Previously, some Snake River cutthroats were introduced in the river; they have hybridized with the rainbows, but occasionally a nearly pure cutthroat may be found. Natural reproduction of both species is poor. Brown trout are rarely caught, but they are more common in the lower reaches. Currently, these browns are not stocked but are wild fish spawned in the river. For smaller fish, average growth rates are about 6 inches per year; growth rates for larger fish are a bit less. The typical fish caught in the San Juan average 14–20 inches.

Because of stable water levels and temperatures, the San Juan resembles a large spring creek with significant algae growth and large populations of aquatic insects. Unlike other large tailwater fisheries, freshwater shrimp (scuds) are not a significant food source nor are there extensive weed beds in the river. The fish in the San Juan are accustomed to seeing a lot of insects of a relatively few species throughout the year. As a result, they are selective in their feeding behavior in regard to pattern, size of the imitation, and its presentation, making the San Juan different from nearly all other New Mexico rivers. These fish rarely feed opportunistically, and the most successful fly fishermen will match the predominant food organism, presenting it accurately and without drag. In spite of its reputation as a "nymph fishing river," the San Juan offers some of the best dry-fly-fishing in New Mexico.

Due to their vast numbers and year-round availability, midges (Diptera) are an important food source. Fish feed on all stages of the midge during its life cycle. Midge larva and pupa imitations, in sizes 18–24, fished on 6X and 7X tippets, are consistent producers. Depending on where the fish are feeding, midge patterns should be fished dead-drift at depths varying from the bottom to the surface film. When riseforms are visible, fish may be feeding on pupa in or near the surface film, on emerging insects, or on single or clusters of adults. Use floating pupae, emergers, or, when groups (clusters) are present, a Griffith's Gnat or similar pattern. It is essential to carefully observe insects and fish to determine which stage you should imitate.

The fish in the San Juan will feed on midges in areas of quieter water, frequently in early morning and late evening. In a group of rising fish, different fish may be feeding on different stages. You will be most successful if you select patterns and methods that are consistent with the observed feeding behavior of an individual fish in a group. Or you may choose a pattern and method (such as a floating midge cluster) and seek out fish whose feeding behavior suggests that they might take the imitation.

Mayflies provide exceptional dry fly and nymph fishing from mid-spring through late fall. Blue-winged Olives *(Baetis)* have peak hatches in April, May, and June and again from October to December. Good patterns that imitate the immature stage include Pheasant Tail and Gold-ribbed Hare's Ear nymphs, size 18 or 20; imitations should be fished on the bottom. During the hatch, which usually occurs in mid-afternoon, these imitations can also be fished successfully in the surface film. When riseforms are first seen but before the fish are clearly taking the duns, mayfly emerger patterns such as an RS2 or floating Pheasant Tail nymph are valuable. As fish move to feed on the subimago or dun stage, patterns such as Blue-winged Olive or grey Comparadun, sizes 16–20, are effective.

Pale Morning Dun *(Ephemerella)* mayfly hatches occur in late July through early October. Nymphs of these larger mayflies are imitated by size 14 or 16 Pheasant Tail and Gold-ribbed Hare's Ear or other generic light tan nymphs. As the hatch progresses, you should follow the techniques for the *Baetis* hatch. Duns are effectively represented by size 14 or 16 Light Cahills, Sparkle Duns, or similar light-colored pattern. As with midges, a careful observation of insects and feeding fish is essential to determine which stage should be imitated. The best areas of the river to find good mayfly hatches are in riffles and on the flats immediately below riffle areas. Spinner falls of both species of mayflies are insignificant.

Caddisfly *(Trichoptera)* hatches are of relatively recent importance on the Quality Waters, and they may not be well enough established as an insect group to be consistently available to the fish. Hatches were excellent in the summer of 1988, but they were almost nonexistent in 1989 except in the lower reaches. A successful pattern is a size 18 brown Elk Hair Caddis. (Oddly enough, this pattern is also sometimes effective during either of the mayfly hatches; it may represent an emerging, crippled, or stillborn mayfly.)

Other important aquatic foods include aquatic worms (annelids)

183

and trout eggs. Worms are available year-round. Successful patterns include San Juan worms in a range of colors, including red, pink, orange, tan, and brown. *(Large hooks or hooks with a very large gap, like English Baithooks, should not be used for worm imitations; they frequently inflict major damage to the eyes and brain of the fish.)* Leech imitations are effective and include Woolly Buggers and chamois and marabou leeches in black and brown. Egg patterns work well during the late fall and winter spawn, and bright colors like pink, peach, and chartreuse are the most effective. Because forage fish are not an important food source for San Juan trout, streamer flies (other than Woolly Buggers) are not usually successful.

This is not meant to be an exhaustive list of insects or fly patterns for the San Juan, just those that consistently work well at particular times of the year. If you tie flies or you come from a different part of the country, don't hesitate to concoct your own patterns or use your own local favorites.

Locating fish on the San Juan is never much of a problem. Trout are everywhere in the river, and newcomers are amazed that they find fish wherever they look. Certain types of water will contain concentrations of food and, consequently, will hold more fish. Riffles are major food "factories," producing large volumes of mayfly nymphs, aquatic annelids, and caddis larvae. Quiet backwaters with silty bottoms produce enormous quantities of midges. Depressions and deeper holes in the large flats are prime holding and feeding areas. The depth and accessibility of many of these areas change dramatically according to flow rates, making it difficult to accurately predict and describe their locations. For instance, many of the side sloughs fill and drain as river flow rates change. The area descriptions below indicate some general areas of riffles, pools, and flats, but successful fishermen locate feeding fish in a variety of water types, not just in the more obvious and popular ones.

Never hesitate to explore new water and use new techniques on the San Juan. Push the limits of your ability. Far too many anglers fish the same places with the same methods. They may catch fish, but they are not likely to learn anything new or fish different water. And that is what this sport is about.

The following areas are given descriptive names only. Each area may be known by several other names.

The No-Kill

The No-Kill area on the San Juan extends from the Navajo Dam downstream to the no-kill boundary cable, approximately one-quarter mile. This section contains some wonderfully diverse water: long, deep runs; shallow flats; and small, deep pools and riffles. The No-Kill is typically midge water, though some Blue-winged Olives and Pale Morning Duns may appear. Stalking the flats and the quiet water is the best way to find midging fish. In the warmer months, watch the riffles in the afternoon for any mayfly activity. Fishing the long, deep run down the center with a Woolly Bugger can also be productive. You can easily spend an entire day fishing this short stretch of river.

The Cable Pool

The Cable Pool begins at the no-kill boundary cable and goes downstream about 100 yards to below the islands. Three distinctly different types of water are found in this reach of the San Juan. To the north is a deep channel, which is best fished on the bottom with Woolly Buggers or mayfly nymphs. The extreme northern bank, with its back eddies, can be the site of some fine dry-fly-fishing during a midge or mayfly hatch. The riffles right below the cable are prime mayfly habitat. Fish this water with mayfly nymphs when a hatch is not on; during a hatch, switch to emergent patterns or dry flies. Blue-winged Olives are the predominant mayfly, though occasionally Pale Morning Duns will appear. The water to the south is slow and calm, making it prime midge territory. As fish feed in the clear shallows, watch for quiet rises throughout this area.

The Upper Flats

The Upper Flats is a wide section of river beginning below the islands at the foot of the Cable Pool, ending in a deep fast run next to the north canyon wall and in a myriad of islands and shallow riffles that stretch across the rest of the river. Water depths in this area are dramatically affected by flow rates, making it easy to wade in the low water (600 cfs or less) and almost impossible to wade in higher water (1000 cfs or more). Watch for the depressions, small pockets, and shallow bars that are scattered throughout the Upper Flats. Fish will sit in these depressions, waiting for food to float by. Mayfly hatches are prolific here and midges are abundant, especially in the shallower, slower water near the south bank and tight against the river's north edge. Even when there is no hatch, the flats are productive when fished with a variety of nymphs, San Juan worms, and leeches.

The Islands and Channels

Under moderate and high water conditions (over 1,000 cfs), the braided water between the Upper Flats and the Texas Hole provides an incredible amount of good fishing with both nymphs and dry flies. Mayfly hatches are dependable, and surprisingly large numbers of fish of all sizes inhabit the small pools below each riffle, moving into very shallow water to feed on midges, mayfly nymphs, and adults. The fishing is fun here, because you often have a clear view of the individual fish you are after. Wading is relatively easy, though smooth and slotted sandstone ledges can be slippery with algae. Under low water conditions (less than 600 cfs), only a few of the pools in this area are deep enough to hold good fish. The deep, fast channel on the far (north) side of the river holds good fish, but it is difficult to fish and even more difficult to land large fish because of the swift current. Wading is treacherous, so be very cautious. An effective method is to drift a small Pheasant Tail or Hare's Ear nymph along the bottom at the edge of the heaviest current. Also, look for fish feeding in the small side eddies.

Kiddy Pool and Texas Hole

Kiddy Pool and Texas Hole, two very popular and often crowded spots, are adjacent to the San Juan Point parking area (also known as the Church Lot or Texas Hole Lot). Both pools contain amazing numbers of fish. During a fall 1989 survey, the New Mexico Department of Game and Fish found about 4,000 fish in Texas Hole alone. Kiddy Pool, just upstream from the parking area, is a large flat pool with two small shallow riffles at its head. Fish in the pool routinely feed on midges here and in the "beaver pond" behind it. Texas Hole, an enormous pool across from the parking area, has several concrete handicapped fishing ramps on the near side. At the pool's head are two large rapids, one on the near side and one next to the far bank. A large back eddy at the head of the pool acts to "recycle" the enormous populations of midges and mayflies, attracting large pods of feeding fish. During a good hatch, huge numbers of midges gather on the north side of Texas Hole, and anglers equipped with midge cluster patterns, such as Griffith's Gnat, can be in for some terrific action. The body of the pool, which cannot be waded, is best fished very deep with Woolly Buggers and leech and worm patterns.

Lower Texas Hole Riffles

The Texas Hole ends in a series of riffles and pockets before coming to Jack's Hole farther downstream. This series of riffles holds many large fish that are difficult to reach due to deep water and fast currents. Effective patterns include San Juan worms and mayfly imitations. This stretch often has heavy Blue-winged Olive hatches.

Jack's Hole

Jack's Hole begins below the lower Texas Hole riffles and precedes downstream ending in the riffle above the Lower Flats. Jack's Hole is a long, deep run that is difficult to fish from shore, yet it holds some of the largest fish in the upper river. The riffle at its head can be fished effectively with leech and worm patterns. The run cannot be crossed by wading, so the most effective way to fish it is in a boat, using leeches and Woolly Buggers fished deep. During low water years, the riffle at its tail can be crossed to gain access to the back side of the hole. On this bank (the north side), you will often find good fish midging in the small back eddies.

The Lower Flats

In the Lower Flats, you will find some of the best fishing on the river. The riffle at its head is the home of many thousands of mayfly nymphs and aquatic annelids. Prolific hatches of Blue-winged Olives and Pale Morning Duns will occur in this riffle from early spring to late fall. Occasionally strong caddis hatches will also come off the water. Throughout the body of the pool are many depressions, where most of the fish will be waiting. In high water years, the depressions can make for tricky wading. Midges live in the silty bottom of the flats, in the slough to the southeast, and in Jack's Hole. During good hatches, these tiny diptera float through the flats and fish concentrate on them, creating excellent midge fishing.

Lunker Alley and Below

Lunker Alley begins below the flats and continues downstream about one-half mile. Often deep, this run is difficult and at places impossible to wade. Along the edges, however, a wading angler can locate large fish holding tight to the bank, feeding on mayflies and midges from the flats above. If you see no feeding fish, fishing deep with standard San Juan patterns is recommended.

Lower Slough

The Lower Slough, one of three significant sloughs in the San Juan's Quality Water, begins at the tail of the Lower Flats. For anglers who want to concentrate on midge fishing, this is one of the most consistent pieces of water available in which to practice this art. Even during low water years (when flows drop below 1,000 cfs), good populations of fish will reside here, especially in the deeper water toward the head. Slow, braided currents, which give fish plenty of time to look while also allowing plenty of time for your imitation to drag, demand the utmost skill from fly fishermen.

The Bluff Corner to E.T. Rock

The slow, deep water in this reach is not often fished by wading anglers, except where the lower slough re-enters the main channel. Banks are steep, dropping off quickly into the river. Floating anglers, however, can find good midge and mayfly fishing here, especially if it is not windy; otherwise, this stretch calls for Woolly Buggers and leech patterns fished deep. When hooked, the fish in this area are often quite powerful, since they are not pestered by anglers as often as their brethren in the river above. For those fly fishermen hoping to catch a brown trout in the San Juan, the river from here downstream holds promise. When the fishing is slow, this is an especially good area to enjoy the river's abundant waterfowl.

Simon Canyon to the end of the Quality Water

At the mouth of Simon Canyon, heavy riffles provide good fishing both with nymphs and dry flies during hatches and with leeches, San Juan worms, and Woolly Buggers when no hatches are in progress. The Simon Canyon section also experiences some of the heaviest caddis hatches in the Quality Water. In late 1988, during a heavy rainstorm runoff, the river bottom immediately below the normally dry canyon mouth was buried in sand, covering much of the insect habitat and fish-holding areas. This condition will probably prevail until high river flows flush the sand away.

Farther downstream, to the end of the Quality Water, the San Juan becomes flat and featureless. This stretch generally has no riffles or pools to concentrate the fish. Caddis and occasional Golden Stoneflies inhabit this area. There are fish here, and angling pressure is very light. This area is a prime candidate for extensive stream rehabilitation.

Egg Pattern

Conejos River and Rio de Los Piños

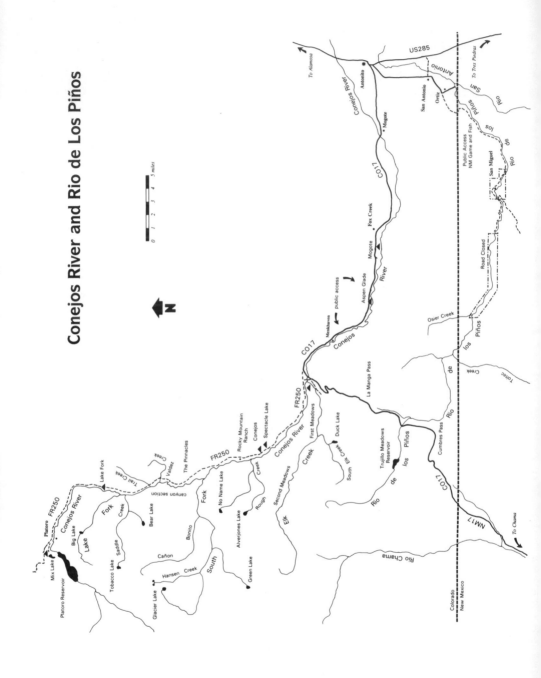

CHAPTER EIGHTEEN

Into Colorado: Conejos River

Mark Gruber

> **Location:** San Juan Mountains of south-central Colorado,
>   Rio Grande National Forest
> **Altitude:** 7,200 to 10,500 feet
> **Type of Water:** classic western freestone, riffles, large pools
>   some pocket water
> **Best Times:** early July to late October
> **Hatches:** caddisflies, mayflies, small and large stoneflies
> **Patterns:** Elk Hair Caddis, Peeking Caddis, Adams, Humpys,
>   Wulffs, Hare's Ear, Dark Stonefly Nymphs, Bitch Creeks
> **Localities Map Location:** E2
> **USGS Quadrangle Maps:** Platoro, Red Mountain, Spectacle
>   Lake, La Jara Canyon, Osier, Fox Creek

THE CONEJOS RIVER HOLDS SOME OF MY FONDEST fishing memories. I started fishing the river in the fall of 1968, when my father took me there. It was the first place in the Southwest we fished together. In the autumn, the river is beautiful, as the banks and surrounding mountain slopes glow honey-gold with aspen and cottonwood highlighted against the purple-blue sky. Crunching through fallen leaves or resting in the shade of an ancient cottonwood, I can still smell my father's pipe and remember his story of the huge brown trout he hooked and lost in the corner pool.

The Conejos River (the name means "rabbits" in Spanish) flows entirely in Colorado. It heads in the high country beneath Conejos Peak, flows out of Platoro Reservoir, runs through the broad Conejos Valley, then out across the San Luis Valley to join the Rio Grande near Antonito, Colorado, approximately 75 miles from its source.

The Conejos is a classic, western freestone stream that flows through narrow canyons and across valley floors and meadows. It is a medium-sized stream ranging in width from 20–60 feet, with the deepest pools reaching over 10 feet deep. Flows are affected by snowmelt, downstream irrigation needs, and heavy rain conditions. Generally, the river cannot be fished in late spring and early summer due to high water. In winter, low water temperatures slow the fishing—or at least the catching. The bottom is polished granite cobbles and boulders, which make for slippery wading. Felt-soled wading gear is always recommended, and more adventuresome fly fishermen wear chest waders for better access.

The Conejos and its tributaries contain rainbow, brown, and cutthroat trout. The river is heavily stocked with fingerlings and catchable-sized rainbows. Stocking is done at many locations from Platoro to Mogote, except in the "fly-fishing only" stretch from Menkhaven to Aspen Glade. This 3.5 miles of river is managed as Wild Trout Water, although rainbows in this stretch are not necessarily wild fish, as some stocked fish certainly swim in from up or downstream. Brown trout are not stocked in the Conejos because of an apparent lack of adult winter habitat, but native Rio Grande cutthroats are found in the river's small tributaries. A portion of the Lake Fork of the Conejos has been designated a no-kill area to protect stocks of Rio Grande cutthroat. The fish in the Conejos average 10–14 inches, with a good fish considered to be over 16 inches.

The Conejos River contains fine populations of all the major aquatic insect families, including mosquitoes. Throughout the season, nymph fishing is an effective way to catch trout. The river holds free-living and cased caddis, various mayflies, and large *Pteronarcys, Pteronarcella,* and other large stoneflies. Nymphs such as caddis larva imitations, large Hare's Ears, Pheasant Tails, and dark stonefly patterns in sizes 8–14 work well.

Some of the best hatches occur toward the end of the runoff. Around Father's Day until the beginning of July, there are good hatches of small caddisflies, large Western Grey Drakes, and yellow stoneflies. During this period, dry-fly-fishing is productive, especially when the trout are taking Gray Drakes with reckless abandon. Use size 10 or 12 Gray or Brown Wulffs or an Adams. Unfortunately, high water flows from snowmelt sometimes coincide with these hatches, making wading difficult and dry-fly-fishing tough.

Later in the season, from mid-summer until mid-fall, attractor dries and terrestrials are effective when the water temperatures are optimum, which on the Conejos range from 50–60 degrees. Good summer dry patterns include Adams, Wulff, Humpy, Elk Hair Caddis, and hopper, ant, and beetle imitations in sizes 12–16. A Blue-winged Olive (*Baetis* sp.) hatch occurs in the fall, so it is wise to have Adams and grey Comparadun patterns in sizes 16 or 18 to represent this important mayfly.

Public access along the river is clearly marked. The area around Platoro Reservoir, Lake Fork Campground, Conejos and Spectacle Lake Campground, and Elk Creek Campground are popular access sites along the dirt FR 250 northwest of Colorado 17. There are 3.5 miles of public access between Aspen Glade Campground and Menkhaven. This section is designated fly-fishing only. Most of the river below Mogote Campground is privately owned, and you must obtain permission to fish water flowing through private land.

The Platoro Reservoir is a 990-acre lake, which, at 10,000 feet, is the highest man-made lake in North America. It is very cold and deep and contains brown and rainbow trout. The lake is fed by two small creeks, the Adams Fork and the Conejos River. The creeks are located in the San Juan National Forest and are only accessible by trail from FR 250 beyond the reservoir, so they receive little fishing pressure.

For several miles below the reservoir, the river meanders through a flat valley, where the meadow water has plenty of undercut banks. Below the meadow, the river enters two distinct canyons, Lake Fork and South Fork, named for the tributaries entering the Conejos within their reaches. The canyon water comprises about 6 miles of pocket water and small rapids. The lower canyon is deep and narrow, with access only at the South Fork and Valdez Creek. The section of river from South Fork to Saddle Creek is currently under special regulations. Only artificial flies and lures may be used in this stretch, and a limit of two fish over 16 inches is in effect.

Native Rio Grande cutthroats have been re-established in the Lake Fork. For several years, the fork of the river was closed to fishing, and now it is no-kill water from its headwaters at Big Lake to within one-quarter mile of its junction with the Conejos. Big Lake is included in this special three miles of water. Please remember that the Conejos' tributaries are small and cannot sustain much fishing pressure. In order to protect these valuable resources, practice catch-and-release as much as possible.

From the South Fork to the Highway 17 bridge, the river again reverts to mostly meadow water. Riffles, pools, and runs slide between banks lined with cottonwoods, willows, and sometimes thick alder stands. A small stretch of public water, which is excellent for brown trout, is found near Spectacle Lake and Conejos campgrounds. Most of the remaining stretch crosses private land owned by Rainbow Trout Lodge. Anglers who want to fish this section should obtain permission from the lodge.

Elk Creek, the largest tributary of the Conejos, enters the river near the Highway 17 bridge. Access to the creek, its tributaries, and high mountain lakes is good along maintained hiking trails. Two major meadow stretches are reached by taking Trail No. 731 out of Elk Creek Campground. First Meadows is about 3 miles from the campground, and Second Meadows is about 4 miles farther upstream. With camping, easy access, good trails, and plenty of fish, Elk Creek is ideal for families.

Below Elk Creek, downstream to the town of Mogote, the river becomes much larger, with many stretches that are too deep to cross. Here the river is a classic western trout stream, with large pools, riffles, and deep bends running through a valley thickly forested with pine and aspen. Between Menkhaven and Aspen Glade Campground lies a stretch of public water designated fly-fishing only. This excellent water has many riffles and pools and holds plenty of rainbows up to 16 inches. Two nearby Forest Service campgrounds, Aspen Glade and Mogote, are perfect for weekend fishing trips. Most of the rest of the river downstream to Mogote is on private land.

All of the water from Mogote to the Rio Grande is on private land. As the river flows across the ranchlands of the San Luis Valley, it is bounded by heavy stands of cottonwood. The water here is typical western freestone. If you want to fish this water, you must get permission from the landowners.

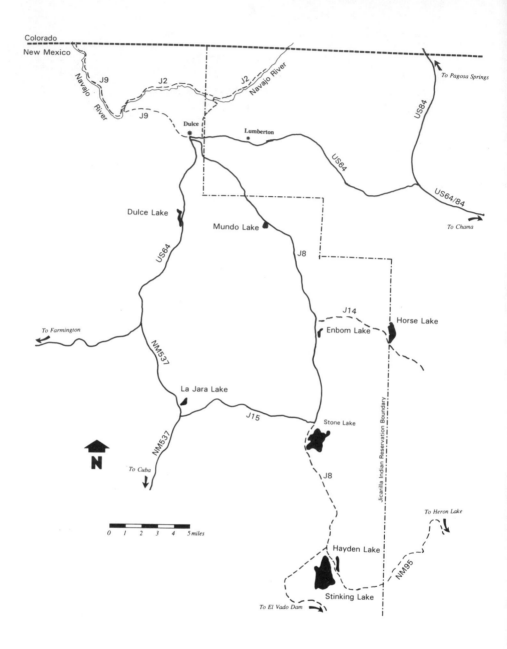

Waters of the Jicarilla Reservation

CHAPTER NINETEEN

Jicarilla Apache
Indian Reservation Waters

Bert Tallant and Joe Hussion

THE JICARILLA APACHE INDIAN RESERVATION IN north-central New Mexico is home to some of the finest fly-fishing in the state. Five lakes, ranging from 30–75 acres in size, together with 13 miles of the Navajo River provide an excellent opportunity for cutthroat and rainbow angling.

The 750,000-acre Jicarilla (hick-a-ree-yah) Reservation is located west of Chama, extending from the Colorado state line south for 75 miles. With mountains and mesas, the terrain is typical of northern New Mexico. The northern half of the reservation is mountainous and timbered with spruce, Douglas fir, ponderosa pine, and scrub oak. The southern half is open with plains and rolling hills covered with piñon pine, juniper, ponderosa pine, and sagebrush.

Dulce, New Mexico, headquarters for the Jicarilla Apache Tribe, is located west of Chama and east of Farmington. Take US 64/84 for 13 miles west of Chama; turn left at the Broken Butt Saloon (where US 84 heads north to Colorado), and then continue another 13 miles on US 64 to Dulce. From Farmington, go 87 miles east on US 64.

Dulce has many conveniences for the traveling angler. There is a reasonably priced modern motel with a restaurant and lounge and a general store with camping supplies and groceries. A small amount of fly-fishing equipment is available at the store, although most of the flies offered for sale are Woolly Worms. Gas is available at several stations in the area, and the Conoco station in Dulce has a coin-operated air pump available 24 hours a day for inflating float tubes. The Jicarilla Game and Fish Department is located in the Natural Resources Building on Narrow Gauge Street, off US 64 at the south end of town.

Fishermen on the reservation must purchase a tribal fishing permit. Permits are available 24 hours a day at the Best Western Jicarilla Inn and during business hours at the General Store and the Tribal Game and Fish Office in Dulce. Tribal permits are also available at some fishing shops and sporting goods stores in northern New Mexico. Fees vary depending on the season and the number of days you want to fish. An adult (12 years and over) Open Water Fishing Permit, which is valid from April 1 to November 30, costs $40 per season, $5 per day, or $20 for 5 days. A permit for senior citizens (55 years and older) costs $10. The fees for children under 12 are $20 for the year or $2 per day. A one dollar service charge per permit is in effect at all locations except the Jicarilla Game and Fish office. Camping and boating are free with a valid fishing permit. A New Mexico fishing license is not required to fish on the reservation. Visitors to the reservation are subject to all current tribal and federal regulations. As guests on the reservation, please respect the customs and traditions of the tribe. When purchasing a permit, take the time to read the regulations, and remember that fishing reservation waters is a privilege, not a right.

The reservation is bisected east and west by US 64 and north to south by NM 537. These are paved roads and are passable in most weather conditions. Many roads on the reservation are dirt and can be impassable or hazardous when wet. Be sure to check local conditions before traveling on the back roads.

NAVAJO RIVER

Location: Jicarilla Apache Indian Reservation
Altitude: 6,500 to 7,000 feet
Type of Water: freestone, riffle and pool
Best Times: May to June, September to October
Hatches: dragonflies, caddisflies, mayflies, terrestrials
Patterns: Elk Hair Caddis, Assam Dragon, Woolly Bugger,
         Letort Hopper, Black Ant
Localities Map Location: D3
USGS Quadrangle Maps: Wirt Canyon, Dulce

STREAM FISHING ON THE JICARILLA RESERVATION MEANS FISHING THE
Navajo River. The headwaters of the river are in the San Juan Mountains of south-central Colorado. Downstream, the river dips into New
Mexico and cuts across the northeast corner of the reservation before
re-entering Colorado, only to return to New Mexico to join the San
Juan River, a stretch now inundated by Navajo Lake. The river on the
Jicarilla Reservation is a classic freestone and mountain meadow stream,
characterized by riffles, shallow runs, and pools and bordered by willows, grasses, and wildflowers. A few beaver ponds are found in the
meadows. The water is often off-color due to erosion of the stream
banks; sediment in the gravel beds is so heavy that trout are unable to
spawn. Fortunately, several tributaries provide spawning beds for the
wild trout in the Navajo River.

At its widest points, the river is an easy roll cast to the far bank,
and you can wade it with hip boots. Wet wading is possible during the
summer months. Fishing is best when the water is clearest; avoid the
river during runoff and after a heavy rain.

The usual complement of stoneflies, mayflies, and caddis are found
in the Navajo River. Of particular interest is the occurrence in flowing
water of a large dragonfly in the family Libellulidae. These ugly, grey-
brown nymphs are about an inch long, with huge heads and squat

bodies. It is hard to believe that this unsightly monster turns into the eye-catching, crimson adult dragonfly. Many terrestrial insects, including beetles, grasshoppers, and ants, are also common food sources for the trout in this stream. A local fisherman told us that trout were plentiful in the river but that the residents don't like to fish it because they have to catch grasshoppers for bait!

Fishing the Navajo River can be feast or famine. The river will disappoint if it is very murky, and you will have better luck fishing the lakes instead. If the water levels are low and the stream is clear, good fishing can be had in the spring and fall with Woolly Buggers and other streamers. In summer, early mornings and late evenings can bring hatches of mayflies and caddis, and size 14 or 16 Elk Hair Caddis or a simple attractor like an Adams or Royal Wulff are good pattern choices to use. In the heat of the day, try a beetle or an ant, or slap a grasshopper along the grassy edges and undercut banks. If nothing is working, try fishing a dark grey or brown Woolly Worm along the bottom. Another excellent pattern choice is Charlie Brooks' Assam Dragon, which imitates the common dragonfly nymph.

To reach the Navajo River from Dulce, turn right off US 64 onto Hawks Drive (just past the Jicarilla Inn) and drive up the hill about three-quarters of a mile. Turn right on River Hill Road (J2) and travel about 2 miles to the bridge. A dirt road, J2 parallels the river for about 5 miles and joins J9, which is also dirt. Turn left on J9 to return to Dulce or turn right to continue along the river into Colorado. There are numerous pullouts along the river for parking, along with several picnic and camping areas.

Crayfish

JICARILLA LAKES

> **Location:** Jicarilla Apache Indian Reservation
> **Altitude:** 6,500 to 9,000 feet
> **Type of Water:** lakes
> **Best Times:** late April to May, September and October
> **Hatches:** dragonflies, damselflies, caddisflies, crayfish
> **Patterns:** Dragonfly Nymph, Olive Woolly Bugger, Brown
>   Woolly Worm, Crayfish
> **Localities Map Location:** D3
> **USGS Quadrangle Maps:** Wirt Canyon, Dulce, Cordova
>   Canyon, Cedar Canyon, Apache
>   Mesa, Horse Lake

THE JICARILLA APACHE INDIAN RESERVATION IS BEST KNOWN FOR ITS lake fishing. Of the many lakes on the reservation, fly fishermen need to be concerned with only five. Other lakes on the reservation are either off-limits or are unsuitable for trout fishing.

The 75-acre Dulce Lake is located 5 miles south of the town of Dulce on US 64. Facilities include a pier with handicap access, a boat ramp, a toilet, picnic tables, and campsites. Because the lake is right off the highway, it is often crowded in the summer and fall is considered the best time to be on the Dulce. Be sure to release any grass carp you may accidentally catch.

La Jara Lake is reached by traveling 10 miles south of Dulce on US 64 and turning left on NM 537. Make a left turn onto a dirt road that skirts the north side of the lake, where you'll find parking, camping, and lake access. You can reach a second entrance to the south side of the lake by traveling another half-mile on NM 537 until you reach J15, a paved road. Follow J15 for a half-mile and turn left onto the dirt road to the lake. This 56-acre lake is excellent in spring, from ice-out to early June.

Mundo Lake is 5.3 miles southeast of Dulce on J8, which is a paved road. Facilities include a small pier for handicap access, toilets, picnic tables, and campsites. Because it has open shores and less weed growth, Mundo has the best bank fishing of all the Jicarilla lakes. Crayfish are abundant, and crayfish imitations or large brown Woolly Worms fished along the bottom are effective. Farther along J8, 12.6 miles southeast of Dulce, is Enbom Lake, where there are picnic and camping facilities.

Hayden Lake is located 24 miles southeast of Dulce via J8. Turn left on the dirt road 6 miles south of Stone Lake just before Burford (Stinking) Lake. Follow this road for one mile and turn left to Hayden Lake. Facilities include a picnic table and a toilet. Unlike most of the Jicarilla lakes, Hayden is well-protected from the wind, but willows and grasses along the banks can make casting from the shore difficult.

The Jicarilla Game and Fish Department maintains an excellent stocking program for trout. Most stocked fish are rainbows in the 10–14-inch range. Cutthroats are regularly stocked, and brown trout and brook trout are occasionally planted. Most of the fish caught in the lakes are 12–14 inches, but a few fish of all species survive the rigors of winter and grow to over 20 inches.

Early in the season, all of the Jicarilla lakes can be fished from the banks; later in summer, as weed growth increases, a boat or a float tube is necessary. Although the weed beds are a nuisance, they create a fertile hatchery for aquatic insects, crustaceans, and minnows. The large invertebrate and forage fish populations lead to an incredible growth rate for the stocked fish. The trout are estimated to grow as much as one inch per month during the peak season. In the winter, these same weed beds decompose beneath the frozen lake surfaces, depleting oxygen supplies in the water and leading to winterkill. The tribe works hard to alleviate this problem by periodically harvesting the weeds during the summer and pumping gases into the lakes during the winter. Grass carp have been stocked in Dulce Lake in an experiment to control weed growth.

All of the reservation lakes have fine populations of insects, including caddis, mayflies, midges, dragonflies, and damselflies. For fly fishermen, the most important insects are the dragonflies that are found in incredible numbers in the weed beds. (Locally, these nymphs are known as hellgrammites). The most common dragonfly is of the family Aechnidae; the nymphs are bright green in color with a 2-inch hourglass-shaped body. The adults are bright blue with clear wings and can be up to 4 inches in length.

Spring brings excellent fishing to the Jicarilla lakes. Ice-out occurs anytime from early to late April, and this is the perfect time to try the lakes. Hungry trout, some as large as 20 inches, cruise along the retreating ice-edge waiting for insects to drop off into the water. Fish the ice-edge with dry attractor or terrestrial flies cast onto the ice and slowly pulled over the edge. When the ice is gone, dragonflies, Woolly Buggers, and other streamers are effective.

During the summer there are good evening rises to caddis and mayfly hatches. The often heavy *Callibaetis* hatch occurs on all the lakes during the late morning. But the best bet for fishing these lakes in the summer is a dragonfly or damselfly nymph imitation. Use a realistic pattern like a Kaufmann Dragonfly or something impressionistic like Olive Woolly Buggers or Woolly Worms, sizes 6–10. A good technique is to fish at varying depths to find where the fish are feeding at a particular time. Begin by fishing your pattern right on the bottom of the lake with a weighted fly and a sinking line. Cast out and let the fly sink to the bottom; then begin a slow retrieve, varying the speed from slow hand twists to short jerks. If this fails, try fishing at mid-depth, keeping the fly from sinking to the bottom before beginning your retrieve. Finally, try a floating line with a long leader, and fish the pattern just under the surface. A floating line is particularly useful when you fish over the weed beds.

For additional information and a copy of the latest fishing regulations, write the tribe at:

Jicarilla Apache Tribe
Department of Game and Fish
P.O. Box 546   Dulce, New Mexico 87528   (505) 759-3255

CHAPTER TWENTY

Trout Lakes of Northern New Mexico

CABRESTO LAKE

Location: Sangre de Cristo Mountains, Carson National Forest
Altitude: 9,200 feet
Size: 15 acres
Best Times: mid-May to September
Hatches: damselflies, midges, budworms (pine moth), *Callibaetis*
Patterns: Marabou Damselfly Nymph, Scud, Midge Emerger,
    Woolly Bugger, Budworm, Adams
Localities Map Location: G3
USGS Quadrangle Maps: Latir Peak

CABRESTO LAKE IS AN EXCELLENT HIGH-COUNTRY lake with cutthroats and brook trout. The deep water is in the southern two-thirds of the lake nearest the dam. At the north end near the inlet, the water is shallow and supports extensive weedbeds. Casting from the banks is difficult except near the inlet and on the north-west shore where limited wading is possible. A float tube or canoe will provide access to the entire lake and will allow you to comfortably cast to weedbeds and the drop-off near the inlet. Attractor nymphs and Woolly

Buggers are effective near the inlet; terrestrial patterns like the budworm (pinemoth) are an excellent choice under the brushy areas on the east bank. The weedbeds provide cover for a large number of trout. Cast damselfly nymphs to the weedbeds during the day, and use midge pupa during the large evening midge hatch. The mid-morning hatch of Speckle-wing Quills (*Callibaetis*) can be matched with a size 14 Adams. Fishing is best in the morning and evening and after a cooling summer afternoon rain. Ice-out usually occurs in early May.

To reach Cabresto Lake, go east on NM 38 out of Questa toward Red River. In a quarter-mile, take a sharp left at an intersection marked for Cabresto. This road goes up a small hill and then through a housing area before becoming Forest Road 134. Follow this well-maintained gravel road about 3 miles to the turnoff to Cabresto Lake. FR 134A is rough, rocky, and usually a single "lane." If you are careful, you can drive it with a passenger car, but a high clearance vehicle is recommended.

EAGLE NEST LAKE

Location: Sangre de Cristo Mountains
Altitude: 8,100 feet
Size: approx. 1,500 acres
Best Times: May to early July, September to October
Hatches: midges
Patterns: Woolly Bugger, Muddler Minnow, Midge Pupa, Griffith's Gnat, Marabou Leech, Crayfish
Localities Map Location: G4
USGS Quadrangle Maps: Eagle Nest

EAGLE NEST LAKE LIES AT THE MIDDLE OF THE LONG, BEAUTIFUL Moreno Valley. Above the valley floor, grasses give way to forested slopes; above the forest are the highest peaks in New Mexico, often seen with

lingering patches of snow, even in July. The setting is spectacular—
and so is the fishing.

The New Mexico Department of Game and Fish leases the privately owned Eagle Nest Lake for public fishing. The lake is stocked
with rainbow trout, cutthroats, and kokanee salmon, who are protected
from winter freezes by the great depth of the lake. Eagle Nest trout
can grow to legendary sizes; the lake consistently yields more large
trout than any other lake in the state.

Eagle Nest is best fished by boat. Nearly constant winds make
float-tubing dangerous. Bank fishing is best on the west side, where
there is plenty of room for a backcast and where the wind will add
distance to your casts. Eagle Nest is a wet fly and nymph lake. Insects
can be sparse, but midge fishing on windless summer evenings is quite
good. At other times, forage fish, leech, and crayfish patterns are the
most effective.

Access to Eagle Nest Lake is easy compared to most New Mexico
lakes. Take US 64 out of Taos or NM 38 from Red River; both roads
drop into the Moreno Valley. There are Game and Fish access roads
on the west and north sides of the lake. These short roads are gravel
and dirt and may be muddy after rains. There is no camping on the
lake, but good campgrounds are located to the east of Eagle Nest along
US 64 in Cimarron Canyon.

FENTON LAKE

Location: Jemez Mountains, Fenton Lake State Park
Altitude: 7,800 feet
Size: 30 acres
Best Times: May, September to November
Hatches: midges, dragonflies, damselflies
Patterns: Midge Emerger, Griffith's Gnat, Lake Dragon
Localities Map Location: D5
USGS Quadrangle Maps: Seven Springs

FENTON LAKE IS FORMED BY AN ARTIFICIAL DAM ON THE RIO CEBOLLA. Currently under management as a State Park, the west bank of the lake offers fishing and camping for a daily fee; the east shore is day-use only, and no fee is collected. Access is on NM 126 by way of NM 4 and La Cueva. The road is paved to within a mile of the lake and can be easily negotiated by any vehicle. Fenton is often crowded, with the banks lined with fishermen casting for the lake-bred browns and heavily stocked rainbows. The shorelines are shallow, and casting is easy from the dam and the east bank. Float tubes are not necessary, but they allow better access to areas away from other anglers.

Ice-out on Fenton Lake occurs from mid-March to mid-April, and flies pulled off the receding ice-edge will often bring browns to the surface. May is warm and windy, and midges, dragonflies, and damselflies are active. Surface midge patterns can be effective, but subsurface fishing with dragonfly and damselfly nymphs is more productive. By mid-summer, weeds are a problem throughout the lake, and oxygen depletion brings fishing to a halt. But by September, the crowds have gone and the water temperature has cooled. Casting streamers in the deep water near the dam or hopper patterns in front of rising trout is certain to attract trout. Fly-fishing remains good on Fenton Lake until early November.

HOPEWELL LAKE

Location: Tusas Mountains, Carson National Forest
Altitude: 9,750 feet
Size: 14 acres
Best Times: May to September
Hatches: midges, damselflies
Patterns: Midge Emergers, Griffith's Gnat, Damselfly Nymph
Localities Map Location: E3
USGS Quadrangle Maps: Burned Mountain

THE MIDGE HATCHES ON HOPEWELL LAKE ARE LEGENDARY. AS THE SUN sets on summer evenings, the entire surface of the lake seems to boil with rising trout. Bait fishermen are frustrated by so many trout that are so uninterested in salmon eggs. Most fly fishermen frantically try pattern after pattern, only to watch the trout take the unseen insects from the surface. But these fish can be caught with tiny midge emerger or midge adult patterns in sizes 18–22.

Griffith's Gnat

The shoreline of Hopewell Lake is steep. Fortunately, the banks are open, and casting from them is not a problem. The inlet end of the lake is shallow and reedy; the deeper water is near the dam. Ice-out occurs from mid-April to May. Spring fishing is best with midges and damselfly nymphs. Summer days are slow, but they often lead up to fantastic evenings. As September temperatures cool, fishing during the days improves. The lake is usually frozen by late October.

Hopewell Lake is located directly off of US 64, about 20 miles east of Tierra Amarilla and 16 miles west of Tres Piedras. A campground with limited facilities is located on the east side of the lake.

LAKE KATHERINE, SPIRIT LAKE, STEWART LAKE

Location: Sangre de Cristo Mountains, Santa Fe National Forest
Altitude: 11,700 feet, 10,800 feet, 10,200 feet
Size: 12 acres, 7 acres, 5 acres
Best Times: June to August
Hatches: Speckle-wing Quills (*Callibaetis*), midges
Patterns: Timberline Nymph, Light Cahill, Griffith's Gnat,
         Midge Emerger
Localities Map Location: F6
USGS Quadrangle Maps: Aspen Basin, Cowles

LAKE KATHERINE, SPIRIT LAKE, AND STEWART LAKE ARE THE MOST accessible of the high-country lakes in the Pecos Wilderness Area of the Sangre de Cristo Mountains. All three lakes can only be reached by trail. The trailhead in the Pecos area is at the Windsor Creek Campground, up FR 121 from Cowles. From here the Windsor Trail ascends the ridges to Stewart Lake in 6 miles, to Spirit Lake in 7 miles, and to Lake Katherine in about 8 miles. The lakes can also be reached by taking the Windsor Trail from the Santa Fe Ski Basin; Lake Katherine is 7 miles from this trailhead.

Although the wilderness surrounding these lakes is beautiful, it can also be dangerous. The terrain is extremely rugged, the elevations are high, thunderstorms with lightning are daily occurrences, and August snowstorms are not uncommon. Be prepared for extreme conditions when traveling to these lakes. Consult the hiking guides listed in the bibliography for detailed descriptions of the routes to these lakes. Also note that camping is not permitted on any of the lake shores.

All three lakes are natural. Set beneath the peak of Santa Fe Baldy, Lake Katherine is a perfect example of a glacial lake. Spirit and Stewart lakes sit in shallow depressions below timberline. All of the lakes host both stocked and lake-bred rainbows and cutthroats, and summer fishing is excellent. Spirit Lake is the most shallow of the three lakes, and Lake Katherine is the deepest. Casting is easy in places from the banks. Weeds are important in Spirit and Stewart, where damselfly nymphs are effective throughout the summer. Speckle-winged Quill (*Callibaetis*) hatches are most important on Lake Katherine, and spinner falls bring the largest trout to the surface. Midges are important on all three lakes.

LATIR LAKES

Location: Sangre de Cristo Mountains, private land
Altitude: 7,500 to 11,700 feet
Size: from 1 acre to 9 acres
Best Times: June to September
Hatches: midges, mayflies, caddisflies, scuds
Patterns: Midge Pupa, Dark Olive Scud
Localities Map Location: F3, G3
USGS Quadrangle Maps: Latir Peak
Contributed by: Van Beacham

THE LATIR LAKES ARE A SERIES OF NINE NATURAL LAKES CONNECTED by Latir Creek. Individual lakes have no names but are known by numbers, with Lake No. 1 being the lowest and Lake No. 9 the uppermost. All of the lakes are on private land managed by the Rio Costilla Cooperative Livestock Association (RCCLA). Fishing permits are available from the RCCLA office in the town of Costilla, the RCCLA shack at the entrance to Latir Creek (which is often closed), or by mail (RCCLA, P.O. Box 111, Costilla, NM 87524). If you have any questions, call RCCLA at (505) 586-0542.

The Latir Lakes are reached from Taos by heading north on NM 518 to the town of Costilla. Turn east on NM 196 toward Amalia and Valle Vidal. About 6 miles past the turnoff to Ski Rio is the RCCLA guard shack and the unpaved road leading to the lakes. The 6-mile road into the lakes is rough, and four-wheel drive and an experienced driver are required. The road ends at Lake No. 3. From the parking area, trails lead up and down Latir Creek to the other lakes. The hike from Lake No. 3 to Lake No. 9 is about 1.5 miles, with a climb of about 1,000 feet; it takes about an hour.

Most of the fish caught in the lakes are Rio Grande cutthroats or cutthroat-rainbow hybrids averaging 15–20 inches. The top six lakes have recently been stocked with Snake River cutthroats.

The Latir Lakes are particularly known for their large native cutthroats. In 1982, the state record cutthroat (24 inches long and over 10 pounds) was caught in Lake No. 9. In the mid-1980s, the lakes experienced a mysterious decline in the number and size of fish, but a renewed management effort is bringing the lakes back to their former status. As of early 1990, the top six lakes were closed off to allow them to make a comeback. This temporary closure should be lifted in the near future. Call the RCCLA office for the latest information.

Most of the lakes cover only one to three acres. Lakes No. 3, No. 4, and No. 9 are larger, in the 6–10-acre range. Lake No. 9 is close against the high peaks in a rocky, barren bowl, and the level of nutrients is low. Moving down from No. 9 to No. 1, the lakeside forest thickens and the amount of nutrients in the lakes increases. Because of the surrounding forest, it is more difficult to cast from the banks of the lower lakes than the higher ones. All lakes are great for float tubes.

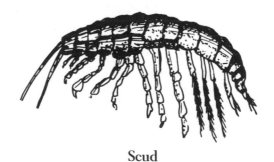

Scud

Due to the lakes' high elevation and northern exposure, the area is inaccessible until June. The lakes are closed each year until about June 20 when the Rio Grande cutthroats finish spawning. Throughout the summer, the lakes produce the usual assortment of high-country insect hatches. The evening midge hatches are particularly important; they are best fished with midge pupa patterns just below the surface. Scuds are another important food source in all of the lakes. The best overall pattern is a size 16 dark Olive Scud. Fish these nymphs along the banks, near the inlets and outlets, and over weedbeds. Note that snows and the hunting season require the RCCLA to close the lakes on about October 1.

Scud

McALLISTER LAKE

Location: Las Vegas National Wildlife Refuge
Altitude: 6,300 feet
Size: 100 acres
Best Times: April to October
Hatches: damselflies, dragonflies, *Callibaetis*, midges
Patterns: scuds, damselfly nymphs, dragonfly nymphs, Woolly
  Buggers, Adams
Localities Map Location: G6
USGS Quadrangle Maps: Las Vegas
Contributed by: Mark Gruber and Jan Gruber

MCALLISTER LAKE HAS A DOUBLE IDENTITY. THE LAKE IS PART OF THE Las Vegas National Wildlife Refuge, managed jointly by the U.S. Fish and Wildlife Service and the New Mexico Department of Game and Fish. Its winter habitat is crucial to wildlife, and it attracts large numbers of birdwatchers who come to observe the amazing variety of ducks, geese, and raptors, including both golden and bald eagles. To protect the waterfowl and birds of prey, the lake is closed to fishing from October 31 through March 1.

When spring arrives and the wintering birds move north to their breeding grounds, McAllister reveals its character as a fine trout lake. Stealthy people with binoculars are replaced by others with fly rods and float tubes. Float-tube occupants enjoy the summer wildlife, the whistling of ducks overhead, the soaring flights of eagles and ospreys, and even the sight of antelope bounding on the tall grass plains surrounding the lake. But most of their attention is focused on the finny residents below the water's surface.

McAllister is one of the most nutrient-rich lakes in New Mexico. The stocked rainbows here have extremely high growth rates. There are plenty of fish in the 9–13-inch range, and the lake is famous for its great numbers of fish from 17 to over 20 inches.

With 100 acres, the lake is a float-tubing paradise. Boats traveling at trolling speed are also permitted. (When float-tubing, it is a good idea to wear a brightly colored hat to make yourself easily visible to boaters.) Shaped as a broad, shallow dish sloping to the west, the lake's maximum depth is less than 20 feet in the center. The banks are covered in reeds, and the many weedbeds growing near shore make it difficult to fish the lake by wading. The west shoreline can be fished with chest waders, while the east shoreline is marginal in waders. It is often windy here on the edge of the Great Plains, and at times casting is difficult.

The great variety of insects in McAllister creates fantastic fishing throughout the open season. Dry flies, nymphs, and some streamers are all effective at certain times. Damselfly and dragonfly nymphs are major spring and summer patterns. Peacock and brown damselfly nymphs are particularly effective, as are black and olive Woolly Buggers. Cast and strip the patterns into and along the edges of the weedbeds, or try harling (trolling) damselfly nymphs or Woolly Buggers across the lake. Harling is also an effective method when it is too windy to cast. Scuds are another major food source for the trout. Fish gray scuds in sizes 16–20 along the bottom and in weedbeds. There are no forage fish in the lake.

Dry flies are also effective at certain times. A summer damselfly hatch calls for an adult blue damsel pattern. The lake has good surface activity just at dark, and a size 14 Adams can be effective at this time. Another good method is casting a small Pheasant Tail nymph to rising fish, a technique that often brings a quick hit. Floating snail patterns will also take trout on the surface. In late summer and early fall, a heavy *Callibaetis* (Speckle-wing Quill) hatch brings a lot of fish to the top at mid-day.

The abundance of food and the consequent high growth rates of the trout make McAllister an exceptional lake. Special regulations are needed to prevent overharvesting of big fish by bait fishermen. Fly fishermen are encouraged to help maintain the high quality of the fishery by treating the lake as no-kill water or by keeping only fish less than 15 inches.

To reach McAllister Lake from Las Vegas, New Mexico, take the NM 104 exit from Interstate 25 and travel east. After about 2 miles, turn right on NM 281 and travel south 4 miles to the Refuge Headquarters. Continue on the gravel road about 2 miles to the lake. This road can become impassable after a heavy rain.

MIDDLE FORK LAKE (RED RIVER)

Location: Sangre de Cristo Mountains, Santa Fe National Forest
Altitude: 10,800 feet
Size: 6 acres
Best Times: June to September
Hatches: caddis, stoneflies, gnats, termites, scuds
Patterns: Dark Elk Hair Caddis, Renegade, Olive Scud,
            Brown Winged Ant, Black Ant, Woolly Buggers
Localities Map Location: F4
USGS Quadrangle Maps: Wheeler Peak
Contributed by: Van Beacham

GETTING TO MIDDLE FORK LAKE IS HALF THE FUN OF FISHING THERE. The trip starts innocently enough on NM 38 in the town of Red River. Travel west to the junction with NM 578, turn right, and continue 5.5 miles until the pavement ends. Turn right onto FR 58, following signs pointing toward Middle Fork. In one mile, at the crossing of Middle Fork Creek, Middle Fork Road (FR 487) heads south to the lake. If you are equipped with four-wheel drive and have a healthy sense of adventure, continue driving up the road. If you are without four-wheel drive or are a cautious driver, park here and begin the one-hour, 2-mile hike to the lake.

Middle Fork Road is perhaps the worst road in all of New Mexico. There are 23 switchbacks from bottom to top. Drive the first one going forward, and then back up to the second switchback. Continue this alternating pattern of driving until you reach the top. Although the short 2 miles to the top is filled with spectacular scenery, there is precious little time to enjoy it.

Several jeep tour companies in Red River will take you to and pick you up from the lake for a fee. These are not fishing guides, but provide transportation only. In order to learn the road, it is recommended that you take your first trip with a tour company.

Camping is permitted at the lake, and many excellent sites are available. Camps must be at least 100 feet from the lakeshore. Vegetation near timberline is fragile and firewood is scarce, so bring along a gas stove for cooking.

Middle Fork Lake is in a glacial cirque nestled at the foot of Bull-of-the-Woods Mountain. Waterfalls plunge down the mountain's face, filling the lake. The lake covers about 6 acres and has a maximum depth of about 25 feet. The banks are heavily forested except near the inlet. A float tube is required to reach most of the fishing spots, although some nice fish are found near the inlet where you can cast from shore.

Most of the trout in Middle Fork Lake are cutthroats in the 14–15-inch range, with some up to 20 inches. Due to heavy use by bait fisherman, rainbows are irregularly stocked. Overwintering rainbows grow to about 15 inches. Some brook trout are also found in the lake, and they often grow to over 20 inches.

Ice-out usually occurs in early June. The first month of fishing is best with sowbug patterns or scuds. Try size 16 olive scuds fished from a float tube inward toward shore. Three dependable and exciting hatches occur in June. A little brown stonefly hatch lasts from sunrise until about 11 a.m. at the outlet end of the lake. It is best to fish this hatch from a float tube, spotting cruising trout and casting 15–20 feet ahead of the last rise. Use a Brown Winged Ant (termite) pattern, size 16 or 18, or any favorite small brown adult stonefly imitation. In the evening, the action shifts to the middle of the lake as the trout feed on an aquatic insect (probably a gnat) that looks like an ant. Fish can be fooled with a size 20 black ant fished dry. In late July and August, evening hatches of a large brown sedge (caddis) can be thick. These

Winged Ant

insects can be effectively matched with a size 10 or 12 Dark Elk Hair Caddis. The hatch is scattered across the lake, and fishing from the bank near the inlet can be excellent.

In September, most of the summer crowds have gone but the fishing remains excellent. This is the best time to try for the large brook trout that hide in deep water for most for the season. Use black or olive Woolly Buggers, fishing them carefully among the submerged logs on the inlet end of the lake. Fall fishing can continue through mid-October, when the first cold fronts arrive.

SAN GREGORIO RESERVOIR

Location: Jemez Mountains, Santa Fe National Forest
Altitude: 9,400 feet
Size: 30–40 acres
Best Times: April to May, September
Hatches: midges, damselflies
Patterns: Midge Pupa, Woolly Bugger, Elk Hair Caddis,
　　　　　Damselfly Nymph
Localities Map Location: D5
USGS Quadrangle Maps: Nacimento Peak

SAN GREGORIO RESERVOIR IS A SMALL ARTIFICIAL POND IN THE JEMEZ Mountains. Despite the half-mile hike necessary to reach the lake, it is a popular spot. Two approaches will take you to San Gregorio. The route with the least amount of dirt road enters from Cuba. From the center of town, follow NM 126 east into the mountains. After about 7 miles, the road turns into an all-weather gravel road. Continue another 3 miles to FR 264; turn left, and follow the signs to the trailhead parking area. An alternative route is from La Cueva. Go west on NM 126, past Fenton Lake and Seven Springs, about 20 miles to FR 264. Sections of this road can be difficult in wet weather. Once at the trailhead, follow the signs to the lake, a short half-mile walk through a cool and shady forest.

San Gregorio is in a small depression surrounded by forest. The lakeshores are clear of vegetation, and casting is easy from almost everywhere. The shoreline is shallow, except along the dam, and you can wade out from the banks. The inlet is shallow and offers no holding lies for trout. In summer, thick weeds grow in the shallow waters on the entire north and west banks. Fishing is best in the deep water along the dam, and a float tube is a real asset on this water.

The lake is regularly stocked with rainbow trout, most of them fingerlings, and a few cutthroats are also found here. Ice-out occurs in mid- to late April. In the early season, fishing can be good all day, with Woolly Buggers or large dry flies fished near the retreating ice-edge. Early summer fishing is best during mornings or evenings with midge patterns or small Elk Hair Caddis. Dragonfly and damselfly nymphs work well in the weedbeds on early summer mornings. During mid-summer, water temperatures are often too high for trout to survive. Fishing picks up again in the fall and continues good until late October.

VERMEJO PARK LAKES

Location: Sangre de Cristo Mountains, private land
Altitude: 8,200 to 10,000 feet
Size: total of 308 acres
Best Times: June to September
Hatches: dragonflies, damselflies, *Callibaetis*, caddis, midges
Patterns: Woolly Buggers, Damselfly Nymph, Adams,
           Griffith's Gnat, Dave's Hopper
Localities Map Location: G3
USGS Quadrangle Maps: Van Bremmer Park, Ash Mountain,
           Vermejo Park, The Wall
Contributed by: Richard Wilder and Martha Noss

THE NAME VERMEJO PARK IS GIVEN TO A LARGE AREA OF THE FORMER Maxwell Land Grant that remains under private ownership. Fishing the Vermejo Park lakes is restricted to guests of the Vermejo Park Ranch. At over $200 a day, with lodging and meals included, fishing these lakes is expensive but always worth the price. It is a unique experience to fish all day, dine in the Victorian dining room, and sleep in spacious accommodations amid elegant period furnishings.

The Vermejo Park Ranch holds 21 lakes, ranging in size from 2 to over 40 acres. Each lake has its own character. The ranch provides john boats for guests to use at most of the lakes. Some lakes are stocked, and others hold only wild fish. Rainbow, brown, brook, and cutthroat trout are found throughout the Vermejo Park lakes, and large fish are the rule rather than the exception. The fish are healthy, full-bodied trout that fight hard and jump freely.

Bernal Lake is the lone lake on the ranch that is managed solely for fly fishermen. At 10 acres, it is perfect for float-tube fishing. At 40 acres, Mann Lake is one of the largest lakes on the ranch. Mann is known for its large rainbows, some over 24 inches.

A variety of lake fishing techniques will be successful for alert fly fishermen who adapt their methods to the conditions. Summer mornings and evenings bring fish to the surface for *Callibaetis*, caddis, and midge hatches. The fish often refuse dry flies at these times, but fishing emergers just under the surface on a greased line will usually end the frustration. Mid-day fishing is still good with Woolly Buggers, nymphs, and snail patterns fished near the bottom. Dragonfly and damselfly nymphs, fished with a start-and-stop retrieve, are other effective mid-day patterns. Grasshoppers and damselfly adults are often found over the weedbeds near the shore in surprisingly shallow water. Dry imitations cast near the shore and allowed to sit motionless will often be sipped by a cruising fish.

For more information about fishing the Vermejo Park Lakes, get in touch with the Vermejo Park Ranch at (505) 445-3097; P.O. Drawer E, Raton, NM 87740.

CHAPTER TWENTY-ONE

Common Aquatic Insects
of Northern New Mexico

Compiled by Gerald Jacobi, Mark Gruber, and Craig Martin

A BASIC KNOWLEDGE OF THE INSECTS AND OTHER food organisms that make up the diet of trout is important to the success of any fly fisherman. Using attractor fly patterns or simply choosing a pattern that looks good to the fisherman but perhaps not to the fish leaves too much to chance. As in other areas of the West, anglers in New Mexico, particularly on heavily fished rivers such as the San Juan and the Pecos, will frequently find fish that feed selectively on specific hatching insects. In these situations, the angler who knows about insects has greatly improved his chances for success.

The following is a list of the important aquatic insects found in northern New Mexico. While not complete, the list will help serious fly fishermen understand and identify the aquatic insects in New Mexico's streams and lakes.

The pattern guide can be used by anglers at all levels of insect knowledge. The listing of generic patterns will help beginning fly fishermen select fly patterns that have proven to be effective in New Mexico. For anglers who can distinguish mayflies, stoneflies, and caddisflies, the guide can help determine the best patterns for each of the families. For anglers who can recognize genera or even species of insects, the guide gives suggested patterns for those species found in the state.

Fly tiers will find the recipes for the patterns listed in the guide in Hafele and Hughes' excellent basic primer, *Western Hatches*; Ernest Schwiebert's detailed treatise *Nymphs*; Randall Kaufmann's *The Fly Tyers Nymph Manual*; Jack Dennis' *Western Trout Fly Tying Manual*, volumes 1 and 2; Dave Whitlock's *Guide to Aquatic Trout Foods*; and Eric Leiser's complete *The Book of Fly Patterns*.

EPHEMEROPTERA (Mayflies)

GENERIC MAYFLY PATTERNS

Adults	*Nymphs*
Dark and Light Cahill	Pheasant Tail Nymphs
Adams	Hare's Nymphs
Blue-wing Olive	A.P. Nymphs
Comparadun	
Humpy	
Wulff	

SPECIES SPECIFIC INFORMATION

Scientific name: *Siphlonurus occidentalis*
Common name: Grey Drake
Dates of hatch: August and September
Time of hatch: mid-morning
Patterns: nymph: Gray Drake #10–12 (Parker)
dun: Gray Wulff #10–12
Adams #10–12
spinner: Gray Drake Spinner #12–14

Scientific name: *Baetis tricaudatus*
Common name: Blue-winged Olive
Dates of hatch: early spring through fall
Time of hatch: all day

Patterns: nymph: Pheasant Tail #16–20
                   Baetis Nymph #16–20 (Swisher and Richards)
        dun: Blue-winged Olive #16–20
                   Baetis Comparadun #16–20
      spinner: Baetis Spinner #18–22 (Swisher and Richards)

Scientific name: *Baetis insignificans*
Common name: Blue-winged Olive
Dates of hatch: early spring through late fall
Time of hatch: all day
Patterns: nymph: Pheasant Tail #18–20
                   Baetis Nymph #18–20 (Swisher and Richards)
        dun: Blue-winged Olive #18–22
                   Baetis Comparadun #18–20
      spinner: Bactis Spinner #18–22 (Swisher and Richards)

Scientific name: *Callibaetis* sp. (common in lakes)
Common name: Speckle-wing Quill
Dates of hatch: late May through October
Time of hatch: early morning
Patterns: nymph: Hare's Ear #14–18
                   Timberline #14–16
        dun: Adams #12–16
                   Callibaetis Compara-Dun #14–20 (Caucci and Nastasi)
      spinner: Callibaetis Spinner #12–16

Scientific name: *Ameletus* sp.
Common name: none
Dates of hatch: early spring, fall
Time of hatch: sporadic
Patterns: nymph: Isonychia Bicolor #8–10
        dun: none
      spinner: none

Scientific name: *Centroptilum* sp.
Common name: Sulphers
Dates of hatch: summer
Time of hatch: sporadic

Patterns: nymph: Pheasant Tail #16–18
dun: Grizzly Wulff #16–18
spinner: none

Scientific name: *Isonychia* sp.
Common name: Great Western Lead-Wing
Dates of hatch: late May to September
Time of hatch: late afternoon to evening
Patterns: nymph: Velma May #10 (Brooks)
Isonychia Velma Nymph #6–8 (Rosborough)
dun: Large Mahogany Dun #12–18 (Swisher and Richards)
spinner: Isonychia Velma Spinner #10–12 (Rosborough)

Scientific name: *Rhithrogena robusta*
Common name: Western Red Quill
Dates of hatch: July and August
Time of hatch: morning
Patterns: nymph: Pheasant Tail #12–14
Rhithrogena Clinger Nymph #12–16 (Jorgensen)
Western Red Quill #12–14 (Schwiebert)
dun: Red Quill #14–18
March Brown #14–18
March Brown Compara-Dun #14–18 (Caucci and Nastasi)

Scientific name: *Epeorus longimanus*
Common name: Western Quill Gordon
Dates of hatch: late June, July
Time of hatch: mid-morning, early afternoon
Patterns: nymph: Epeorus Nymph #14–18 (Jorgensen)
dun: Quill Gordon #16–18
spinner: Red Quill Spinner #16–18

Scientific name: *Epeorus* sp.
Common name: Little Yellow Mayfly, Little Blue Quill
Dates of hatch: April to September
Time of hatch: mid-morning to early afternoon
Patterns: nymph: Epeorus Nymph #14–18 (Jorgensen)

dun: Grizzly Wulff #16–18
           Light Cahill #16–18
           Pink Lady #18–20
spinner: clipped dun patterns

Scientific name: *Cinygmula* sp.
Common name: Blue-winged Red Quill
Dates of hatch: June
Time of hatch: late morning
Patterns: nymph: Cingymula Nymph #16 (Schwiebert)
          dun: Red Quill #16–18
          spinner: Red Quill Spinner #16–18

Scientific name: *Heptagenia* sp.
Common name: Western Pale Evening Dun
Dates of hatch: late May to late August
Time of hatch: late afternoon and evening
Patterns: nymph: Little Gray-winged Dun Nymph #14–16
              (Schwiebert)
          dun: Light Cahill #14–16
               Heptagenia Compara-Dun #14–16
          spinner: Cream Compara-Spinner #14–16 (Caucci and
               Natasi)

Scientific name: *Paraleptophlebia* sp.
Common name: Western Blue Quill, Little Western Red Quill
Dates of hatch: June through August
Time of hatch: all day
Patterns: nymph: Hare's Ear #16–18
              Western Blue Quill Nymph #16–18 (Schwiebert)
          dun: Red Quill #16–18
               Dark Blue Quill #16–18 (Schwiebert)
          spinner: Red Quill Spinner #16–18
               Blue Quill Spinner #16–18

Scientific name: *Seratella tibialis (Ephemerella tibialis)*
Common name: none
Dates of hatch: June through September
Time of hatch: mid-day

Patterns: nymph: Hare's Ear #14–18
           dun: Gray Wulff #14–16
           spinner: none

Scientific name: *Drunella doddsi (Ephemerella doddsi)*
Common name: Western Green Drake
Dates of hatch: early July through late August
Time of hatch: late morning to early afternoon
Patterns: nymph: Hare's Ear #14–18
           dun: Green Drake Wulff #12–14
                    Green Paradrake #12–14
           spinner: Green Drake Spinner #12–14

Scientific name: *Drunella grandis (Ephemerella grandis)*
Common name: Western Green Drake
Dates of hatch: mid-June to early September
Time of hatch: late morning to early afternoon
Patterns: nymph: Great Lead-wing Olive Drake Nymph #8–10
                    (Schwiebert)
           dun: Green Drake Wulff #10–12
                    Green Paradrake #10–12
           spinner: Green Drake Spinner #10–12

Scientific name: *Drunella coloradenis (Ephemerella coloradensis)*
Common name: Little Slate-wing Olive
Dates of hatch: early July to late August
Time of hatch: mid-day
Patterns: nymph: Little Slate-wing Olive Nymph #16–18
                    (Schwiebert)
           dun: Blue-wing Olive #16–18
                    Comparadun #16–18
           spinner: none

Scientific name: *Ephemerella infrequens*
Common name: Pale Morning Dun
Dates of hatch: July and August
Time of hatch: mid- to late morning
Patterns: nymph: Pale Morning Dun Nymph #16–18 (Swisher and
                    Richards)

dun: Pale Morning Compara-Dun #20 (Caucci and Nastasi

spinner: Pale Morning Dun Spinner #20 (Swisher and Richards)

Scientific name: *Tricorythodes minutus*
Common name: White-winged Trico, White-winged Curse
Dates of hatch: early June through mid-September
Time of hatch: early to mid-morning
Patterns: nymph: Tricorythodes Nymph #20–22
          dun: Trico Dun #20–22
          spinner: Poly-wing Spinner #20–22

PLECOPTERA (Stoneflies)

GENERIC STONEFLY PATTERNS

Adults	Nymphs
Salmonfly	Golden Stone
Golden Stonefly	Girdle Bug
Yellow Humpy	Kaufmann Stone
Stimulator	Bitch Creek
	Hare's Ear
	Woven Stone

SPECIES SPECIFIC INFORMATION

Scientific name: *Zapada cintipes*
Common name: Little Sepia Stonefly
Dates of hatch: February to September
Time of hatch: sporadic
Patterns: nymph: Little Sepia Stonefly Nymph #16 (Schwiebert)
          adult: Little Brown Stonefly #16 (Rosborough)

Scientific name: *Malenka californica, Malenka coloradensis*
Common name: Little Western Stonefly
Dates of hatch: June to November
Time of hatch: sporadic
Patterns: nymph: Little Western Stonefly #12–14 (Schwiebert)
          adult: Little Brown Stonefly #16 (Rosborough)

Scientific name: *Taeniopteryx (pecos)*
Common name: Early Brown Stonefly
Dates of hatch: February to April
Time of hatch: sporadic
Patterns: nymph: Dark Hare's Ear #14–18
adult: Little Brown Stonefly #16 (Rosborough)

Scientific name: *Capnia* sp. (about 15 species in New Mexico)
Common name: Little Winter Stonefly
Dates of hatch: January to June
Time of hatch: sporadic
Patterns: nymph: Early Black Stonefly Nymph #12 (Schwiebert)
adult: Little Black Stonefly #12–14

Scientific name: Leuctridae
Common name: Needle Fly
Dates of hatch: February through September
Time of hatch: sporadic
Patterns: nymph: Needle Fly Nymph #16 (Schwiebert)
adult: Little Black Stonefly #18

Scientific name: *Pteronarcys californica*
Common name: Giant Stonefly, Salmon Fly
Dates of hatch: early May to July
Time of hatch: late afternoon and evening
Patterns: nymph: Montana Stone #2–8 (Brooks)
Kaufmann Stone #2–8
Box Canyon Stone #2–8 (Barker)
adult: Bird's Stonefly #4–8

Scientific name: *Pteronarcella badia*
Common name: none
Dates of hatch: early May and July
Time of hatch: late afternoon and evening
Patterns: nymph: Montana Stone #2–8 (Brooks)
Kaufmann Stone #2–8
Box Canyon Stone #2–8 (Barker)
adult: Bird's Stonefly #4–8

Scientific name: *Hesperoperla pacifica*

Common name: Golden Stonefly
Dates of hatch: April to September
Time of hatch: late afternoon and evening
Patterns: nymph: Montana Stone #2–8 (Brooks)
Kaufmann Stone #2–8
Box Canyon Stone #2–8 (Barker)
adult: Bird's Stonefly #4–8

Scientific name: *Isoperla mormona* (about 7 other species)
Common name: Western Yellow Stonefly
Dates of hatch: May to August
Time of hatch: late evening
Patterns: nymph: Little Yellow Stone Nymph #12–14 (Rosborough)
Partridge, Yellow and Fur Thorax Soft Hackle
#12–14 (Nemes)
adult: Yellow Bucktail Caddis #12–14
Little Yellow Stone #12–14 (Rosborough)

Scientific name: *Sweltsa* sp.
Common name: Little Green Stonefly
Dates of hatch: mid-April to August
Time of hatch: late afternoon and evening
Patterns: nymph: Pheasant Tail Soft Hackle #16–18
Partridge and Green and Fur Thorax Soft Hackle
#16–18 (Nemes)
adult: Green Bucktail Caddis #18–20

TRICOPTERA (Caddisflies)

GENERIC CADDIS PATTERNS

Adults	*Larva*
Elk Hair Caddis	Green Caddis Larva
Hemmingway Caddis	LaFontaine Caddis Larva
King's River Caddis	Cased Caddis Larva
	Peeking Caddis
	Red Squirrel Caddis

SPECIES SPECIFIC INFORMATION

Scientific name: *Chimarra* sp.
Common name: Fingernet Caddisfly
Dates of hatch: mid-summer
Time of hatch: afternoon
Patterns: larva: Little Orange Caddis Larva #16–18 (Schwiebert)
            adult: Gray Elk Hair Caddis #16–18

Scientific name: *Wormaldia* sp.
Common name: Micro Caddis
Dates of hatch: April through September
Time of hatch: evening
Patterns: pupa: Pale Microcaddis Pupa #18–22 (Schwiebert)

Scientific name: *Hydropsyche* sp.
Common name: Spotted Sedge
Dates of hatch: May through September
Time of hatch: late afternoon
Patterns: larva: Cream Caddis Larva #12–16
                Latex Caddis Larva #12–16 (Jorgensen)
            pupa: Cream Sparkle Pupa #12–16 (LaFontaine)
                March Brown Soft Hackle #12–16
            adult: Elk Hair Caddis #12–16

Scientific name: *Cheumatopsyche* sp.
Common name: Little Western Sedge
Dates of hatch: July
Time of hatch: late afternoon
Patterns: pupa: Little Western Sedge Pupa #14–16 (Schwiebert)

Scientific name: *Rhyacophila* sp. (at least 5 species in New Mexico)
Common name: Green Rock Worm
Dates of hatch: May through September
Time of hatch: afternoon
Patterns: larva: Rhyacophila Caddis Larva #10–16 (Kaufmann)
            pupa: Partridge and Green #10–16 (Nemes)
            adult: Dark Bucktail Caddis #10–14

Scientific name: *Brachycentrus americanus*
Common name: American Grannom

Dates of hatch: May through September
Time of hatch: late afternoon and evening
Patterns: larva: Herl Nymph #10–16
           pupa: American Grammon #10–14 (Schwiebert)

Scientific name: *Limnephilus coloradensis*
Common name: Orange Sedge
Dates of hatch: June through October
Time of hatch: evening and night
Patterns: larva: Cased Caddis #12–14 (Bodmer)
           pupa: Medium Cinnamon Sedge Pupa #10–12
                     (Schwiebert)
           adult: Orange Bucktail Caddis #10–12

Scientific name: *Mystacides* sp. (uncommon)
Common name: Black Dancer
Dates of hatch: summer
Time of hatch: evening

DIPTERA (True Flies: Midges, Mosquitos, Black Gnats and Crane
       Flies)
Family: Tipulidae
Common name: Crane Flies
Dates of hatch: April through October
Patterns: larva: Muskrat #8–10 (Rosborough)
                     Western Crane Fly Larva #10–12 (Schwiebert)
                     Woolly Worm #10–12
           adult: Ginger Spider #10–16
                     Ginger Variant #10–16
                     Darbee Crane Fly #8–10

Family: Culicidae
Common name: Mosquitos
Dates of hatch: June to September
Patterns: larva: Mosquito Larva #14–20
           adult: Adams #14–20
                     Mosquito #14–20

Family: Chironomidae
Common name: Midges
Dates of hatch: all year
Patterns: larva: Brassie #18–24
Midge Larva #18–24 (Whitlock)
pupa: Chironomid Pupa #18–24 (Kaufmann),
brown, black, olive, gray
Emerging Pupa #18–24 (Whitlock),
black, brown, green
adult: Parachute Midge Cluster #14–18
Fore-and-Aft Midge Cluster #14–18
Griffith's Gnat #18–24
Bobber Midge Emerger #18–24
Adams #18–24

Family: Simuliidae
Common name: Blackflies
Dates of hatch: April to September
Patterns: adult: Black Gnat #16–18

ONDONATA (Damselflies and Dragonflies)

Zygoptera (Damselflies)

GENERIC DAMSELFLY PATTERNS

Adults	Nymphs
Blue Damsel #12	Marabou Damsel #10–12 (Kaufmann)
Ginger Damsel #12	Filoplume Damsel #10–12 (Armstrong)
	Brown or Green Damsel #10 (Rosborough)

GENUS SPECIFIC INFORMATION

Genus	Nymph Pattern (from Schwiebert)
Hetaerina	Great Olive Damselfly Nymph #8–10
Lestes	Speckled Olive Damselfly Nymph #10–12
Ischnura	Pale Olive Fork-Tailed Nymph #12–14
Enallagma	Speckled Olive Damselfly Nymph #12–14
Argia	Purple Damselfly Nymph #12–14

Anisoptera (Dragonflies)

GENERIC DRAGONFLY PATTERNS

Adults	*Nymphs*
Dragonfly #8–12 (Bailey)	Carey Special #8–12
	Brown, Olive Woolly Bugger #8–12
	Assam Dragon #8–10 (Brooks)
	Lake Dragon #6–10 (Kaufmann)

GENUS SPECIFIC INFORMATION

Genus	*Nymph Pattern (from Schwiebert)*
Anax	Green Darner Dragonfly Nymph #4–8
Aeshna	Giant Dragonfly Nymph #2–8
Libellula	Ten-spot Dragonfly Nymph #6–8
Gomphus	Riffle-burrowing Dragonfly Nymph #8–10

HEMIPTERA (True Bugs: Backswimmers)

Species: *Notonecta* sp.
Common name: Backswimmer
Patterns: Backswimmer #12–14 (Troth)
    Gray-winged Backswimmer #14–18 (Schwiebert)

MEGALOPTERA (Alderflies and Dobsonflies)

Family: Sialidae
Common name: Alderflies
Patterns: larva: Brown Woolly Worm #10–14
       adult: Wet Alder #10–12
          Quill-wing Alderfly #10–14

Family: Corydalidae
Common name: Dobsonflies
Patterns: larva: Hellgrammite #6–10 (Prince)
          Brooks Stonefly #6–10

Where To Go For
Additional Informaton

CLUBS

National

Trout Unlimited
P.O. Box 1944
Washington, D.C. 20013

Federation of Fly Fishers
P.O. Box 1088
West Yellowstone, MT 59748

Local

Sangre de Cristo Fly Fishers
P.O. Box 922
Santa Fe, New Mexico 87504

New Mexico Trout
P.O. Box 8553
Albuquerque, New Mexico 87198

San Juan Fly Fishers
P.O. Box 6474
Navajo Dam, New Mexico 87419

Mesilla Valley Fly Fishers
P.O. Box 2222
Las Cruces, New Mexico 88004

Rio Grande Fly Fishers
P.O. Box 4006
Taos, New Mexico 87571

SHOPS

Many businesses throughout New Mexico specialize in fly-fishing equipment or have a staff knowledgable in the ways of fly fishermen. These friendly people are generally more than willing to take the time to answer whatever questions you may have concerning fly-fishing in their local area. Don't hesitate to use this resource!

NATIONAL FORESTS

Carson National Forest
P.O. Box 558
Taos, New Mexico 87571

Santa Fe National Forest
P.O. Box 1689
Santa Fe, New Mexico 87504

NEW MEXICO DEPARTMENT OF GAME AND FISH

New Mexico Department of Game and Fish
P.O. Box 25112
Santa Fe, New Mexico 87504

Bibliography

Black, William. *CreekCraft: The Art of Fishing Small Streams.* Boulder, Colorado: Pruett Press, 1988.

Black, William. *Flyfishing the Rockies.* Boulder, Colorado: Pruett Press, 1976.

Borger, Gary. *Naturals.* Harrisburg, Pennsylvania: Stackpole Books, 1980.

Borger, Gary. *Nymphing.* Harrisburg, Pennsylvania: Stackpole Books, 1979.

Brooks, Charles. *The Trout and the Stream.* New York: Nick Lyons Books, 1974.

Dennis, Jack. *Western Trout Fly Tying Manual.* Jackson Hole, Wyoming: Snake River Books, 1974.

Dennis, Jack. *Western Trout Fly Tying Manual.* Vol. 2. Jackson Hole, Wyoming, Snake River Books, 1980.

Fothergill, Chuck, and Bob Sterling. *Colorado Angling Guide.* Aspen, Colorado: Stalker Publishing, 1989.

Hafele, Rick, and Dave Hughes. *Western Hatches.* Portland, Oregon: Frank Amato Publications, 1981.

Hughes, Dave. *Handbook of Hatches.* Harrisburg, Pennsylvania: Stackpole Books, 1987.

Kaufmann, Randall. *The Fly Tyers Nymph Manual.* Portland, Oregon: Western Fisherman's Press, 1986.

La Fontaine, Gary. *Caddisflies.* Piscataway, New Jersey: Winchester Books, 1982.

Leiser, Eric. *The Book of Fly Patterns.* New York: Alfred A. Knopf, 1987.

McCafferty, W. Patrick. *Aquatic Entomology.* Boston: Jones and Bartlett, 1983.

Migel, J. Michael, ed. *Masters on the Dry Fly.* Garden City, New Jersey: Doubleday and Company, 1977.

Migel, J. Michael, ed. *Masters on the Nymph.* Garden City, New Jersey: Doubleday and Company, 1979.

Piper, Ti. *Fishing in New Mexico.* Albuquerque: University of New Mexico Press, 1989.

Schwiebert, Ernest. *Matching the Hatch.* New York: Macmillan, 1955.

Schwiebert, Ernest. *Nymphs.* Tulsa, Oklahoma: Winchester Press, 1973.

Schwiebert, Ernest. *Trout.* New York: E.P. Dutton, 1978.

Sierra Club. *Day Hikes in the Santa Fe Area.* Santa Fe: Sierra Club, 1990.

Sublette, James, Michael Hatch and Mary Sublette. *The Fishes of New Mexico.* Albuquerque: University of New Mexico Press, 1990.

Swisher, Doug, and Carl Richards. *Fly Fishing Strategy.* New York: Nick Lyons Books, 1975.

Swisher, Doug, and Carl Richards. *Selective Trout.* New York: Nick Lyons Books, 1971.

Trotter, Patrick C. *Cutthroat, Native Trout of the West.* Boulder, Colorado: Associated University Press, 1987.

Whitlock, Dave. *Guide to Aquatic Trout Foods.* New York: Nick Lyons Books, 1982.

About the Authors

Van Beacham, founder and co-owner of Los Rios Anglers in Taos, is a fourth generation New Mexican with plenty of fly-fishing in his blood: one grandfather built the Lisboa Springs Hatchery in the Pecos, the other ran Santa Fe's only hardware store and fishing shop during the 1940s. Van is in his eighth year of managing his shop and guide service and recently founded the Rio Grande Fly Fishers. In spite of his busy schedule, Van remains active in many conservation organizations in northern New Mexico.

Barrie Bush was born in Utah, lived most of his adult life in California, and has spent the last 4 years in New Mexico. A fly fisherman for 45 years, many of Barrie's activities center on the sport. His latest projects included producing fly-fishing videos and founding Fish New Mexico, a group dedicated to promoting and preserving the quality fisheries in the state.

Jerral Derryberry grew up in a variety of places known for excellent hunting and fishing: Florida, Texas, Colorado, and West Virginia. Although a fly fisherman on and off for 30 years, Jerry did not get serious about the sport until 12 years ago when he discovered he could catch tarpon in Galveston Bay with a fly. Working as a fine artist in Santa Fe, Jerry is very active in the Sangre de Cristo Fly Fishers and is a founder of Fish New Mexico.

Marcus Garcia is a native of Santa Fe, moving away only to obtain a degree in natural resources from New Mexico State University. He has been a fly fisherman for 15 years, concentrating on the streams of the Pecos Watershed. An excellent fly tier, Marcus also serves as Communications Committee Chairman for the Sangre de Cristo Fly Fishers and is responsible for publishing the club's monthly newsletter.

Jan Gruber was born in central Minnesota, where she grew up fishing for anything in any kind of water. She has been fly-fishing for more than 25 years and has fished all over the world. Since 1985, Jan has run Santa Fe's High Desert Angler with her husband, Mark. She is also a founder and past president of the Sangre de Cristo Fly Fishers.

Mark Gruber began tying flies at the age of 9, using them to catch pan fish in the ponds of Michigan. His interest led him to a degree in wildlife biology. A New Mexico resident for the past 14 years, Mark has spent the last 5 years operating the High Desert Angler in Santa Fe with his wife, Jan. Mark was a founder and first president of the Sangre de Cristo Fly Fishers. His deep respect for trout and the environment keep Mark active in many conservation projects.

Joe Hussion learned to fly-fish on the small streams of his native West Virginia. He came West in 1976, and his job as a pharmacist with the Public Health Service has enabled him to live in a variety of rural areas with excellent fishing. Joe is a founder and past president of the Sangre de Cristo Fly Fishers.

Gerald Jacobi is a professor of Environmental Science at New Mexico Highlands University. Gerry learned to fly-fish as a kid growing up in Colorado, an interest that led to studying insects, particularly stoneflies, at Colorado State University and at the University of Utah. He has been collecting insects and fly-fishing for trout in New Mexico for 12 years.

Dirk Kortz, a native of New Jersey, has been living and fly-fishing in New Mexico for 25 years. He makes his living as an artist and a screen writer and was formerly a co-owner of a guide service, Troutfitters of Santa Fe. Dirk's political awareness and activity have been important factors in preserving the quality fisheries on the Rio Chama.

Ron Lujan is a lifelong resident of Santa Fe who has been fly-fishing for the past 5 years. Ron has combined his interest in insects with his skills as an artist to produce illustrations not only for this book but also for *The Fly Fishing Directory* and the Sangre de Cristo Fly Fishers newsletter. A mechanical designer by trade, Ron's many talents include art, woodworking, building musical instruments, and designing and making jewelry. He also designed the Sangre de Cristo Fly Fishers logo.

Craig Martin, a native of Pennsylvania, never caught a trout until his thirty-third year, but since then fly-fishing has been his insatiable passion. Formerly a naturalist with the National Park Service and a junior high school science teacher, Craig now devotes his time to raising a daughter and a son.

Martha Noss is a native of New Mexico where her father and grandfather taught her spin-fishing as a child. But fishing did not become a habit until 4 years ago when she learned to fly-fish; since then, she has spent almost every weekend on the water. When not working at the School of American Research, fly-fishing is just one of the many excuses Martha uses to spend time in the mountains.

Taylor Streit hails from upstate New York, where smart trout on heavily fished waters taught him the fine art of fly-fishing. Taylor moved to New Mexico in 1968 and began his fly-fishing business a few years later, first owning the Taos Fly Shop and more recently guiding under the name of Taylor Streit Fly Fishing Service. He also ties flies commercially. When not guiding, Taylor loves to spend time with his kids and is helping his 10-year-old learn to fish and tie flies.

Bert Tallant was raised in a small Oklahoma town where he learned to fly-fish for bluegills on the local stockponds. His work as a clinical laboratory scientist with the Public Health Service gives him frequent opportunity to fish on the Jicarilla Indian Reservation. Recently, Bert and his wife Marie published *The Fly Fishing Directory,* a comprehensive list of national fly-fishing resources.

Bob Widgren was born in Ohio and lived in many parts of the country before settling in northern New Mexico. In 1980, after years of fly-fishing and building rods as a hobby, he and his wife, Lee, founded Los Piños Rods and began creating custom fishing rods. First based in Antonito, Colorado, Bob had plenty of time to explore the Rio de los Piños. Today, Los Piños is in Albuquerque. When not building rods or rod cases, Bob and Lee enjoy traveling around the West.

Richard Wilder, a landscape contractor in Santa Fe, spent most of his childhood moving around the country. If any one place was home it was Wisconsin, where his grandfather started him on fly-fishing at the age of 5. He has been fishing in New Mexico for 15 years. Richard travels not only with a fly rod but also with a camera. His excellent photographs are testimony to his special love for New Mexico.

Based in Santa Fe, the Sangre de Cristo Fly Fishers is northern New Mexico's largest fly-fishing organization. Established in 1986 to promote conservation of trout habitat and resources, it now has more than two hundred members. Beyond its monthly meetings, sponsored events include a spring rendezvous and a day-long seminar on the Pecos River for novice fly fishermen. The Sangre de Cristo Fly Fishers participates in the public hearing process for regulatory and management policies for state trout fisheries, and members are active in habitat improvement projects, clean-ups, and assisting the New Mexico Department of Game and Fish to stock brown trout. The group also publishes a monthly newsletter, *The Flypaper*.

Index